S0-BRA-302

INCIDENT AT BIG SKY

The True Story of
Sheriff Johnny France
and the Capture
of the Mountain Men

**Johnny France
and Malcolm McConnell**

PUBLISHED BY POCKET BOOKS NEW YORK

POCKET BOOKS, a division of Simon & Schuster, Inc.
1230 Avenue of the Americas, New York, N.Y. 10020

Copyright © 1986 by Johnny France
Cover photo copyright © 1987 Mort Engel Studio

Published by arrangement with W. W. Norton & Company, Inc.
Library of Congress Catalog Card Number: 86-5398

ISBN: 0-671-63924-2

First Pocket Books printing July 1987

10 9 8 7 6 5 4 3 2 1

POCKET and colophon are registered trademarks
of Simon & Schuster, Inc.

Printed in the U.S.A.

Kidnapping. A person commits the offense of kidnapping if he knowingly or purposely and without lawful authority restrains another person by either secreting or holding him in a place of isolation or by using or threatening to use physical force.

Montana Criminal Code

PROSECUTOR: "There's no question is there, that on July 15th, 1984, that you restrained Kari Swenson?"

DON NICHOLS: "No."

PROSECUTOR: "And there's no question that you did that by secreting her or holding her in an isolated place?"

DON NICHOLS: "I don't know what you mean by isolated. All everywhere we ever go is isolated. . . ."

PROSECUTOR: ". . . Okay, so where you were camped that night, as far as you are concerned, was a place of isolation?"

DON NICHOLS: "Yes."

Trial of Donald Boone Nichols
July 10, 1985
Virginia City, Montana

Kari realized that the men wore holstered pistols and thick-bladed hunting knives. The older man's face was almost hidden beneath a matted gray beard and the brim of a greasy cowboy hat. But his intense blue eyes frightened her. Even on first sight, she realized that he was not normal.

Then she saw the younger man staring at her body, his lips grim. Her T-shirt was plastered sweaty tight across her chest. Kari was suddenly shaky and dry-mouthed.

"Please let me go," she cried.

For a moment, no one spoke. Finally the old man asked, "Well, Danny, shall we keep her?"

The boy nodded decisively. "Yeah. Let's keep her."

Kari screamed, and the old man turned and clubbed her hard with his fist. Then he was on top of her, gripping her in a painful necklock. "You keep screaming like that," he shouted, "and we're gonna beat you up." He cranked her head sharply, and she bit into the side of her own cheek.

Kari stopped screaming . . .

Preface

Remembering a tragedy is painful; recalling the exact words and details of a violent and tragic crime is a challenge for victims, participants, and witnesses. Therefore, when the authors faced the challenge of re-creating the events that began with Kari Swenson's brutal kidnapping in July 1984 and ended on the snowy ridge above the Cold Springs Ranch five months later, we were fortunate to have available a body of evidence, court testimony, and official records to consult when human memory failed.

Kari Swenson and Jim Schwalbe provided a wealth of detail on her kidnapping and Alan Goldstein's murder during their sworn court testimony. Obviously, the terrible events of that crime were seared into their memories because their vivid re-creations of actions, emotions, and conversations hardly vary from one testimony statement to the next during their multiple court appearances.

The details of the long, often confusing manhunt and eventual capture were less accessible. But all major crime investigations leave a trail of records; in this case, law enforcement communications logs, investigation reports, and operational plans supplemented the memories of the principals involved, allowing us to re-create events with confidence. Incredibly, Dan Nichols himself kept a diary during the early weeks of the manhunt, and this document served as the basis for discussions of these events between him and Sheriff Johnny France. Don Nichols also provided details of the manhunt months and capture to both authors, particularly to Sheriff France on the long car trips to and from court appearances during the eight-month legal process that ended in Deerlodge Prison last fall.

Finally, of course, the authors spent weeks at the vital, unglamorous drudgery of interviews, tape-recording participants as we studied maps and police reports with them, sifting valid detail from faulty memory.

The end product of this effort, we hope, is an accurate record of one of modern America's most bizarre crimes.

Johnny France, Malcolm McConnell

PART 1

A Place of Isolation

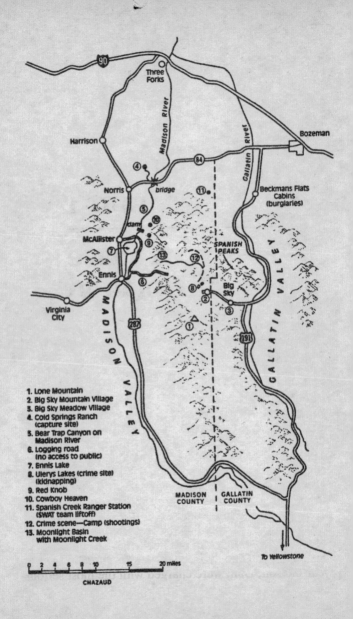

1. Lone Mountain
2. Big Sky Mountain Village
3. Big Sky Meadow Village
4. Cold Springs Ranch (capture site)
5. Bear Trap Canyon on Madison River
6. Logging road (no access to public)
7. Ennis Lake
8. Ulerys Lakes (crime site) (kidnapping)
9. Red Knob
10. Cowboy Heaven
11. Spanish Creek Ranger Station (SWAT team liftoff)
12. Crime scene—Camp (shootings)
13. Moonlight Basin with Moonlight Creek

0 2 4 6 8 10   15   20 miles

CHAZAUD

1

Madison Range, Montana

July 15, 1984

THE MADISON COUNTY COURTHOUSE IS OLD BY MONTANA standards. It has stood on a lean, treeless slope in Virginia City for over a century. The graceful red brick and white portico are topped by a fretted cupola, evocative, perhaps, of a more settled civilization thousands of miles to the east of the violent mountain frontier where the structure was built.

But to the citizens of the sprawling county, the courthouse represents more than a colorful landmark, dating from the Alder Gulch gold boom of the 1860s. The cathedral-like building is a tangible symbol that the rule of law firmly governs the affairs of men. Road agents and cattle thieves, vigilantes and ambushes in the muddy streets are flamboyant history.

In the spring and summer of 1985, the handsome courtroom on the building's second floor was the scene of two widely publicized criminal trials. A middle-aged man named Donald Boone Nichols and his twenty-year-old son, Dan, were charged with the most serious

3

offenses in Montana's criminal code, kidnapping, armed assault, and deliberate homicide.

During the course of emotionally charged testimony, the witnesses, the surviving victim, and the participants in these crimes detailed the bizarre and tragic events of the previous summer.

In the words of the state's key witness, a striking young woman with auburn hair, the crime began on the hot afternoon of July 15, 1984.

Kari Swenson ran alone through the dry heat. Above her left shoulder rose the heavy angles of Lone Mountain. The dark tree line, giving way to stone and, above, vestigial snow. Ahead stood the massive Spanish Peaks. The dazzle of a glacial lake cut through the lodgepole pines. Then the trail rose into thick timber and the lake was gone. Sudden green shadow, cicadas, and aromatic pitch in the windless afternoon.

Coming up on one mile. The Forest Service trail dipped to join Jack Creek logging road. Kari's cleats pounded on hardened truck ruts. She skidded on bark trash and gravel and lengthened her stride for the level.

A mile and a half. The sun was a weight on her neck and arms. Her long braid slapped below her shoulders. The terry cloth headband kept the sweat from her eyes. To the left, Lower Ulerys Lake had disappeared in the jumble of blowdown lodgepoles. Her feet struck the ruts. The slope rose before her. Almost two miles. Camp robber jays squawked in the bright Montana sky. She shortened her stride, pumping with her elbows.

Sunday was a long day for the summer restaurant staff at Lone Mountain Ranch. Brunch lasted from ten till two, and set-up for dinner began at five. Some of the other waitresses napped in the afternoon. But today Kari ran through the dry mountain heat, up the logging roads of Jack Creek, away from the Jacuzzis and satellite dishes of the Big Sky resort and into the Pleistocene wilderness of the Spanish Peaks. As Kari often told her friends, she did not simply "go jogging" in her free time. This was a training run, six miles at altitude, a circuit of rugged trails around the two pothole lakes hidden in the steep forest. Six miles was almost exactly ten kilometers, her best distance.

Four months earlier, at the women's world championship biathlon at Chamonix, Kari had placed fifth overall in the ten-kilometer final. Her performance was the best ever for an American biathlete in postwar international competition. At age twenty-two, Kari had suddenly become America's strongest Olympic contender in the brutally demanding composite sport that combines Nordic trail skiing with rifle marksmanship.

Biathlon evolved out of Scandinavian army training and has been dominated since the war by the military "amateurs" of Eastern Europe. Before the war, the endurance and martial skills needed for the sport were considered by some Olympic officials impossible for a woman to master. Now Kari Swenson, a recent graduate of Montana State University in nearby Bozeman, ran through the heat of these isolated mountains toward the goal of a biathlon medal at the next winter Olympics.

Coming up on two miles. The trail cut to the right, along an alpine meadow bright with asters and columbines. Kari was now cut off from the Gallatin Valley below to the east. The Jack Creek drainage, as this canyon was called, divided the southern Madison Range from the Spanish Peaks wilderness area ahead to the north. When she had parked her car at the trailhead she could still distinguish the miniature log lodges of Big Sky. That was Resort Montana, an all-season recreational preserve for wealthy Easterners and the tanned Calvin Klein set some of the old ranchers called

"Californicators." Down there, the meadows were cut with tractor mowers and gardeners tended even the quaking asps.

The dark mountains ahead did not offer gondola cars or chair lifts. In the Spanish Peaks, the trails were cut by elk and moose. Mule deer made ruts in the mud up there, not logging trucks or snowmobiles, and the ponds were designed by beavers, not landscape architects. At every trailhead entering the roadless wilderness, the Forest Service had posted signs instructing hikers how to avoid grizzly bear attack. The Madison Range was not a park; only the previous summer, a camper had been dragged from his tent up near Quake Lake and eaten by a grizzly.

That morning, Bob Schaap, the owner of Lone Mountain Ranch, had told Kari about the grizzly signs he'd seen while hiking on Jack Creek Road yesterday.

"I've never sighted a grizzly in the wild," Kari said. "I'd die to see one." And so she'd decided to "go training" up here today on the chance she might sight that grizzly bear.

Although she had spent the first nine years of her life in Philadelphia, Kari could be considered a native Montanan. Bob Swenson, her father, was a professor who had brought his family back to his home town of Bozeman to take over the chairmanship of the Montana State University Physics Department in the early seventies. There was an unwholesome urban environment back East, and he and Kari's mother, Jan, wanted their kids to experience the natural outdoor childhood they'd had in the West.

Kari had flourished in Montana. In May, she had received an honors degree in microbiology from MSU. Sometime in the next few years, she planned to start the grueling slog of veterinary school, but not before she trained to peak performance level and led the U.S. Biathlon Team to the next winter Olympics.

The meadow steepened, and the trail ahead climbed toward the timbered ridge that should mark the rim of Upper Ulerys Lake. She had never run this particular trail, but she wasn't afraid of getting lost. This was the edge of the wilderness, but the forest was, despite the grizzlies, a managed area.

With small adjustments in breathing and stride, she found the proper pace for the incline. Kari was a disciplined woman, self-directed and confident. From her parents, she had learned that a person could control a complicated life involving scholarship, athletics, and a vigorous attachment to the mountains. Her joint careers of scientist and athlete were right on schedule. If she continued to work hard and stayed healthy, there was very little that could stop her.

The trail grew steeper as she neared the ridgetop. Then the trees opened, and she saw the shimmering blue lake below her. Although Kari knew trout fishermen often hiked in here after the big cutthroats and browns, the lake looked untouched, primitive. The slope before her was so steep and jumbled with blowdowns that she couldn't be sure of the trail. But Kari saw the faint path, snaking down through the brush to the right, and she dug in her cleats for the descent.

Here in the thick brush, mosquitoes whined around her sweating face. There were swarms of deer flies. Her shoes hit gummy black turf as the trail reached the lake level. Animal tracks pocked the mud, and she slipped in the craters. To her left, the chill water gleamed in the sun. Then there was a movement in the dense lodgepoles across the lake. A man standing in the trees. Kari's feet pounded the mud, and she gazed down at the track before her, wary of twisting an ankle. Probably a fisherman, just another dedicated angler, willing to put up with the steep hike and the mosquitoes and flies to land a big one.

Kari was halfway around the small lake now. The trail was hardly wider than a deer path, and steep, following the sharp contour of the pothole lake shore. She splashed through a stream and puffed up a sharp rise. Here the pines were even thicker than up on the ridge. But ahead, to the left, the trail opened again, a clear route, cutting up the slope among the dense deadfalls to rejoin the ridge. That should be Jack Creek Trail, and if she followed it, her route would cross the logging road again, and she could head back to the trailhead where she'd parked her car.

Just before the end of the lake, the trail climbed another rise into dense timber, and Kari stared intently at the ground to avoid injury in the roots and stones.

Two men appeared, not ten feet away. The older man stood to the left, one foot on the trail. The younger man was half hidden in the trees to the right, five feet off the path. Her first reaction was surprise, then apprehension. These men were dirty; they did not look like fishermen from Big Sky. And they stood very still, watching her with flat dark eyes, expressionless, just staring at her body. Now she saw their green backpacks, propped against a tree at trailside.

Kari slowed, breaking stride. Two rifles leaned against the tree near the packs. July was a long time before any legal hunting season, and these two guys with their grungy beards and sooty clothes sure did not look like wardens from the Fish and Game. As she stumbled ahead, she realized that they both wore holstered pistols and thick-bladed hunting knives.

The older man's face was almost hidden beneath a matted gray beard and the brim of a greasy cowboy hat. But the intense blue eyes frightened her. ("Feral" was the word they used when a domestic animal went wild. That was the word for his eyes.) Even on first sight, she realized that he was not normal.

She slowed more when she saw the younger man was staring at her body, his lips grim. The Day-Glo Sasson jogging shorts billowed over her hips, but the old blue T-shirt was plastered sweaty tight across her chest. He bore a certain resemblance to the older man, but his beard was blond and thinner. His eyes were deep brown.

Kari was shaky and dry-mouthed. But she did not panic. These two men were definitely grungy, some kind of rough misfits, but they had not actually attacked her. She did not intend to give them the chance. She decided to run right past them, up the ridge and back to the Jack Creek logging road where there might be hikers.

Without a word, the older man stepped onto the trail, blocking her way. Kari stumbled to a stop, but still overcame the natural panic reaction rising inside her. Maybe, she thought, if I just ask directions, I can keep the conversation short, then turn around and leave.

"Hi," she began, keeping her tone normal. "Is this the trail to Jack Creek?"

"Yeah," the old man answered. He formed a quizzical smile. "This is the Jack Creek Trail all right."

"Thanks," Kari blurted out, then spun to dash back along her original route.

Before she could complete her turn, the older man

9

seized both her wrists in a grip so tight she felt her bones might crack.

"Please let me go," she cried.

"No. We don't want to let you go." The old man's voice was amazingly calm, as if he were discussing the weather.

Kari struggled against his grip, twisting her weight right and left. "What do you want?" she demanded, anger overcoming her initial fear. "Why won't you let me go?"

"Well," he began, "we don't meet many beautiful women up in the mountains, and we just want to talk to you for a while . . ." He shrugged. The boy remained silent, staring. "Just to carry on a conversation," the older man added.

Kari was not taken in for a moment. She understood exactly what they wanted from her. "Well," she said coldly, "I sure don't want to talk to you. Let me go."

Again she twisted. Again the old man held her tight. They were so close together that she was engulfed in his stale, smoky odor.

"All we want's some conversation," the old man said.

"I know what you want." Kari's outrage grew as her fear and frustration mounted.

"Well," the old man said, almost indignant himself now, "we're not going to rape you, if that's what you're worried about."

"I don't believe you," Kari said. "What do you really want me for?"

The old man formed a lopsided smile beneath his beard. "Just for conversation . . . like I said."

Kari had stopped struggling momentarily, but now she resumed. Once more, his grip defeated her. He did

10

not appear to be exceptionally strong, but she realized his lean frame was deceptive.

"What's your name?" His voice seemed more relaxed now.

Kari was not about to give this creepy scarecrow her real name, and she was prepared to use the question to her advantage. "Sue," she muttered.

"You work down at Big Sky?"

"Yeah," Kari added. "I work in a kitchen."

He leaned closer to watch her eyes. "You married?"

Kari did not hesitate. "Yes, I'm married."

"So what's your husband's name?"

"Bill Soa," Kari answered, this odd name springing to her mind. Perhaps she might have thought that the name had a rugged working-class ring to it, evocative of a vengeful young husband.

"Where's your wedding ring?" he demanded, twisting her left hand open to examine the fingers.

"I . . . don't wear a wedding ring," she said. "Working in the kitchen with those machines and all, a ring could get caught and rip your finger off."

The old man examined her hand more closely. "I don't believe you. It doesn't look like you've ever worn one." There was a cold, bullying dogmatism to his manner now, as if he were being rational and Kari herself was creating a problem.

"No," Kari said desperately, "I don't wear one, and my husband doesn't either because he works in the kitchen, too."

"You believe her?" The old man turned to the boy.

For the first time, the young man spoke. "She's lying. All women lie." His voice was flat, a bizarre copy of the old man's.

The boy moved closer now, and she could smell the same rancid, smoky odor as the old man's. But he

11

didn't seem as calm about this whole nasty business as the older man. The boy was searching about to get a better view through the trees both back down the trail and up across the ridge. Clearly he was worried that a hiker or fisherman might stumble on them, out here in the open on the lake shore trail.

"Please let me go," Kari said, looking up again. "You don't want to get involved in something like this."

The old man did not answer.

She turned to directly address the boy for the first time. "You're young," she pleaded. "You don't want to get involved in this. It doesn't make sense."

Mosquitoes swarmed on her legs and arms now, but she was powerless to brush them off. For an uncertain moment, no one spoke. Finally, the old man asked: "Well, Danny, what do you think, shall we keep her?"

The boy nodded decisively. "Yeah. Let's keep her."

Kari thrashed out with her elbows and lurched backward, but the old man was not taken off guard. "All right," he shouted, "get the rope, and let's tie her up."

When she saw the boy extend a dirty white nylon cord, she screamed and dragged backward from the old man's grip.

His reaction was fast and shocking. Seizing both her wrists in one hand, he turned and clubbed her hard with his fist, striking her near the left temple. His blow knocked her to the ground, where she lay, stunned silent by pain and outrage. Never before had Kari been struck in anger. She came from a social world where people did not employ physical violence. But before she could protest, he was on top of her, his sweaty green sleeve across her throat as he gripped her in a

painful necklock. Kari kept her wits. Instead of exposing her arms to the boy's extended rope, she thrust her
hands beneath her to hide them. The old man dragged
her head harder to the left. Twisting her mouth, she
tried to find exposed flesh to bite, but he only cranked
her head more sharply, and she bit into the side of her
own cheek.

"You keep screaming like that," the old man
shouted, "and we're gonna beat you up. You want a
couple black eyes, a broken nose? Is that what you
want?"

Wordlessly, Kari shook her head.

"Wouldn't matter to me at all that you're a woman,"
he went on in his bullying way. "I'll do it anyway . . .
no problem."

Kari stopped screaming.

"We want you to come up in the mountains with us
for a couple of days," the old man said in an almost
normal tone. "We just want you to come on up and try
living with us."

The boy had several tight hitches of nylon line about
her right wrist now. They dragged her to her feet, and
the boy added two more hitches, then turned to the old
man for instructions. Without speaking, he nodded to
the boy's own wrist, and the young man wrapped the
cord tightly about the cuff of his Levi jacket.

"Why do you want to take me with you?"

"Well," the old man began, smiling nervously again,
"we never get any female companionship up in the
mountains. I was married back a few years and I could
never talk my wife into coming up and even trying it up
in the mountains. . . . "

The shock of the struggle started her shaking.

But the old man didn't seem to notice. He just
babbled on. "See . . . we need a woman for Danny.

13

That's the only way he'll travel with me up here. If we get him a woman, he'll stay on. . . . "

"Don't you know that there'll be people looking for me, tonight, when I don't show up at work?"

Now the old man's voice reverted to his bullying flatness. "We don't care if people are looking for you. We are going to take you off in the mountains anyway."

During this exchange, the younger man became increasingly agitated, jumping back and forth on the path to scan the lake shore trail in both directions.

"Come on," he finally shouted. "Let's get our gear and get out of here before someone comes along."

The old man nodded, and they struggled awkwardly into their packs. The boy had to untie the line from his own wrist to shoulder his large green backpack, but the old man gripped Kari tightly again while this maneuver was completed. When they were ready for the trail, the old man again nodded silently, and the boy dragged Kari ahead. Instead of following the trail, however, he struck off directly through the brush and deadfall trees, up the slope of the pothole lake, away from the trail, away from the managed sections of this wilderness.

Kari had no choice but to follow, bound like an unwilling Siamese twin. Behind her she could hear the old man puffing as they struggled up the incline toward the ridge. Ahead, there was only tangled timber and distant sky. They were heading northeast, she realized, into the forest of the Spanish Peaks.

Two hundred yards from the pine thicket where Kari Swenson was seized, the trees opened on a sunny glade beside Upper Ulerys Lake. Bark had been cut from the trunk of a tall, straight lodgepole that stood alone

in the corner of the glade. On the smooth exposed surface of the wood someone with a bold but disciplined
hand had written these words with indelible artist's
marker:

Dan

and

Don

Nichols

Live in

These Mts.

July 14, 1984

2

Ennis Lake Shore Lodge

July 15, 1984

JOHNNY FRANCE POURED HIMSELF A GLASS OF WINE FROM the green jug on the picnic table and sat back in the lawn chair. Pete and Bonnie Cox had one of the best sites in the campground. Their shiny Airstream trailer was a fixture here under the tall cottonwoods, at the edge of the water. There was deep shade on an afternoon like this, but they still had a view of the mountains rising across the lake.

The Coxes pulled their trailer up from Oklahoma every summer. They took real pleasure in the cool valley evenings around their campfire. And they also enjoyed some of the best trout fishing in the country. But most of all, Johnny suspected, they looked forward to the casual social life and genuine hospitality of the Madison Valley. Over the years, Peter Cox's birthday in mid-July had become an annual celebration among the half-dozen regular couples who parked their trailers along this shore.

Hands down, Johnny and Sue France were the most truly Western couple at the party. They lived in nearby Ennis, with a population of six hundred, the largest town in the Madison Valley. Ranching was the primary industry here, with summer tourism and outfitting for the fall elk hunters pretty far behind. Madison County was still an authentic corner of the American West.

As a young man, Johnny had been a cowboy. And he knew a thing or two about the pain and pleasure of the rodeo circuit. Mostly the pain. For the past three years, though, he had served as sheriff of Madison County. And, as the people drinking gin and tonic and chablis around the Coxes' fireplace could attest, he certainly looked the part of a Western sheriff.

At forty-four, Johnny France was lean and wiry. His face was lined from decades' exposure to the high country sun. His hands were strong, calloused, and rippled with accumulated scars. He probably owned a dozen wide-brimmed cowboy hats, and he was not usually seen by anyone other than Sue and the kids when he wasn't wearing one.

But Johnny's most notable feature was his eyes. Pale blue and luminous, they were seldom still. Johnny had grown up on ranches, just down Beartrap Canyon from Ennis Lake. From the time he was a little kid, he'd spent a lot of time out in the open, working cattle, fixing fences, trapping and hunting. All his life, Johnny had looked for things . . . stray calves, coyotes, an eagle across the canyon, a sow grizzly up a timbered draw. Before he'd been in law enforcement, Johnny made a living breaking horses and riding rodeo. He had learned young to look real hard at horses. As a young town constable and later as a deputy, he discovered that his life might depend on exactly what he saw, how quickly he saw it, and what his mind did with that visual information.

People who didn't know Johnny well sometimes thought that he wasn't attentive to conversations because his eyes ceaselessly scanned his surroundings while he spoke. But that was just his way. He always

17

heard what you were saying and responded appropriately. He just liked to see what was going on around him.

This afternoon, for example, Johnny was simultaneously aware of the couples before him in their lawn chairs and of the fishermen in that aluminum boat a quarter mile up the shore, and of the pickup truck's dust plume on the Cedar Hill Ranch road, three miles across the lake. He was also conscious that Bonnie Cox was about to remind him that he'd promised to tell the story about the big gray horse in Helena who had stamped on his face during his last summer of rodeoing.

"Johnny," she began with mock affront, "you never did tell me about that old belt buckle you always wear."

Johnny fingered the cool metal buckle. The sterling and gold oval was large, rich, but not gaudy. Out here, it was about as proud a possession as a man could own.

"Montana Rodeo Association," Bonnie read, prompting him. "Champion Bareback Bronc Rider, 1967."

Sue was up at the trailer, helping Linn with the appetizers, so Johnny decided to have a little fun with Bonnie. She was an attractive blonde with a sardonic sense of humor who truly did enjoy a party. Back home in Oklahoma Bonnie worked with victims of sexual abuse, so he understood her fondness for jokes and laughter. She surely didn't get too much of that in her job.

"Yeah, well . . . ," Johnny began, "you shouldn't put too much stock in belt buckles."

"Oh, no?" Bonnie replied, rising to his bait. "Didn't you do anything heroic to earn that one?"

Johnny gripped his chin in his thumb and index finger as he often did when asked to talk about himself. "No," he said quietly, as if owning up to a somber truth. "Fact is I had an old boy in jail one night . . . pretty good old cowboy from up around Missoula . . . seems he had a little too much whiskey and drove his truck off the road. Yeah, well . . ." He paused for effect here, aware that he'd actually ensnared most of those around the fireplace, not just Bonnie, then continued in his best cowboy drawl. ". . . old boy had his hearing before the J.P. and couldn't make his fine. So I allowed as how I might be able to help him out with some cash if he could cut loose of that there fancy rodeo buckle." Johnny gazed at Bonnie with his pale blue eyes, waiting for her to speak.

"So?" she finally exploded, "what happened?"

"I bought it off him for twenty bucks." Johnny remained as deadpan as he could. "Old cowboy hated to give her up, but he had his back right to it, you know." He nodded sharply, as if at some unpleasant, but morally edifying memory. "I took to wearing it when I was out of town, so as my friends wouldn't see me with it. Then, well . . . guess I just got fond of it because I . . . "

Bonnie saw now what he was doing. "Johnny France! You rotten . . ." She threw a slice of lime at him, but Johnny ducked and let his pent-up laughter burst.

"Well . . . yeah," Johnny smiled warmly at Bonnie and rubbed the belt buckle. "I guess maybe I got a little lucky that year." He knew that he would have to talk some about his rodeo career, that people kind of expected it. Unconsciously maybe, people who came up here in the summer were looking for the real West, for Cowboy America, a civilization distilled from childhood Bob Steele matinees and adolescent years of "Gunsmoke" and "Bonanza."

"I hear you got a little lucky the year before that, too," Pete Cox offered.

"Yes, sir," Johnny answered, "I . . . ah, I took the all-around championship that year." Beneath the cottonwoods the circle of faces turned expectantly, and Johnny slowly recited his impressive list of rodeo titles, accepting the fact that he fulfilled a certain symbolic function, combining as he did two of America's mythical heroes in one person. A real cowboy and a real Western sheriff.

He finished his recitation, dumped some more ice cubes in his glass to chill and dilute the wine, and chatted his way out of the group. Johnny could work a crowd with natural grace. That was part of his job. In rural Montana, a sheriff was elected not just to enforce the criminal code and assure public safety, but also to serve as a tangible symbol of legal authority, proof that legally structured civilization prevailed in this isolated corner of the West.

In a little while he would rejoin the group but right now he saw Sue coming down from the trailer and he wanted to have a few minutes alone with her, to enjoy a quiet glass of wine and the chance to speak quietly with his wife in the shade by the water's edge. He would use part of this peaceful Sunday afternoon to examine the week past and make plans for the week ahead. That was a luxury he and Sue had not been able to enjoy for a while now.

In theory, the sheriff was free of duty obligations from noon Saturday until eight Monday morning. That was the theory. In reality, the summer tourist rush always overwhelmed the limited personnel at his disposal, and Johnny found himself working weekends from early June until after Labor Day.

This year the Ennis Rodeo on the Fourth of July had started a crush of work that had Johnny on the go from dawn until after midnight each day. He not only had the department to run, but also his river-float business was entering the busiest part of the season. Johnny was one of only two outfitters licensed to work the nearby

Beartrap Canyon, just below Ennis Lake on the Madison River, one of the most exciting and dangerous stretches of white water in America.

But his obligations as sheriff did not end just because he had to spend seven hours a day out on the river with his clients . . . not to mention another two or three hours servicing the boats for the next day's group.

One of the problems with the department was that Madison County was over thirty-five hundred square miles, almost as big as the whole state of Connecticut. And Johnny only had himself and seven full-time deputies to enforce the law, twenty-four hours a day, every day of the year. In summer, the tourists spilling up from Yellowstone en route to Glacier Park and the rafters and trout fishermen swelled the county's population. During the rodeo, the drunken college kids always took on the local cowboys, so drunk and disorderly arrests shot up. All summer his officers had to contend with a much higher rate of DUI's, traffic accidents, stranded motorists, and sundry other headaches that people expected the sheriff to handle for them.

Today he'd told Vicki Hudson, his dispatcher, not to bother him unless there was a real emergency. He and Sue had been working hard all spring and early summer, and they hadn't had a chance to just relax, away from the telephone and the police radio in the car. Beyond Johnny's responsibilities as sheriff and Sue's job at the McAllister Inn, there was the riverfloat business. Johnny's skill on the river and his friendly way with clients brought him a lot of repeat customers and a regular stream of new people recommended by the old ones.

Normally, that would be fine. By working long hours, he could juggle the demands of both jobs. But above the pressure of their seasonal workloads, Sue and Johnny were deeply involved with their "place," the small piece of valley range land they had bought the previous year and christened the Circle Four Ranch. For years they had wanted some land of their own, where they could keep their horses and build the big, handsome log home that was their dream. Just before the July Fourth rodeo, Johnny had finished the well and drainage ditches, and now J.T., their oldest son, was almost done with the fencing.

Johnny bit back a yawn and ducked under a cottonwood branch to reach the water's edge. He was tired, but he didn't want Pete and Bonnie to see him yawning. In a minute, he knew, Sue would join him here, and they could talk about what was on her mind.

It was J.T., he realized. Not that the boy was a problem in any way. J.T. was a year out of high school and eager to pull his share of the load. Johnny had promised to train J.T. to take over the Beartrap Canyon trips this summer. In fact, he'd promised the boy he'd have him ready to lead the trips scheduled for late July. That would free Johnny up to work on the place.

But Johnny simply hadn't had enough time to get out on the river with J.T. and run the canyon, over and over in the big rubber Avon riverboat. It was one thing to ride the river, hanging on and whooping and hollering with the rest of them when they were sucked down into the spray and spewing hydraulics of that big set of rapids called the "kitchen sink." But it was something altogether different to control the boat, to actually sit there up on the high rowing frame with those two long fiberglass oars in your hands, watching the green curves of the current, the bulges of water that signaled dangerous suction.

The Beartrap was a new river every day, depending on how much water the power plant was letting through the turbines to meet the irrigation load downstream in the Missouri headwaters. He couldn't simply explain to J.T. about the eddies and the setups for each section of the rapids. Johnny would have to be there in the boat, coaching him through. And, until he did, it was too dangerous to send J.T. out there.

Beartrap Canyon could kill you real quick, if you didn't understand the river. Every year, it seemed, at least one inexperienced floater was drowned. And he was determined that would not happen to J.T. or to any of those who placed their trust in the boy's abilities. Johnny knew that his son understood his concern. But J.T. was anxious to learn. He was a normal nineteen-year-old boy, a little bigger than some, certainly smarter than many. He wanted to make his own way as an adult. J.T. had learned a sense of quiet responsibility from Johnny, a pride in paying his own way, in doing his job well. Now he just wanted a chance to demonstrate those qualities, and Johnny couldn't fault him for that.

"What's up?" Sue asked, slipping between two trees to join him on the grassy shore. "You look so darn serious."

Johnny rubbed his face, and muttered, "Yeah, well, about J.T. . . ."

"He has been asking again." Sue nodded. "I told him I'd remind you."

"Tuesday," Johnny said. "We can get out there all day on Tuesday. Then work the Wednesday trip together, and . . ."

They talked slowly, each listening carefully to the other. For almost twenty-five years, they had worked through their problems this way, sorting out the possibilities, weighing their opportunities. They made a pretty good team. When they'd married, neither one had been much older than J.T., and Johnny's worldly

23

possessions didn't amount to much more than a saddle and a quarter horse mare he'd bought off his Uncle Joe.

In the reflected sunlight Sue's long black hair, the dark warmth of her eyes, and her slender grace in peasant blouse and jeans evoked the girl he'd married . . . nearly a quarter century ago. Johnny only had to look at Sue for a while to understand that life had been pretty good to him, all in all, and that there was still a lot left to enjoy.

He toed the grass with his boot and felt the familiar blade of pain from his ankle. He hadn't been much older than J.T., either, when he'd busted that ankle, at the Bitterroot Rodeo, early in the '64 season. He'd drawn a big rank gray saddle bronc, and they'd had trouble with him in the chute. The arena was muddy and the ground pretty badly chewed up from the earlier events.

Trouble happens fast with a big horse. His neck rope snagged in the gate, and he had nowhere to go. So he threw Johnny sideways across his head and Johnny came down feet first in that gummy mud. He actually heard the ankle snap when he hit.

He'd hobbled out of the ring to find Doc Wheeler, his friend the vet, out by the stock pens. Doc sprayed the black, swollen ankle with some freezing chemical, taped it up tight, and helped Johnny pull his boot back on.

"Gotta ride the remount," Johnny said between his teeth. "Need the money real bad."

"She'll take a cast, Johnny," Doc warned. "You don't get a cast on her, you're gonna get crippled up, years from now."

Johnny finished the day with his ankle taped and drew first money in the saddle bronc event.

And he completed the season without a cast. Every Friday night before he left for the weekend rodeo,

Johnny visited Old Doc and got his ankle retaped. That's when he was working as a cowboy over near Dillon. Kathy was three and J.T. was just a baby. He had a family to support on a wrangler's pay. He needed that rodeo prize money. He had responsibilities. And that was something Johnny France took very seriously.

Now J.T. felt the same sense of responsibility. And Johnny could not fault him for that.

The lake was flat calm in the windless afternoon. Here at the northern edge, the massive heights of the Madison Range, from the Spanish Peaks above Beartrap Canyon, all the way down past Sphinx Mountain to the south, were nicely reflected in the water. He started past Sue, to the timbered silence of the mountains. On the other side of those rock summits was Big Sky—developed, Leisure Montana.

But this valley was still relatively untouched. He was proud to have been raised here, and proud that he and Sue could raise their own kids here. They'd certainly had their share of money worries and hard work, but they sure as hell didn't want to live anywhere else.

"Well, Susie," he said, summing up the way he felt. "Things'll work out. You know me, I always find some way to get things done."

"That's the truth," Sue smiled. "Lord knows how sometimes."

"Yeah, well . . . maybe things'll quiet down now at the office, and I'll get some time with J.T. out on the river."

Sue France gazed up at the silent mountains. "Well," she said, "let's hope so."

3

Moonlight Basin

July 15, 1984

THEY MUST HAVE MADE A STRANGE PROCESSION THROUGH the tangled lodgepole forest, but there was no human present to observe their progress. The blond youth took the lead, with Kari stumbling along beside him on her short tether. Behind them, the old man guarded the rear, his rifle unslung as he scanned the trees.

Once they had crested the ridge, Kari saw that their route seemed to lead almost due north, paralleling the Jack Creek Trail toward the drainage called the Moonlight Basin. But, five minutes later she could no longer be certain of their direction because the timber was so thick. The dense geometry of the deadfalls cross-hatched the view around her, combining with the uneven terrain of ridges and draws to prevent easy orientation.

This difficult country did not seem to bother the two men, however. They picked their way skillfully through the tangled brush, avoiding open areas where the ground looked soft and they might leave obvious tracks. The ridge sloped into a hollow, and they negotiated an especially difficult area of deadfalls. On the far side, a small grassy swamp marked the course of a stream. Kari felt that they were getting further from any trail or logging road as they crossed this thicket. Soon it would not matter if they left tracks because they would be so far into the trailless country that no search party would ever find her. She also realized that every delay she could cause would increase her chances of eventual rescue. It was after three o'clock now, and Bob Schaap would no doubt start a search for her within two hours.

Kari dug in her cleats, scuffing a mole mound. She breathed heavily, as if winded by the trek from the lake. "Can we . . . can we sit down a minute and talk about this?"

The old man was beside her. His face was mottled from the exertion of the climb, and he seemed almost relieved to be stopping. "Sure," he said. "We'll get a drink of water."

Again they repeated the awkward process of unlashing the line from the boy's wrist. Kari now knew that the young man was named Danny, but she had no clue as to the old man's identity. Once the packs were off, the old man scanned the green circle of the swamp and pointed out a shallow pond, twenty yards to the left.

Handing the line to Danny, he strode toward the pond, unconcerned that he was leaving clear boot tracks in the soft ground. "I'll get some water."

Kari stared at the sluggish stream, at the gummy compost of the swampbed. "Don't you worry about drinking the water?" The question was obvious to her. Most of these swamps were infected with protozoan parasites, especially the debilitating giardia.

The old man stopped. "Why worry about the water?"

"Well," she said, trying to sound sincerely concerned, "you can get very sick from drinking the water up here . . . from giardia."

As she spoke, the old man assumed an expression of annoyance. "Oh, no, no, no," he scolded, shaking his head impatiently. "We don't worry about that kind of thing."

He was wrong, of course, but she saw that there was no sense arguing with him. This man was a tyrant, even about something as obvious as infected swamp water. When he answered her, it was as if she had had no right even to comment about conditions in these mountains, as if, somehow, he and the boy were specially privileged. They did what they pleased up here, when it pleased them to do it, and that included shooting game out of season, drinking bad water . . . and taking any woman who happened to come along the trail.

When each man had gone to drink, Kari kept her place, seated on the grass. The longer she stalled them, the greater her chance at rescue. "Look," she finally said, "you really do plan on raping me, don't you?"

"No, no, no," the old man insisted, impatiently shaking his head. "That's not what we're interested in at all."

He spoke in normal tones. "We just want a female to be with us in the mountains, that's all." He sounded as if his demand was absolutely justified, as if they deserved to have a female to share their weird life.

Danny had already pulled on his pack. Once more, it was he who was most concerned about making their way deeper into the forest. "Come on," he said, "we'd better keep moving because we're not very far from the lake yet."

The old man rose from his squat and dragged on his own pack, then jerked Kari to her feet. Her right hand was puffy blue and her wrist numb from the tightly hitched line. "Could you, you know . . . loosen the line a little? It's getting very uncomfortable."

28

"No, no, no," the old man muttered. "She'll be able to wiggle away from us."

Once more, Kari literally dug in her heels, both to show her resistance and to leave clear tracks in the swampbed. "You know people are going to start looking for me," she said, not trying to hide her outrage, "so I don't understand why you guys are keeping me. They are going to find me."

The old man spun on her, his own stubborn anger obvious now. "You just better keep quiet," he hissed. "If anyone comes up on us that's looking for you—" He shook his head, his eyes hot. "—or anyone just happens to walk into our camp, we'll shoot them." He thrust his face close to hers. "Anyone tries to rescue you or comes up on us, we'll shoot them, understand? We'll kill them."

Before Kari could answer, they tugged the line, dragging her forward into the dense timber.

After ten minutes crisscrossing the ridgetop and clawing through draws choked with young fir and deadfalls, Kari was more confused about their route. The sun was behind the shoulder of Lone Mountain, so they now moved in the shadows of the higher ridges. Mosquitoes and sticky buffalo flies were a nasty presence. But she was more preoccupied with what lay ahead when they reached the "camp" about which the old man had spoken.

There were more snaking mole tunnels right before her. Without obviously looking down, Kari kicked the clods aside and ground her distinctive cleat marks into the exposed earth. To any experienced search team, such a track would be like her signature.

"Hey!" the old man shouted from behind her. "Let's stop that right now. Remember what I said. You really don't want any of your friends finding you. We'll shoot anybody who comes after you."

He scuffed aside her footprints and churned up the dry mole mound with his rifle butt, as if an animal had been rooting for the mole. "You watch her now, Danny," he called. "We don't want her doing that."

The boy yanked on the line, cutting her wrist as she lurched ahead into the brush.

Only a few hundred yards further along the ridge, the old man called a halt. "I'm getting dizzy," he muttered, removing his greasy hat. "We'd better set here for awhile."

Indeed, he did look pale and queasy, his blue eyes sunken deeper into his bony face. He breathed slowly, as if his chest pained him.

Beside her, the boy looked anxiously back along the route they had traveled.

After dumping his pack, the old man wiped the sweat from his face with his sleeve and flopped to the ground. "Kind of dizzy," he repeated to Danny. "Don't know what's wrong with me all of a sudden."

"Well," the boy began, "how far you figure we can travel today?"

They spoke in seemingly calm terms about the best way to thwart a search team, discussing Kari as if she were a piece of burdensome, but valuable equipment they'd been entrusted to move across these mountains.

"So," the old man concluded, "camp the night up ahead there, then cross the logging road real early before any hikers are on it. Then we can just head on up toward the Jack Creek cache."

Danny wriggled his shoulders in his packstraps. "Well, come on," he said. "Let's keep moving."

But the old man still seemed winded, dizzy.

Kari took the opportunity to delay them again. "How far will we have to go tomorrow?"

The boy smirked, as if her question was predictably stupid.

"Oh," the old man said, considering the question, "sometimes we travel thirty, forty miles on a good day. I'll tell you one thing, we sure want to get you far away from here, if there really are gonna be people out looking for you."

"Can you actually travel forty miles in one day?"

Again, the boy smirked at her question, but the old man treated it seriously. "Well, we've lived up here for a few years and we know this country real well. We know how to travel, too. We've got our caches buried here and there, and we've got some real nice camps . . . winter or summer. Got one big old hole in the ground that's real comfortable. You can sit out a blizzard in there and never be cold. There's gardens and extra gear . . . you'll be surprised how well we live in these mountains."

"Yeah," the boy volunteered, "we don't have to go down much for supplies, just once and awhile to Ennis or Big Sky."

"You . . . you shoot your meat?" She was pleased to be stalling them so well and wanted to keep the conversation moving.

"Nothing at all wrong with shooting your own meat in the mountains," the old man said emphatically. "Those game laws are just for the bureaucrats. People have been living in the mountains a long time before they started the laws . . ." He glared at her with his chill blue eyes. "We don't take anything we don't need."

Around them, the forest was deeper in shadow. In a

31

few hours it would be dark and they would have her in their camp.

Ten minutes later, they pushed their way through some dense beetle-kill lodgepoles, and Kari let her bright terry cloth headband fall to the ground.

Almost without breaking stride, the old man bent to scoop up the red band and thrust it into the pocket of his stained work trousers. "Danny," he called, "you gotta keep your eye on her better than that."

Kari stared back at the old man and he spoke with slow, menacing tones. "You shouldn't be doing that kind of thing, Sue." He shook his head in disgust. "Someone might find us. Remember, one of your rescuers might just walk in on us, and we'll shoot him."

It was probably after six when they made camp. But Kari had no way of telling the exact time because they had confiscated her watch during their last rest. She'd been able to convince them to shift the nylon tether to her left wrist, and, during the transfer, she had dropped her digital watch to the pine-needle floor of the forest. But, as with the headband, the old man had instantly discovered her ploy and had again warned her against leaving behind "clues."

Kari was surprised at their choice of camp. They had come down a wide draw, choked with deadfall, following a mossy streambed. Ahead, there was a low hummock that dominated the draw. All around, the forest was dense lodgepole and spruce. Once again, the combination of uneven terrain within the larger land form of the draw, as well as the confused angles of the naked gray deadfall trunks, made easy orientation impossible. But instead of seeking out the natural camouflage of the thickets, the two men dragged her up to the small grassy clearing on the rise above the stream.

"Looks fine to me," the old man said, eagerly dropping his pack. He glanced around the open rise and pointed to a tall lodgepole behind him. "Let's chain her to this tree."

Kari wasn't certain she had actually heard the word "chain," but then she saw the old man retrieve a heavy dog chain from his pack. At the end of the chain hung a thick brass padlock.

But they were almost blasé about chaining her; obviously, they had discussed this practicality, and the actual act of chaining a human being as they would a dog or a domestic animal did not seem to affect them. With a sense of bizarre unreality, Kari found herself standing in her jogging shorts and her old blue T-shirt, her back to the rough bark of a tall pine, a thumb-thick chain wrapped about her waist and the tree. She was somewhere up on the Moonlight Drainage, she imagined, but, given the thick timber and the confusing lie of the land, she might just as well be in the middle of the Amazon jungle.

The chain around her waist was not a work chain, a normal woodsman's tool. They had bought this chain and lock specifically to chain a prisoner. Maybe they'd used it before, on other young women, girls they'd taken back here to rape and murder.

While she watched, the two men set to work constructing their spartan camp. The old man unloaded sooty plastic food canisters from his pack and began mixing biscuit batter in a greasy, fire-blackened skillet. While he worked at this chore, the boy stooped into a hollow thicket of small Christmas tree firs across from her and began smoothing the pine needle floor of the alcove into a soft sleeping platform.

When Danny finished with the sleeping chamber, he strode around the nearby trees, snapping off the dead lower branches people called "squaw wood." This would burn with a hot, smokeless flame and quickly produce cooking embers.

Danny took out a stained and patched mosquito net and rummaged deeper in his pack. "Here," he said, offering Kari what appeared to be a rolled-up magazine.

She leaned forward to take it, slightly wary of the offer. When she unrolled the tattered book, she found herself staring at the idiotic grin of Alfred E. Neuman. Danny had given her a *Mad* magazine to read. Silently, she leafed through the pages.

The sun had disappeared now, even from the surrounding treetops. Kari was cold; the sweat had stiffened on her T-shirt, and the mosquitoes were nasty again. Near her feet, the old man squatted on his haunches, tending the coals around his biscuit skillet. The young man had been gone ten minutes, stalking a mule deer they'd heard crossing the stream forty yards below their camp. To Kari, it seemed fundamentally cruel to kill a two-hundred-pound animal, just to provide them a few pounds of meat. But the old man had dogmatically insisted that they had a right to "kill any animal that we want to eat."

A few minutes later, they heard a shot, and then a large animal thrashed through the brush to their left, down the draw from the camp. Danny reappeared, his rifle slung, muttering that he had "just grazed" the doe, and that she had gotten away.

Neither man seemed at all concerned about tracking down the wounded animal. Instead they squatted before her and ate their wedges of scorched biscuit. Kari had worked the chain down the tree trunk, so that she could sit. She clutched the burnt crust of her biscuit, pretending to pick at the soggy interior.

The two men made domestic small talk as they chewed their food, but Kari did not join the conversation.

Then they heard the distant shout, a faraway human voice, faint but unmistakable.

Instantly, the old man was on his feet, scuffing out the fire with his boot sole. Danny grabbed his rifle and knelt at the far side of the camp clearing, peering intently toward the hidden ridge from which the yell seemed to have come. When the fire was dead, the old man took his rifle from its green nylon case and cocked the action.

He approached Kari and spoke again in a low, threatening voice. "You just better hope that's not about you." Because if anybody tried to come in here after her, he said, they would shoot him.

Sometime later, they heard the airplane. It was flying low, a single-engine plane, circling the surrounding ridges. Although the sun was hidden by the flank of Lone Mountain to the southwest, there was probably still enough light for an airborne observer to spot them in the clearing. As the plane circled lower and closer, the two men showed their first real apprehension.

The old man seized Kari's wrists again, while Danny unchained her. Then they pushed her under the cover of the low firs that sheltered the sleeping alcove. When the aircraft pressed nearer, they threw their sleeping bags and packs into the hollow of fir trees after her.

"You must be pretty important," the old man called from his hiding place at the edge of the clearing. "They already got a plane out looking for you."

"Yes, I am," Kari called back, letting defiance ring through her voice. "And there's going to be a lot of people out looking for me."

"Makes no difference to us," he answered from the shadows. "Anybody finds you with us, they get themselves shot."

Kari crouched in the dark thicket, listening to the airplane.

Mosquitoes tormented the darkness. The moon was rising, but did not cast enough light for Kari to see much detail around her. It had been a long time since she'd heard the airplane or the distant calls of the search team. They had chained her back to the tree when the airplane flew away, and sometime later Danny had given her a long-sleeved shirt and a pair of wool socks to ward off the chill.

When the sky was truly dark, they offered her a musty green sleeping bag to pull around her legs. She sat now with her back to the tree trunk, the chain biting tight around her waist.

The old man spread the second sleeping bag on the pine needles inside the alcove. "Might as well turn in," he called. "It's too dark for anything now."

Kari found herself exchanging an involuntary chorus of "good nights," just as if this were some family camping trip. She sat, stiff and uncomfortable, the bark scraping her back, the stones bruising her legs through the thin sleeping bag. After the two men had bedded down beneath their mosquito netting, she struggled to test the chain and the lock one more time. It was no good; she was securely chained to this tree, like a heifer to the slaughterhouse rail.

Sleep was not possible. She understood that the old man and the boy were intelligent and crafty, that they were cruel and stubborn, and that they considered these mountains and everything and everybody in them to be available for their pleasure. Either they would wait until she fell asleep to spring out of that dark hollow in the firs and rape her, or they would do it in the morning. Probably, when it got light, they would just announce that it was time for her to become Danny's "female." When that happened, Kari knew, she could expect no more compassion than they'd shown to that poor wounded doe.

Later, she heard the distant whine of a trail bike, a long way off in the darkness. Someone was out there, Kari realized, searching for her along the logging roads and trails, calling her name, shining a light. But she understood with terminal sadness that no trail bike could penetrate the thick timber of this draw to find her tonight.

The branches above creaked in the chill breeze. Night birds called. Kari Swenson crouched alone, waiting through what was probably the most terrible night of her young life.

4

Ennis

July 15, 1984

THE MOON WAS BRIGHT ON THE LAKE. BUT A COOL BREEZE had risen, and the remnants of the party—"the hard core," according to Bonnie—had moved into the trailer for a nightcap.

Johnny and Sue were wedged into a molded sofa at the end of the small living room. He was still tired, but the long, relaxed meal and the company had helped him forget his obligations and workload for a few hours. They'd say their good nights here in a few minutes, and be home in bed before midnight. A good sleep, he knew, would complement the pleasant evening, and he'd be able to dig in tomorrow and face another couple weeks of eighteen-hour days.

A light rapping on the door and Linn Kreig, the co-owner of the Lake Shore Lodge, ducked inside the trailer. Linn and Kevin had just left for the lodge. Their empty brandy glasses were still on the table. "Sorry, Johnny," Linn said, brushing back her blond hair as she leaned forward to hand him a pink telephone message slip.

Johnny scanned the slip, frowning. The first call from Vicki had come in at 2200, over an hour before.

And there were two more. "Call the office. Emergency."

Linn was clearly chagrined. "They were on the answering machine . . . If anybody had been up there to answer the phone, they'd have come right down."

Johnny was already on his feet. Sue went into the trailer's small kitchen to gather up her cake pans.

"Anything serious?" Pete asked.

Again, Johnny frowned. Three calls from Vicki since ten o'clock. Merlin Ehlers, his sergeant, was on duty this weekend. Whatever was happening had to be too urgent for Merlin to handle on his own. "Yeah, well . . ." Johnny nodded to Pete, "it would appear so."

Johnny's small office at home is just off the living room. The decor is masculine and Western—antlers, gun racks, a rolltop desk, and an antique safe.

After Linn had delivered her message to him at the lake front, he had decided to go home to call Vicki. Whatever she had for him, he knew, would probably involve his contacting Merlin and other deputies. And he didn't have enough range in his car radio to reach everyone he might need. That would mean he'd have to have Vicki serve as relay, a slow, clumsy procedure that would tie up the dispatcher's radio channel in an emergency.

There was another reason, which neither Sue nor he had discussed on the fast drive back from the lake to Ennis, but which they both understood. Johnny's heavy guns were at home. Off duty, he only carried a small .38 snubnose. His .45 automatic and his long-barreled .44 magnum hung in their holsters from the mounted steer horns above his desk. Any situation that merited three emergency calls might well require a bigger gun than his .38 snubnose.

Out of long practice, Sue went straight to the kitchen and put on the coffee pot. Johnny opened his rolltop desk, got out his yellow pad, and called the office. It was just after midnight, so he wrote 7/16/84 on the top of the sheet.

"What you got, Vicki?"

"Johnny," she replied, with obvious relief. "I'm glad I got you. This place has been kind of crazy."

Johnny frowned, waiting for the bad news.

"An ATL," Vicki said, her voice going flat as she got down to business. An ATL was an "attempt to locate" a missing person in layman's parlance. "White female, twenty-three. Up at Big Sky. First call came from Gallatin County Sheriff's office at . . . 1943."

He made brief notes as he listened.

"Gallatin County got a call from Bob Schaap, owner of the Lone Mountain Ranch with an ATL on a girl named Carrie Swenson—"

"Could you spell that, please?"

"C-a-r-r-i-e. She's a summer waitress, very reliable, he told Gallatin County. She was jogging up around Beehive Basin. Left after lunch for a couple hours' run, and didn't show up for work at 1700."

"Okay," Johnny muttered, taking notes. "What else?"

"Mr. Schaap found her car, a green Subaru station wagon, at the Jack Creek trailhead. Locked, just like she'd left it. He's got some men from the ranch up there now with radios, searching for her."

Sue brought in a steaming mug of coffee and Johnny nodded his thanks as he took it. "Okay, Vicki," he repeated, "I'm listening."

"I called Jay Cosgrove at . . . 1945. He said he'd talk to Mr. Schaap and get back to us."

Johnny could visualize the whole area on a mental map. The Big Sky resort area was just inside the

Madison County line. But, because the resort lay on the other side of the mountains from Ennis and Virginia City, until recently Madison County had contracted out law enforcement for the area to the Gallatin Sheriff's Department in Bozeman, but for the past year, Johnny's own resident deputy had been living right there at Big Sky. As Vicki recited the facts of the case, it became clear to Johnny that there was a minor jurisdictional hassle building. Bob Schaap was used to doing business with Gallatin County, not with Jay Cosgrove, the Madison County resident deputy.

"So," Vicki continued, "Jay called back at 2006. I'm afraid there's been a grizzly sighting in the area where the girl was supposed to be jogging. He said that the ranch has quite a few men out searching. He planned to cover all the logging roads with his patrol vehicle, then switch over to his trailbike to get up the back trails and cover more country."

Johnny made a quick note. Jay Cosgrove was an old friend. He knew the area well; he was quiet and dependable, and could take charge without waiting for detailed instructions. He was not worried about Jay. But this business of "quite a few men" from Lone Mountain Ranch up there searching in the dark might be a problem, especially if they were armed and nervous about that grizzly sighting.

"At 2158," Vicki continued, reading from her communications log, "Jay called back. There's been no sign of the girl. There seems to be about a dozen men searching on foot, four or five on horseback, and a few on trailbikes. Jay requests a regular search and rescue effort from the Madison side."

"I got all that," Johnny said. "What else?"

Vicki sighed, and Johnny knew there must be some complications. "Twenty-two thirty-one, I got a call from John Palmer, the assistant fire chief of Big Sky.

He's their search and rescue coordinator, and he wanted to know what was happening up there on the mountain. He'd seen all the activity, and—"

"Nobody bothered to tell him, right?" Johnny could see the problem unfolding.

"Right," Vicki answered. "Anyway, he got himself informed on what was going on, and he says that he'll be able to assist with a search at dawn. He's got a regular team from the Gallatin side and a good communications setup."

"Okay," Johnny said. "I know him."

"At 2250," Vicki continued, "Mr. Palmer called again. Seems the Lone Mountain Ranch got ahold of him and wants him to organize the search and rescue effort in the morning. I told him that we have Merlin Ehlers already coordinating our team for a morning effort, and he said he'd call Merlin."

He heard Vicki turn a page and sigh again. Things must be getting even more complicated. "Mr. Palmer couldn't get through to Merlin because Merlin's phone just went out of order. So I copied a message for Merlin about the airplane they had up today. Civil Air Patrol, pilot named Norm Wortman from Gallatin Field."

"Fine," Johnny said. "What else is there?"

"Mr. Schaap himself called at . . . let's see . . . 2352. He says he's now been in touch with Jay, and that he'll have a couple of tracking dogs available at 0400. I told him that we would be coordinating a regular search and rescue effort from this office and that you'd probably have people up there at first light."

"Is that it?" Johnny already had his Search and Rescue file open and was ticking off the telephone numbers of those men he knew were in town.

"That's about it," Vicki said. "Oh yeah, I finally got ahold of Merlin by phone and relayed all this to him. I said you'd probably be calling."

"Real good," Johnny said. "I'll take it from here." It was after midnight now. His new work week had begun.

By 1:00 A.M. Johnny had contacted his key deputies and the leaders of the Madison County Search and Rescue team. He called for a 6:15 meeting at Bettie's Cafe with Robin Shipman and Steve Powell, two of his best mountain riders.

Even before he'd heard Vicki's full report, Johnny had decided against trying to activate a search and rescue effort before daylight. Johnny had been raised in the foothills of the Madison Range. He had ridden the high summer pastures above Jack Creek many times as a kid, searching out stray cattle. He'd hunted all those drainages for deer and elk since he'd been ten years old. And, since he'd been in law enforcement, he had searched that same wild country several times for lost hunters and campers.

One thing he had learned over the years was that night searches seldom were successful. And, often as not, members of a night search party ended up getting lost themselves. Sometimes they fell and twisted an ankle or dislocated a shoulder. Then they became a bigger problem for the team than the original victim. That country up there was so tangled, so confusing, that people were constantly getting lost in daylight, in good weather. It was never a good idea to send a bunch of men crashing off into that brush in the middle of the night.

But there was another good argument against bringing in his search team before morning. The people from Big Sky were up there right now, bushwhacking the ridges and draws. Many of them were experienced woodsmen, but others were no doubt well-meaning amateurs. And they were probably all armed against the reported bear threat. As any hunter could tell you, a man crashing around that thick timber, or worse, a man on horseback, looked a lot like a grizzly on a moonlit night, especially if you were tired and nervous. Add that risk to the danger of an accidental fall down a rockslide in the dark. His decision was obvious.

Some people might not understand; they might want to charge up there come hell or high water to find the girl, but Johnny had learned a lot about making considered, responsible decisions since taking office three years earlier.

You couldn't please everybody all the time, and you were probably going to get criticized, no matter what you did. So you might just as well do the right thing and get on with your life.

Easier said than done.

Johnny hunched over the phone on his rolltop desk. Jay Cosgrove would call if they found her. Johnny just did not like the idea of that damned bear. This time of year, a sow grizzly probably had cubs with her, either newly weaned winter cubs or, worse, yearlings she was about to turn loose. A sow bear like that would attack in a wink.

Again he scowled. All the more reason not to send out the search team in the dark. Bears were active feeders on a moonlit night. If one of his people spooked a cub and treed it, there'd be hell to pay, no doubt about it.

But . . . Johnny drank more coffee, and his stomach churned. All his life, he'd been plagued with a bad stomach. Maybe it was the hard times he had known as a kid, losing his mother when he was only four, and coming to live with his Uncle Joe and Aunt Eva on the Six Bar Nine, a poor enough little place, even with those high beef prices during the war. Maybe it was a childhood of venison and red beans, seven days a week.

Maybe it was sharing adult worries, taking things so seriously, even as a small kid.

Johnny grinned. Sue always said he was the funniest serious person she'd ever known. That was a pretty fair way to describe him, he had to admit, a friendly, smiling kind of a guy who was real no-doubt-about-it serious, just beneath the surface. And the one aspect of his life that Johnny took most seriously was his sense of duty, the weight of responsibility. You learned that on a ranch, and you learned it young.

When Johnny's aunt and uncle had moved down to a bigger place in Wyoming, he was twelve. He stayed back to live as a foster child with Forrest and Betsy Shirley on the Cold Springs Ranch. They were making a go, year by year, but everybody had to pull his share of the load. Horses and cattle did not take weekends off or give you a summer vacation. If you kept livestock, you became responsible. A cow and her calf were a serious investment. They represented your future, your ability to survive, to maintain an independent life on the land.

And life, Johnny learned long before he acquired the strength and height of a man, was a real serious business.

If that girl was dead up there, or worse, if she was now dying, mauled by the grizzly, alone in some draw where the bear had chased her . . . Well, then he, the sheriff of Madison County, who had the final decision on dispatching the search and rescue team, would undoubtedly take the blame for not having done his duty. And, Lord knew, there were plenty of self-proclaimed wilderness experts on both sides of the mountains who would line up to blast him, if this girl Carrie had gotten herself killed by the bear.

The Madison Range, like all the subranges of the Montana Rockies, had attracted a strange mix of people in the past twenty years. There were unreconstructed hippies, recluse Vietnam vets living on disability checks and marijuana, and all manner of rich Easterners who had followed Chet Huntley's lead to Big Sky and were now buying up ranch and timber country at a crazy pace. There was no shortage of righteous environmentalists, either, with postage-stamp ranches and fat monthly checks from Merrill Lynch who claimed their vision of range and forest management was the only way the mountains could be saved—and anybody who disputed them was a Neanderthal fascist.

And then, there were some downright dangerous people up there, too. Recently, Johnny had received FBI bulletins on right-wing and neo-Nazi groups, reported to be building fortified survivalist "compounds" in the wilderness areas of the mountain West. Outfits like the Posse Commitatus and a lunatic group called "The Order" were said to have formed alliances with the Klan and some whacko anti-Semitic cult known as The Church of Jesus Christ, Christian. They, too, had definite ideas about how this wilderness should be used. And to them, any law enforcement officer who tried to interfere was "an agent of the satanic Jews who controlled America."

If that weird bunch wasn't enough, Johnny had heard stories of some old boys living alone in shacks or abandoned mine shafts up above the canyons, poaching game and stealing an occasional calf, taking the odd potshot at anybody invading their "territory." Sleep was going to be hard tonight. It was not going to be easy to relax, thinking of that poor kid up there, alone in the forest.

5

Moonlight Basin

July 16, 1984, Dawn

ROBBER JAYS SCOLDED AS THE SUNLIGHT TOUCHED THE treetops. On the forest floor, the shadows were deep and chill. Kari tried to slouch lower into the musty sleeping bag bunched around her hips, but the chain cut into her waist. She hunched there in the cold, exhausted from the sleepless night.

In the hollow beneath the firs, the old man dozed under the green sleeping bag. Half an hour before, Danny had left camp with his rifle in search of "meat for breakfast."

Neither man had tried to touch her in the night.

Despite her cramped limbs and the numbness of her shoulders, Kari remained quiet. There was no sense struggling against the chain and attracting the old man's attention. Every minute that he dozed and the boy scouted the forest for deer, the rescue team would be drawing closer.

Kari gazed up at the soft sunlight on the pine boughs and tried to judge the time. By dawn, she knew, her mother and father would have joined the search. There would be forest rangers, the sheriff's people, and lots of volunteers from Big Sky. If the searchers found her now, with the old man still in bed and the boy away from camp, there might be no more violence. But if . . .

The old man rose to an elbow, then thrust aside the folds of the sleeping bag. He called a cheerful greeting, and Kari replied in neutral tones. While he knelt, folding the sleeping bag, he made jolly conversation, again offering the bizarre assurance he had the previous afternoon.

"When all this is over, Sue, just think what great stories you'll have to tell your grandchildren. This is a real adventure."

Kari nodded, but did not reply. If he thought this was an "adventure," he was crazier than the boy.

"How old are you, Sue?"

"Twenty-two."

He frowned. "Oh, well . . . I was hoping for an older woman for my son."

Now she understood the resemblance between the two, and the similarity of their two voices. "Well, why don't you just let me go, if I'm too young?"

He busied himself with the bedding. "No, we're just gonna keep you, and maybe you'll decide on one of us."

A snapping rustle to her right. Danny appeared among the deadfalls, carefully picking his way up the rise toward camp. He carried his rifle in both hands, and she saw no sign of game. As he worked his way through the tangled timber, a pine squirrel chattered shrilly overhead. Without hesitation, Danny raised his rifle, sighted on the treetops and fired. A moment later, a small auburn squirrel tumbled limply onto the pine needles, twenty feet to her right.

Kari was surprised. She knew a lot about rifles and marksmanship; it could not have been easy to hit such a tiny target fifty feet above the ground. But even more surprising was the casual attitude of the boy as he fired his rifle . . . right there at the edge of camp. Either he didn't realize search parties were out, or he simply did not care. And now the old man was pulling on his boots, just as calm as could be. The shot obviously hadn't alarmed him very much, either.

He rose and stretched, then strolled to Danny to examine the dead squirrel.

"Well," the old man called, "let's go see how your woman's doing this morning."

He paused. "I think we ought to move camp under those trees." He pointed to the right, down the grassy rise to a cluster of lodgepoles and large spruce with overhanging boughs. "Better cover over there, in case anybody comes along."

"Okay," Danny answered, hefting the squirrel in his open hand. "Let's get her up and move her over there."

Kari remained silent while they unsnapped the lock and looped the chain back around her waist, this time with the chain's free end doubled through the end ring. She really was being treated like an animal now, Danny leading the way down through the jumble of deadfalls and the old man taking up the rear like a careful herdsman. Kari's legs and shoulders were stiff as she worked her way across the uneven ground. They crossed the soggy moss of the creekbed and climbed again to the level shelf where they planned to pitch the new camp.

In the new clearing she saw that the fir did, indeed, provide excellent cover. The drooping boughs formed a dense conical roof that effectively hid any detail on the ground from aerial observation.

Wordlessly, Danny found the padlock key and motioned for Kari to sit. The ground was a level bed of dry, springy needles. A dead trunk lay against the far side of the tree. A blow-down lodgepole as thick as Kari's arm had fallen at an angle atop the pine trunk.

Kari went to one knee, and Danny looped the free end of the chain around the thin trunk of the dead lodgepole, then snapped the padlock. They handed her the loosely bundled sleeping bag, and she drew the folds up her bare legs against the chill.

While Danny cleaned the squirrel at the stream to Kari's left, the old man ferried down the gear from their overnight camp. Once again, they did not seem concerned about any search team as they chatted back and forth, discussing whether they should travel further, or wait for darkness before moving on.

When he had skinned the squirrel, Danny rolled three large stones from the streambed and built a fire ring. As he had the night before, he built his fire from dry squaw wood twigs to prevent a telltale smoke plume. The old man entered the clearing and took Danny to one side.

But Kari could hear their words. "We gotta do something about those red shorts of hers," the old man said. "They're just too bright, too easy to spot from the air."

Kari went chill inside. Her mouth was dry and once more her limbs trembled. If they took away her shorts, they would rape her. What else would be on their minds at a time like that?

"Let me have your shorts," the old man commanded, reaching down with his bony hand.

Again, Kari protested. "You're going to rape me, aren't you?"

The old man shook his head violently. "No, no, no, no . . . no."

Kari had no choice; she was chained to the deadfall and unable even to sit properly, let alone stand or run.

She pulled the sleeping bag as high as she could and slid off her red jogging shorts.

The old man bunched them in his hand and strode back toward their camp on the rise.

Kari forced herself lower in the sleeping bag, acutely aware of her vulnerability.

Danny knelt only three feet away, calmly feeding dry twigs to the fire.

Kari's exhaustion and fear had reached a terminal point. "Why don't you just turn me loose?" she begged, hot tears coming now for the first time. "You really don't want to get involved with anything like this."

Danny shook his head stubbornly, but did not answer.

"I'm married," Kari sobbed. "I love my husband, and I don't want to be with you. Any chance I get, I'm going to leave."

"No, no," Danny muttered, shaking his head just like his father.

"Please turn me loose."

"No, I won't let you go," he said, again shaking his head. "I want to keep you for myself."

The old man strode back down the rise, carrying her jogging shorts. "Here," he said, bending over her. "They're a lot better now."

He had done a thorough job. Using charcoal from the dinner fire, he'd blackened the bright shorts both inside and out, muting the Day-Glo red to a dull ocher. Kari snatched back the shorts and tucked the fold of the sleeping bag as high above her waist as the chain allowed. It was hard to move her feet and legs inside the bag. Her cleats no doubt snagged on the shorts' mesh liner, and she probably realized they were watching her.

They all heard the dry rustling from the thick timber to the right of camp. Kari swung inside the sleeping bag to get a better view. As she did, the two men grabbed their weapons. Danny had his .22 pistol out of the holster, and the old man gripped his hunting rifle. At the far edge of the clearing, Kari saw a stocky, suntanned young man in a red-and-black lumberjack shirt, kneeling in the tall grass.

Kari did not hesitate. "Watch out!" she screamed. "They'll shoot." The old man spun to face her, but Kari did not stop. "They'll kill you. Don't come in . . . they've got guns."

"Stop right there!" Danny yelled, using both hands to aim the pistol at the kneeling man.

"Is this the girl you're looking for?" the old man called.

"Yes," the man called. "We're looking for her."

"Don't come in!" Kari screamed. "Watch out! They'll kill you."

The old man's face was mottled with fear and anger. "Shut her up, Danny," he yelled, turning to level his rifle at the stranger. "Just shut her up."

When Danny turned back to confront Kari, his eyes were loose with panic. He stumbled toward her, his pistol extended.

Still Kari screamed her warning to the rescuer. "Watch out . . . don't come in, they'll . . ." Danny jerked the cocking slide of the automatic, as if to menace her, and the pistol cracked.

The bullet pounded Kari against the log with the force of a club. Her right side went numb and the bright morning forest around her began to fade to shades of gray.

From her left, another voice called. "Don't shoot. Don't shoot. I'm not a bear."

"I shot her," Danny yelled. "Oh, I didn't mean to shoot her."

"Help me," Kari called, her voice suddenly very small. "Help me, I've been shot." All color was washing from her vision. She realized with ultimate horror that she was badly wounded, that she would die in this terrible forest.

The voices above her echoed, as if the men were calling to her through a dark cave.

"We need some help here," Danny shouted. "The girl's been shot."

"Shut up, Danny," the old man yelled again, his voice hoarse with rage and fear. "Everyone stay out of this camp."

Kari thrashed in the sleeping bag, her right arm hanging awkwardly at her side. She was shot through the right chest, and the bullet had numbed her entire right torso. There was movement above her, and more voices. But the sound echoed badly now, and her vision was darkening with each breath.

Now a young man with a ginger mustache hung above her, reaching down to lift the T-shirt neck from the wound. His face looked familiar. He was from Big Sky. There were rescuers in camp. They had come to help her. But something was very wrong here. The old man had his rifle pointing squarely at the blond rescuer's back as the young man stooped to help her.

Once more the old man turned to level his rifle at the clearing to the left. "I hope you don't have any weapons on you," he yelled.

Kari heard no answer.

Someone was telling her that she'd be okay. Someone was turning her gently, lifting the sticky blue fabric of the T-shirt away from her chest. The world grew darker around her. Kari forced herself more upright.

She would not just give in to the darkness. As she gazed around her she saw Danny and the blond rescuer, leaning close. But they seemed to be high above her, as if peering down from ladders.

"Al," the blond rescuer yelled, "call for help. We need some help."

"Shut up!" the old man shouted.

Now another voice echoed through the twilight. It was the first rescuer, the man in the lumberjack shirt. Her vision steadied and grew bright again. She could see and hear.

"Drop your guns," the rescuer called. He was half hidden behind a thick lodgepole at the edge of the camp clearing. The tree had a large curved snag like a giant's longbow rising along its right side, and the man's plaid shirt was visible between the snag and the trunk. "You're surrounded by two hundred men. You can't get away."

To her left, the old man was swinging his rifle back and forth. Now the blond rescuer was on his feet, his hands raised. "Everything's cool," the blond shouted. "Nobody's gonna get hurt. We don't want any more gunplay."

The blond turned to face the old man, but he stepped back to take cover behind a tree directly across the clearing from Kari. For a splintered moment everybody seemed to shout and move at once. But Kari had a clear view of the old man.

He pressed close to the tree, raised his rifle, sighted down the scope and fired.

The shot stunned everyone into silence. No one moved. Then the blond dashed toward the snag tree. "Al!" he screamed. "Oh, my God . . . Al . . ."

Kari thrashed to her left, straining to see the first rescuer. But all she saw was empty forest.

Movement above her. Danny and his father bent close, but their faces were fading into gray again.

"She's gonna die," Danny moaned.

"No, no, no . . . She's not going to die. I've seen lots of these wounds. That's no big deal."

They bent even closer. Hands fumbled, and she felt the chain dragged free from her back. Straining to clear her vision, she realized that they were jamming their gear into their packs, that they were breaking camp. A deep, waxy chill spread now through her body. She knew that she was going into shock. "You're just leaving me here, aren't you?" Neither man answered. "At least let me have the sleeping bag," Kari pleaded.

They did not reply. Instead, they raised the foot of the bag, flopping her roughly to the damp forest floor. The young man lifted her slightly by her naked hips and pulled the shorts up to her waist. She thrashed now against the mounting pain. There was another blur of movement, and she heard them trudging out of camp, down the streambed to her left.

Kari Swenson lay alone, bleeding steadily into the springy pine needles. The world dulled again to gray, cold, fuzzy gray. Somewhere to her right, a voice squawked on a radio. "Al . . . call for help," the rescuer had shouted. If she could crawl to that radio . . .

It was no good. Her strength was gone, frozen by the crushing chill. She couldn't breathe. There was hot pain inside her numb chest, like a dentist's drill beneath the novacaine. The cold seeped into her body like a fluid. She had to get warm or she knew that shock would take her. Maybe Al was not badly wounded, maybe they could work out some plan together.

But first she needed warmth. Rolling numbly, Kari forced herself the three feet to the stone fire ring. She grabbed blindly for a handful of pine needles, dumped them onto the black ashes and tried to blow. No air entered her lungs. She could not breathe. Instead of normal breath, she heard a liquid suction under her T-shirt that terrified her. She was shot through the lungs, she now realized with awful finality. With a wound like this, she would not survive very long, especially if she slipped into shock.

She had to conserve her body's heat. Rising as high as she could, Kari tried to scan the clearing. She couldn't be sure, but there seemed to be a pair of boots in the grass and wild flowers at the base of the snag tree.

That would be Al. He made no sound. The boots did not move.

Mosquitoes and ants swarmed the wet folds of her T-shirt. They had come to feed on her blood. In their mindless efficiency, the insects had congregated to harvest this dying creature, just as the beetles processed the damaged pines. But Kari was not a tree, not a creature; she was an intelligent, vital human being. Danny and his father had left her to die, alone in this tangled forest. She would not give them that satisfaction.

To her right, she saw a lumpy gray shape. She thrashed in the cold twilight. A large backpack formed under her chill fingers. Maybe there was another radio. It took a long time to drag open the pack and paw through the contents.

There was no radio. But Kari found a down sleeping bag with a shiny red lining. She also discovered a plastic canteen of lemonade and a candy bar in a foil wrapper. Using all her strength, Kari slid her legs inside the bag and wriggled toward the sunny spot at the base of the tree from which the old man had fired. Blood was pooling under her T-shirt. Liquid, she thought, she had to replace the fluids she was losing through hemorrhage. Shock was her mortal enemy. She had to fight. But now the pain was washing up inside her in hot waves. If she gave in to shock to avoid the pain, she would die.

But the forest around her, the entire world was growing so dark and cold. She had to balance herself between pain and numbing sleep. If someone did not find her soon, Kari knew with ultimate sadness, she would die here in this awful clearing.

PART 2

Manhunt

6

Madison County

July 16, 1984

JOHNNY FRANCE DROVE HIS EAGLE DOWN THE LONG incline from the Virginia City Pass. It was after eight, and he was headed from his office at the courthouse, back through Ennis, then on to the logging road in Jack Creek Canyon to join the search team. The last word he'd heard from Big Sky was that there'd still been no sign of the missing girl.

He yawned, squinting into the morning sun through the dirty windshield. Around here in the summer, it was a losing battle trying to keep your windshield washer filled, what with the dusty roads and the grasshoppers.

This stretch of highway dropped due east into the Madison Valley from the barren ridge that separated Ennis and Virginia City. Ahead the Madison Range was arrayed across the horizon like the backdrop of a Charlie Russell painting. The sun was high above Sphinx Mountain. But the cleft of Jack Creek Canyon was still in shadow, the thick lodgepole forest black from this distance. There was a lot of snow above timberline. Johnny knew, though, that it would already be hot on the logging roads and trails. Hot and buggy. In July, the mosquitoes and cloying buffalo flies drove you crazy up there. It always amazed him that people actually liked to hike that country in the summer. Spring and fall, there was no prettier place in the world, but right now, it could get downright miserable in the mountains.

Johnny had been up at dawn, after a night of worry about the missing girl. While Sue and the kids slept, he got together his personal gear for the search and sorted out the portable radios to bring to the six-fifteen meeting with Robin Shipman and Steve Powell.

Bettie's Cafe had been crowded with sleepy fishermen and their riverboat outfitters when Johnny took his place in the end booth—what Sue always called his "Ennis Office." He spread his Forest Service map between their coffee mugs on the formica tabletop and showed the two men the area he wanted them to search. Robin Shipman had his battered old horse trailer parked across the street; their horses were already saddled. Robin and Steve were experienced in mountain searches, and Johnny didn't have to explain things more than once. They both agreed that it looked like a bear attack. But none of them was inclined to dwell on the possibility. Like Johnny, they'd been involved the previous summer in the search for the bear incident victim down near Quake Lake when a grizzly pulled a camper from his tent one night and dragged him off into the forest. When they finally found the man the next day, he was dead. The press and TV made quite a thing about that. But the word had not gotten out very far that the bear had eaten over sixty pounds of the man's flesh.

Now, in the cool sunrise of a Monday in July, Johnny and two of his best mountain riders had to grimly accept the probability that they had another gory recovery job waiting for them before the day was done.

Maybe it was the sleepless night, maybe his worry about the missing girl, but Johnny found himself staring at the familiar breakfast crowd in Bettie's as if he'd never been there before. Most of the trout fishermen were Easterners, middle-age men with money. It wasn't considered polite anymore to say "dudes." "Out-of-stater" was the currently accepted epithet. The deeply tanned outfitters and the quiet, efficient women waiting on tables, of course, were locals. Johnny called everyone by his first name. This morning, he couldn't help but see the difference between his neighbors and the visiting fishermen.

The people from out of state came here to have fun. For them, Montana was a place of amusement. You could play here. For a few weeks each year, you could become a fisherman, or a cowboy, or a hunter of large animals. When your vacation was over, you could return to the supposedly serious world of corporate policy or malpractice suits.

Johnny stared at Steve and Robin's thick, calloused fingers and the knotted muscles of their forearms. Guiding a quarter horse up a thickly timbered slope, searching for a wounded—probably dead—girl, was what he considered serious work. Robin, for example, kept a string of pack mules in a barn right in the middle of town. Visitors thought that was colorful, real old-time West. The fact was, however, that Robin used those mules to earn a living, packing supplies for the Forest Service and provisioning hunting camps. Robin Shipman and men like him were workers, not tourist attractions. Despite the four-color brochures from the Montana tourist board, Johnny understood that the

Madison Range certainly wasn't an "all-season vacation paradise." And when things went wrong, the country required serious people, not vacationers.

For fifteen years as a law enforcement officer, Johnny had cleaned up after visitors' accidents and arguments and sometimes fatal indiscretions.

Once, he and a group of deputies had been obliged to climb Beehive Mountain with a string of mules to pack down the rotting remains of two hefty doctors whose small plane had failed to clear the summit by one hundred feet. The summer before, he'd been obliged to view the grizzly victim in the morgue. He had lifted dead tourists from the mangled remains of their cars at the bottom of mountain gorges, and he pulled their lifeless bodies from the water in Beartrap Canyon.

People came here for fun, to enjoy a manageable adventure in the recently tamed West. To them, the country was simply a composite of good trout fishing, mountain wilderness to hike, colorful locals, and cheap prices. On the Beartrap, Johnny's clients—flushed with the exhilaration of the white water—would often say they wished they could "restructure" their lives so that they could live here all year.

Johnny would answer, "Yeah, well, it's real nice summer country, but the winters here get a little long."

Behind the counter at Bettie's there was a small wooden plaque, the kind you could find in a novelty store or a truck stop. On it was a simple message:

New Incentive Plan
Work or Get Fired

Visitors laughed when they saw it, but the local ranchers who came here every morning for coffee and gossip only smiled. To them, the message was perfectly logical. The country demanded at least that much of you. A natural corollary might be:

Be Careful
Or Get Killed

And this morning, as he folded his map and sent his men on their way, Johnny knew they all had some serious, careful work to do.

Johnny downshifted for the last steep hill before the valley. Ennis was spread before him, a cluster of low buildings and dense cottonwoods. He had to stop for a minute at home to grab a pair of wool socks for his hunting boots and another battery charger for the walkie-talkies he'd just picked up from his Virginia City office. He was running late; he'd be up at Big Sky by nine.

The radio burst static, and he automatically hit the squelch button. It was Jay Cosgrove calling; his voice was excited.

"—confirm a double shooting. Repeat, two people shot. Two victims, possibly both fatal." Jay's voice slowed and Johnny could hear him take charge of his emotions. "Six-one has called for backup. Understand 25-1 is 10-85 this location—"

The transmission became garbled. Jay was calling from up in the mountains and reception was never good down here in the valley.

Instinctively, Johnny hit the gas pedal and glanced at his watch, almost exactly 8:25. He breathed deeply to overcome the initial adrenaline rush. On TV, the cops didn't get excited when they heard such reports. So much for TV. Johnny never got used to it. Never.

Jay was transmitting again, but the signal was too chopped up to understand. Johnny waited until the channel was clear and then punched his mike button to call Kim Hudson. Kim had taken over from his wife, Vicki, at seven. He was a good, steady hand in an emergency, and he'd have copied all of Jay's message.

"Kim," Johnny called, breaking formal radio procedure, "25–1, repeat the message from 25–8."

Kim's voice was overly calm. "Okay, Johnny. Jay confirms a double shooting in the search area. One witness reports the victims are the missing girl, Kari Swenson, and one search team member from Big Sky, name unknown. Copy?"

"Go ahead, Kim, I'm 10–4."

"Stand by a sec . . ." The mike clicked dead, and a few moments later Kim was back up. "Okay, I just received some land line traffic on this, too. We've got a confirmation on the victims and the suspects. Male searcher definitely fatal gunshot wound, according to the witness, a James . . . sorry, can't read the last name. And Kari Swenson, that's K-a-r-i, by the way, wounded by handgun, possibly fatal."

"What's this about suspects?" Johnny interrupted. "Did Jay report this wasn't an accident?"

"That's affirmative," Kim said calmly. "Deliberate shooting. Suspects in incident, two white males dressed in green fatigues. One light-haired, in twenties, one in forties, with gray beard. Confirmed two handguns, maybe one shotgun, maybe more rifles. You 10–4, Johnny?"

Automatically, Johnny grabbed his blue pursuit light bubble and reached out the window to snap the suction cup to the Eagle's roof. "I'm 10–4. What else is there?"

"I copied a weak transmission from 25–8 to other officers advising them to stay off the ridges and to get the search parties back in from the Ulerys Lake and Beehive Basin area."

Johnny hit the lights and siren and sped toward Ennis. His initial impulse was to bypass the town and head straight up the Jack Creek logging road to the scene. But, now he slowed, letting the relayed messages work in his mind. This was no longer a missing person search. A bear attack or accidental shooting was not the problem. There were confirmed shooting victims and at least two armed suspects. For years as a deputy, Johnny's duty would have been to rush to the scene. But now he was the sheriff, not just a deputy. He had to think through the entire tactical situation.

"What else, Kim?"

"Land line from Lone Mountain Ranch. They want a helicopter to search for the victims and evacuate them."

"Ten-four. Have you contacted Bozeman?"

Kim's voice was showing some strain now. "Johnny, Sheriff Onstad's already called in the one available chopper from Central Helicopters over there. It's 10–85 right now with Gallatin County people on board."

Johnny frowned, then tried to relax, to let the dimensions of the problem reveal themselves naturally. Big Sky was much more accessible from Bozeman than it was from the Madison Valley. It was normal for John Onstad to be on the scene already, and Johnny could not fault him for taking the initiative in ordering up that chopper. At a time like this, you didn't worry about the bureaucratic small change of county jurisdictions. But Johnny had no way of knowing for sure if the helicopter John Onstad had commandeered was equipped with a litter to evacuate the wounded girl.

He was coming up fast on the outskirts of Ennis. Then he remembered the seismograph survey outfit that had set up their trailer office next to Hickey's Motel in June. They had two choppers, and he knew one could carry a sling litter.

"Kim," he called, trying to speak slowly and clearly, "we've got an emergency. Alert all the deputies and the reserves to stand by for assignments. Contact Merlin and tell him I'm going to get a chopper from that oil survey outfit and proceed up the mountain." He paused, sorting the details. "Yeah . . . where've they got their command post?"

"On the dirt road near Jay's house . . . in the upper village there, below the trailhead."

"Ten-four, Kim. That's where I fly in . . . ETA, depends on how fast I can get a helicopter. You copy all that?"

"Yes, sir. Any special orders for the deputies?"

Suspects in green fatigues, Johnny thought. Possibly those neo-Nazi crazies the FBI had been warning people about. He couldn't be sure at this stage, but somebody up there was armed to the teeth and shot a girl out jogging, then murdered a cowboy who came searching for her. "Yeah," Johnny said. "Tell them to get their rifles and ammunition together. Explain that we've got armed and dangerous people running around up there."

The lady behind the counter in the seismograph company looked cool, efficient, and potentially stubborn. Johnny could tell that she wasn't going to like the idea of a small-town sheriff taking over one of their helicopters. But he sure didn't have time to fill out any forms and wait for permission.

"Ma'am," he began, without so much as saying good morning, "I need one of your helicopters immediately. We've had a shooting up near Big Sky. One man is dead, and there's a girl up there wounded real bad."

The woman paused, as if preparing to cite all the reasons his request was impossible to accept. But then she nodded silently and reached for the microphone of the large radio beside her on the countertop.

* * *

The helicopter would meet him at the Sportsman's Lodge landing strip in twenty minutes. Johnny sped back up Main Street, trying simultaneously to speak clearly into the radio mike over the wail of the siren and to steer clear of tourists. He was calling Bill Hancock, his reserve deputy sergeant and the owner of the Charging Bear Trading Post, a well-stocked gunstore and Western museum.

If Johnny was going up there after armed murderers in green fatigues, he was going to need more firepower than his .45 automatic.

"Twenty-five–R–3," he called, once he'd made contact with Bill's patrol car, "meet me at your store, ASAP. I'm gonna need one of those assault rifles of yours and lots of ammo."

Bill was just coming off night highway duty and had obviously copied all the radio traffic on the situation up at Big Sky. "I'll be there in five minutes, Johnny."

As it turned out, both cars slid into the dusty parking lot of the log store at the same time. Bill dashed into the building with Johnny behind him.

Bill chose a Ruger GB Mini 14, a lighter-caliber version of the semi-automatic military rifle. This was the police model, with a collapsible metal stock and a flash suppressor. It was not a hunting rifle with a polished walnut stock. The steel parts were intentionally dull to prevent reflection, the tubes and joints of the stock functional, not graceful. The gun evoked Vietnam or Lebanon, not *Field and Stream*.

Johnny hefted the rifle, checked the safety and sighted down the barrel. "Okay," he muttered grimly. "This'll do. How about ammo?"

Bill was a tall gray-haired man with a quiet, precise manner. Without speaking, he peeled back the Velcro pouches of the rifle's black carrying case to reveal four magazines, each holding twenty rounds of .223 ball ammunition.

Johnny muttered, "Okay, Bill, thanks."

"What job have you got for me, Johnny?" There was no question that Bill wanted to be part of the posse that went after the killers, whoever or whatever they were.

Johnny looked at his watch. There were still several things he had to do before he met that chopper pilot at the Sportsman's Lodge. "Call Kim and tell him you're standing by for assignment."

"Good luck," Bill called, as Johnny dashed for his car.

"Thanks," Johnny yelled over his shoulder. "You, too."

Johnny made the twenty-eight-mile round trip from the west side of Ennis to his office in Virginia City and back to his house in under twenty minutes, hitting over a hundred on the few straight stretches. After the last shooting incident Johnny had been involved in, Sue had made him promise to always wear his bulletproof vest, if he had advance warning of potential danger. But this morning, he'd left the vest in his office.

As he roared back into town, he couldn't help grinning, despite the danger facing them all up in the mountains. A twenty-minute round trip "over the hill" to fetch a piece of safety equipment was like paying four five-dollar bills for a twenty-dollar mule and thinking you'd got a bargain.

Sue must have heard his siren because she was standing on the front porch as he pulled up. He dashed past her to grab his extra map case and his big pistol from his office off the living room.

"What's going on, Johnny?"

He could see from her face there was no sense trying to play things down. She knew him far too well for that.

"There's been a shooting up there, Sue." He threw his binoculars and a box of .44 ammunition into a canvas sack. "I've got to run, honey. There's a chopper waiting for me."

"Just a second," she protested, trying to block his way back out the front door. "What shooting, where?"

"Up above Big Sky . . . the girl, and somebody helping to find her . . . Sorry, Sue."

He was down the stairs. The car door was already open, so he threw his bag in, pushed the armored vest off the driver's seat, and jumped behind the wheel. As he sped down the quiet street, he saw women and kids gaping at him from the shady yards beneath the big old cottonwoods.

He had the weird sensation that he was riding off to war.

The landing strip at Sportsman's Lodge stretched across an old hay field behind the motel. There was a prefab hangar, a gas pump, a wind sock, and not much else.

Johnny cut his siren and pursuit lights before he turned into the lodge. Word of the shootings would get out soon enough, without him advertising the emergency any more than necessary. The chopper was sitting right in front of the hangar, its big rotor blades spinning slowly at low idle.

Johnny grabbed an armful of gear and scooted beneath the rotor tips to the open door on the right side of the cockpit. Up close, the turbine whine was loud, and he could only gesture to the dark-haired young man sitting in the pilot's seat. As Johnny returned with the rifle case and his maps, he saw that the pilot had already attached a long sling cable and metal casualty litter to the hoist point on the chopper's belly. This guy was no rookie.

Bill Hancock had traded hats with Johnny, giving him a brown plastic-mesh baseball cap with Madison County Sheriff's Department across the front, so that he'd be able to wear earphones in the chopper. As Johnny snapped himself into the seat belt, he was thankful that he had guys like Bill and Jay backing him up today. It was always the same, going into a deal like this . . . a sagging, lonely kind of feeling down in the gut. Hard to explain to people who'd never felt it, but very familiar to those who had.

Obviously, the pilot belonged to those already initiated to combat. When Johnny had his headset in place and could talk to the young man without shouting, the pilot held up a heavy, long-barreled .357 magnum pistol.

"Hope you don't mind, Sheriff," he said, gazing at Johnny through lightly tinted sunglasses.

From his expression and the tone of his voice, it was pretty clear that he intended to pack the gun, even if Johnny objected.

Johnny hit his mike button. "Yeah, well . . . I'm not really expecting any trouble for you up there."

"That's what they always used to say in 'Nam," the pilot replied. He smiled now, a young man's grin beneath much older eyes.

"Okay," Johnny conceded. "Be my guest."

The pilot nodded abruptly, reached across Johnny to double-check the door lock, then twisted open the throttle grip. Johnny felt the familiar vibration as the turbine howled. He looked back out the window to verify they were clear of obstacles, then gave a thumbs up.

Beside him in the small cockpit, the pilot eased back the control stick and the improbable machine rose gracefully into the morning sky. Johnny pointed toward the dark forested gap of the Jack Creek drainage and tapped the landing area on the pilot's open aerial chart.

"Roger that," the young man called. His expression was alert but not troubled. He seemed happy at the prospect of facing armed men up there.

Johnny could not be certain, but he sensed the young man had flown many times into mountains much more threatening than the dark ridges that now rose before them.

7

Madison Range

July 16, 1984

JACK CREEK CANYON OPENED BELOW THE HELICOPTER. Johnny caught a glimpse of a blue horse trailer and a sheriff's vehicle on the road, just past the Hammond Creek Ranger Station. That would be Robin Shipman's trailer and the patrol car had to be either Jerry Mason or Dick Noorlander. Good; Merlin was getting the troops out to seal off the roads from the mountains.

When Johnny turned to look ahead, he flinched. They were heading straight for a sharp, timbered ridge. The trees seemed to rush down at them, and for a moment his vision spun with vertigo. This kid seemed to have forgotten they were swinging a cable litter beneath the chopper. They cleared the ridge and were climbing again at a hundred knots.

"Sorry about that," the pilot said, smiling. "I kind of like to fly the contours when there's a chance of ground fire."

Johnny nodded and swallowed dryly. He had been a fixed-wing pilot for over fifteen years, but he could never get used to choppers. Flying in a helicopter meant abandoning all the subconscious caution a good airplane pilot acquired with years of experience. Airspeed was sacred in a normal aircraft; in a helicopter it was of little importance. A fixed-wing pilot learned early to strive for altitude and avoid ground obstacles . . . although Johnny had stretched this rule about as far as possible when he flew his battered little Tailor Craft on the rodeo circuit. Helicopters worked slow and low and at all kinds of crazy altitudes. Stall and crash always seemed imminent when Johnny rode in choppers.

Then, too, this guy was obviously of the Vietnam generation who enjoyed taking their aircraft to the limit.

As they climbed the densely forested shoulder of Lone Mountain, it came to Johnny that he didn't even know the pilot's name. At any moment, they might get hit by gunfire from some crazy survivalists hidden below, and he would die beside a nameless young man.

"What's your name?"

"Francos," the kid grinned, reaching across with his free left hand to shake.

At least he hadn't let go of the stick. Even though Johnny wasn't certain if Francos was the pilot's first or last name, he decided not to distract him anymore.

They were on top now, sailing above the unbroken lodgepole forest of the Moonlight Creek drainage. Suddenly blue glacial lakes swept beneath the plexiglas nose. Ahead, a green valley opened, and they could see the dark trench of Gallatin Canyon further east. The lodges and ski lifts of Big Sky shimmered in the midmorning thermal haze.

Dust trails rose from the gravel road above the cabins of Big Sky Mountain Village. Horse trailers, four-by-fours and patrol cars with their pursuit lights flashing soundlessly in the dust. Another helicopter angled down the sky, approaching the parked vehicles from the northeast.

In his earphones, Johnny heard Francos calmly advising the other pilot that they would "hold hover on the base leg of the LZ" until he had landed.

It was their turn. Johnny licked his lips, gazing down at the men on the road who gazed expectantly back at him, as if he had some solution to the tactical problem they all faced. Ever since Vietnam, he thought, we've gotten used to authority descending from the sky in helicopters. It used to be the cavalry, sweeping in with a troop of white horses to rescue the wagon train. Now it was cops with headsets and weird-looking rifles.

Johnny gathered up his gear, unsnapped his belt and dashed low beneath the rotor tips to escape the billowing dust. John Onstad's pickup and horse trailer stood at the head of a line of patrol cars and pickup trucks, the unofficial command post. The road was wide here, three lanes of packed gravel in the last grassy draw before the thick timber of the national forest. This was a good place for a temporary command post, Johnny saw, room to turn the trailers around without backing up, and plenty of space for the choppers. Also, the spot was a safe distance from any potential snipers in the trees above.

The choice of location was typical of John Onstad—thorough, logical, by the book. Sheriff Onstad was one of the most professional officers Johnny had ever worked with. Some of Onstad's men might grumble about his temper, but he'd always been friendly with Johnny.

Onstad was talking on a hand-held radio as Johnny dumped his gear onto the tailgate of a pickup. Grouped along the road there was a crowd of regular and reserve deputies from both the Madison County and Gallatin departments, some tired-looking cowboys from Lone Mountain Ranch who'd been searching all night, and at least five reporters from the Bozeman papers and TV station. Among the deputies, Johnny recognized Bob Campbell, Dave Dunn, and Bob Pearson from Gallatin County. Robin Shipman and Steve Powell were already on the scene. From the look of their horses, they hadn't wasted any time getting up here, once they'd gotten word of the shootings.

"Glad you're here," Onstad said, shaking Johnny's hand. Onstad was a tall brawny guy with linebacker's shoulders and big strong hands. Everything about him was on a larger scale than other men.

A reporter's camera whined and clicked. Johnny nodded, and they turned their backs on the cameras. Onstad braced his arm against the trailer, shielding them from the press.

"What's the situation, John," Johnny asked quietly.

"Not good," Onstad said, frowning. "Our witness is still pretty shook up, and he's not real clear about the location of the crime scene." He tipped his chin toward Bob Campbell, who stood in the shade talking with a deeply tanned young fellow with sandy hair. The young man's jeans were torn and muddy, his face scratched. He definitely looked shaken.

"Name's Jim Schwalbe," Onstad continued. "One of the search team from Big Sky. He saw the shootings, at least the fatal shot. He was teamed up with another guy from the Big Sky search party, name of Goldstein, Al Goldstein. That's our homicide victim. Shot right in the face, according to Schwalbe."

"That why he's so shook up?"

"You bet, Johnny. Goldstein was a close friend of his. Apparently saw the shot hit him, right in the head. I imagine I'd be, too."

Johnny nodded grimly and released a pent-up breath. "What about the girl?"

Onstad gazed up at the dark trees. "Well, she's still up there some damn place. We've been flying the area in the chopper with Schwalbe, but we can't locate the crime scene."

The reporters were edging closer again, and Onstad gestured impatiently to one of his deputies to keep them back.

Johnny led him further down the trailer so they could talk undisturbed. "What have we got for a general location?"

"Kinda vague," Onstad said, pointing toward Beehive Basin. "Schwalbe says it's a clearing, sort of like a little park, with thick deadfall timber around it and a stream running right through the middle." Onstad shook his head slowly. "I don't know if you copied the radio traffic, but he reports they had the girl chained to a log with her pants down when they shot her."

Johnny turned to study Schwalbe. He looked like an honest, straightforward kind of young guy. There was certainly no reason to doubt what he'd seen, as bizarre as it sounded. "Listen, John," he said, still speaking softly, "I've got the roads in and out sealed off on the Madison side. How have—"

"Roadblocks all around," Onstad stated, anticipating Johnny's question. "They won't drive out of here, that's for damn sure. You got Jack Creek campground covered, too? They could make their way down there on foot and steal a car. Or take some hostages. Who knows? We've got some crazy people on our hands, Johnny."

Once more Johnny nodded his grim understanding. "Any idea what we've got for hikers up there, people from Big Sky up fishing or camping?" The danger of a hostage situation was always present in a case like this.

Onstad made a note on his interview pad. "I'll get someone down to Huntley Lodge to find out. I think we ought to contact Bob Morton from the Forest Service, too. There's bound to be a lot of people camping up in the Spanish Peaks this time of year."

"Well, we're gonna have to get some reserve deputies on all those trailheads, John, to warn people off."

As they worked out the seemingly endless but vital details of the initial security operation, more media cars sped up the dusty road from Big Sky. Now there were three television crews, several still photographers, and four newspaper reporters milling around. One reporter was blocking the road with his station wagon, feeding a breathless live report to his station.

If those crazies up there have got themselves a transistor radio, Johnny realized, we're in big trouble.

Johnny's interview with Jim Schwalbe was no more successful than Onstad's. Schwalbe seemed like a nice guy, and it turned out he wasn't as young as he looked. He'd been living at Big Sky for several years, working his own landscaping business. For most of that time, he'd hiked and fished the high country. But despite Johnny and Onstad's gentle prompting, he was simply not able to pinpoint the crime scene on the maps they spread before him on the hood of Onstad's patrol car.

The crime occurred, Jim repeated, above the Jack Creek logging road in an open, grassy clearing, surrounded by "thick country," broken timber, and young trees. There was a shallow draw, and a mossy streambed with a good flow of water. When he'd last seen the girl, she was wounded, inside a green sleeping bag, chained to a log, under a big spruce tree.

The older guy had fired the fatal shot, Schwalbe repeated. He was leaning against a tree to steady his hunting rifle, and he shot Al in the face . . . right in the face. Al was dead, lying on his back in the open, his blue backpack beside him. Jim's red backpack was also in the open, near the stream.

When Jim Schwalbe spoke about Al Goldstein, Johnny could see in his face that there was no sense pushing him for more. Johnny had seen his share of crime victims, and he recognized the emotional impact that the shooting had had on Jim. When a person had witnessed something as horrible as Jim had, you simply had to give him time.

But right now, time was getting away from them. That girl could be bleeding to death up there, and nobody knew where.

Johnny stepped aside from the group of officers around Schwalbe and closed his eyes against the sun-glare. Thick country, a grassy clearing, a mossy stream-bed with running water. . . . That really should not be too hard to locate from the air, if they kept their wits about them.

Given the lay of the land, most of the shallow draws above the Ulerys lakes went west, into the Jack Creek drainage. To the east, Beehive Basin was much steeper. As far as Johnny could recall, there were only about two or three streams up there big enough to have ample running water this time of year. And, if they flew the treetops in those two or three draws, they'd be bound to see bright backpacks lying in the open. If the killers hadn't hidden them, if they hadn't already finished off the girl and buried her in the deep brush.

While John Onstad organized his deputies to alert the Big Sky community and the Forest Service, Johnny studied his maps. Schwalbe was positive there had only been two men, and he was certain they wore military fatigues and jungle boots. But something in his description of them struck a nagging, hazy note in Johnny's memory. Schwalbe had repeatedly used the phrase, "the old man and the boy," as if there was a full generation between the two. And he'd said they were

80

dirty, that their beards were shaggy, unkempt. That just did not sound like spit-and-polish Nazis playing End of the World games up in the mountains.

What it did sound a lot like was two kind of crazy hermits whom Dave Wing, the Forest Service law enforcement officer in Ennis, had been telling Johnny about for the past four or five years. But, for the life of him, Johnny couldn't remember their names, and Dave was off working a forest fire in California; otherwise, Johnny would get on the radio and talk to him right now.

Johnny folded his maps carefully so that he could use them seated in the open door of the helicopter. He stood alone at the side of the patrol car, his lips pursed in concentration. What the hell were those two guys' names? Dave had suspected them of burning down the Cowboy Heaven cabin and also of burning the Spanish Creek ranger station. They were a father and his boy . . . from around here, originally, sort of weird hermits who lived up above Beartrap Canyon, poaching game, maybe even stealing cattle. Dave Wing had never actually caught up with the pair to question them about the arson, but he'd told Johnny enough about them.

But right now, with the newsmen hovering, and the deputies' radios squawking, it was hard to think.

"Sheriff," the pilot called, "I'm all set."

Once the chopper had left the roadside command post, Johnny pulled on his white Teflon bulletproof vest. The TV cameramen had practically climbed into the cockpit with him, and he didn't want to give them anything more sensational than they already had.

While Johnny had been conferring with Onstad, Francos had detached the cable sling from the chopper's belly and taken off the doors. This young guy was good; he'd realized that he would be needed for a low-level recon, and that he couldn't fly too low dragging a fifty-foot sling cable.

Now they headed up past Ulerys Lakes, with the second chopper flying in tail formation. Onstad's deputy, Bob Pearson, flew with the other pilot and Jim Schwalbe. Pearson knew this country pretty well and was experienced in aerial searches. But Johnny wanted someone else to fly with him in the lead chopper, to sit behind him and cover the portside, so that Francos could concentrate on flying. He also wanted to confer with Jay Cosgrove, who'd been on this case since before dark the day before.

Cosgrove's patrol vehicle, a dusty white Blazer, stood on the Jack Creek logging road near a wide spot marking a culvert over Moonlight Creek. The slope was steep on either side, and a huge slash pile of beetle-kill timber took up one end of the clearing.

"I don't suppose you can set this thing down there, can you?" Johnny asked, pointing to the clearing.

"Piece of cake," Francos answered. "What you need?"

"Another set of eyes." Johnny pointed again, indicating Jay and Brad Brisban, Onstad's resident deputy from West Yellowstone. Brad's huge German shepherd, Bear, was barking savagely at the chopper.

Francos squinted into the sun. "Do me a favor," he said casually. "Take the smaller guy. If we have to hover very long with much weight at this altitude, it can screw up my engine."

"What happens then?" Johnny already knew.

"Oh, a stall of some kind. You know, something that'll mess your day up real bad."

"Yes, sir," Johnny answered. "I know about that."

* * *

Getting the helicopter into the clearing was not what Johnny would have classified as a piece of cake. With dust, gravel, and bark trash blasting up from the rotorwash, visibility was bad right next to the ground. On Francos's instructions, Johnny leaned out the open door, shielding his eyes from the flying debris, to judge the tail rotor clearance from the slash pile. When the skids touched down safely, he estimated there was less than a foot between the tail and the jumble of dead timber.

Brad Brisban became Johnny's observer because he weighed less than Jay, and because Jay was needed in the Blazer to act as radio relay between the command post and Johnny's office in Virginia City, thirty miles to the west.

The two helicopters now crisscrossed the timbered slopes that rose toward Beehive Mountain from the depression of Ulerys Lakes and the clear demarcation line of the logging road.

Ten minutes, then fifteen. Twenty-five minutes into the search, and no one had seen a "clearing like a little park in a shallow draw." Johnny hung out of the open door, restrained by the seat belt, his face in the hot wind. As the chopper banked and retraced their earlier route, the heavy stone mountains above them seemed to turn in odd directions. He closed his eyes, instantly aware that he was experiencing a form of disorientation common to aerial searchers. It was for this reason that he had wanted a second observer to relieve the pilot of that responsibility.

Johnny called Bob Pearson in the other chopper. "You guys see anything?"

"Negative, Sheriff, not a thing."

"Sheriff," Francos suggested, "maybe we should fly a little lower and sort of troll for groundfire . . . maybe we can flush 'em out that way."

"Troll?"

"Just an expression we used in 'Nam. It works, you know."

"Yeah, well . . . let's wait on that. Let me think this out a little more."

Schwalbe had reported that Kari Swenson was shot through her chest with a .22 pistol. He thought that the bullet had passed right through her, because he saw blood on her lower back. How long could a person live with a wound like that, up here alone?

Johnny leaned back inside the cockpit to talk to Francos. "Can you set this thing down someplace up high there?" He pointed toward timberline on Beehive. "I want to get out and crawl up on that open ridge there so I can look down on this whole country."

Francos nodded his understanding. "Sure, Sheriff. No problem."

Johnny tugged his seat belt snug. At least Francos had not called it a piece of cake.

From the stony ridge, a thousand feet above Ulerys Lakes, Johnny and Brad had a clear, panoramic view of both Moonlight and Beehive Basins. The second helicopter was working up the logging road, just west of Upper Ulerys Lake. Johnny tried the binoculars, but all he saw was details of treetops. He removed his sunglasses and squinted, but that was no good either. Finally, he let his line of sight just naturally meander up from the lakes as he tried to make the hidden contours of the country reveal themselves.

"We've got two shallow draws in there," he muttered, his words lost in the dying whine of the chopper's engine. He stepped beside Brisban and pointed down the mountainside. "First one seems too close to the lake for their camp," Johnny continued, "but the second one there, that's gotta be it."

Johnny raised his radio. "Bob," he called to Pearson in the other chopper, "I think we've got something. From what Schwalbe said about a shallow draw with water above Ulerys Lake, you should pick it up if you get your pilot to fly due north from your present position and scout the bottom of that little drainage there."

But when Johnny released the transmit button, he heard the chopped-up squawk of simultaneous transmissions. This frequency was so crowded, what with officers from both departments arriving on the scene, that he couldn't be sure Pearson had heard him.

But before he could speak again, the helicopter swung north and Pearson called out in triumph. "There it is," he shouted. "We've got the red pack in the clearing."

Johnny and Brad were already scrambling down the rocky ridge to reach their helicopter. "Find someplace to set down, so we can join up," Johnny called. "We'll be there right away."

They assembled at an outcropping of large orange boulders, a quarter of a mile north of the campsite clearing. Pearson was already there when Johnny and Brad jumped down from the hovering chopper. Less than five minutes later, Murray Duffy ferried John Onstad and his deputy, Bill Pronovost, and two other Gallatin deputies to the rock pile.

Everybody had a rifle and a sidearm, and they all carried radios. Johnny looked around at the men. They were dressed in a motley blend of uniforms and blue jeans. But each had his badge prominently displayed.

"An open point's probably the best assault formation," Johnny suggested.

The others nodded somberly. No one seemed in the mood for small talk.

"Let's keep an even interval," Onstad said, chambering a round in his rifle. "We draw fire, the point man can drop back and we can give him cover fire."

Again, the men nodded their grim acceptance.

Johnny checked his watch. Only 10:50. It seemed like he'd been up here flying around for hours. He licked his lips and rubbed the sweat from his forehead. He'd left his canteen in the chopper. Well, that could wait. There was no sense stalling.

Bob Pearson took the point. Nobody asked him; he just slid down the hot boulders and took up the central position. The others filled the flanks, then stepped as quietly as they could into the hot shade of the forest.

Johnny was on Pearson's left, about twenty yards behind him. As Schwalbe had reported, the country was thick, and visibility was terrible. There was a combination of healthy mature trees and thousands of thinner beetle-kill and gray blow-down deadfall. But Pearson had the streambed, and they were able to move with a steady pace, relatively quietly. Whenever someone stumbled or snagged the cracking branch of a deadfall, they all paused and waited until the chickadees and jays started calling again.

The flies were bad. Mosquitoes whined about their sweating faces. But nobody lowered his rifle to wave off the bugs.

Johnny's mouth was terribly dry. His ankle throbbed, but he gazed into the cross-hatched gray jumble of dead timber with a concentration he'd only been able to achieve at times of extreme danger. He was acutely aware that they were nearing the camp clearing. At this actual moment, one of the killers might have Johnny's face in the crosshairs of his telescopic sight.

He shook his head, both to flick off a biting fly and to banish the fear that was rapidly rising toward panic.

This was what being a lawman always came down to. The gold badge, the uniform, the wide gray Stetson, the pearl-handled .45 . . . that was all well and good. But none of those fancy decorations mattered at a time like this.

What mattered was what a man did, not what he said, not the way he looked. In less than five minutes, they would be on the crime scene. Ten minutes from now, he could be dead. Or the killers could be dead. Or they might find the girl already dead. Or they might find the killers barricaded behind some logs, holding a cocked pistol to the girl's head.

He dreaded a hostage situation with the wounded girl as the pawn almost as much as he did facing a hidden sniper. But he knew such a situation was possible, even probable, if there was an organized group of crazy Nazis out there in the trees, not just some old fanatic and his mixed-up son.

The timber opened up some here, and he could see ahead. Off to the left, the ground rose to meet a ridge, and there seemed to be a similar hillside climbing to the right. Beneath Johnny's feet, the ground was soft with springy bear grass, almost level. They were nearing the end of the draw, and he guessed the camp clearing would be right beyond the next stand of dense timber.

Johnny caught Bob Pearson's eye through the brush and raised his hand to signal a halt. If someone had to be on the point here, it was Johnny's job. This was Madison County, and he was sheriff. Scanning the ground ahead for broken branches, he took several deep breaths, licked his lips, then moved forward. But the open "V" formation had strung out to a line-abreast now; it was hard to say who had the actual point.

When he had assumed the lead, the others followed, their weapons ready.

Somewhere to Johnny's right, a radio broke squelch with a loud squawk. A robber jay screamed, flapping brightly above.

"Help me, please . . ." The girl's voice was weak, close ahead in the brush.

Johnny punched off the rifle's safety and plunged ahead. Men were running to his left and right. The dead branches crashed beneath his boots. He was across the soggy moss of the streambed. Sunlight cut through the green ahead.

"Help . . . me." Her voice was even weaker.

Suddenly, there was the clearing, bright with sunlit bear grass, the pleasant little "park" that Jim Schwalbe had described.

The line of armed officers burst through the trees and across the exposed clearing to take cover.

As he dashed through the sudden crowd of deputies, Johnny tried to scan the surrounding trees for the old man and the boy. Nothing, just gray deadfall and bright green foliage.

"Here," the girl pleaded. "I'm over here."

Onstad's deputies were crouched behind trees, their rifles angled out to cover the perimeter. They all waited, maybe a minute, maybe less. No sound. If the killers were using the girl as sniper bait, there was only one way to find out for sure.

Sheriff Onstad and Sheriff France stood up full height and dashed together across the clearing to the jumbled shape on the ground.

Johnny slung his rifle and bent to pull back the bloody fold of the sleeping bag. Kari's face was horribly pale, her lips tight and blue. She could be dying, right here and now. But there was a solid, unflickering strength in her eyes.

"You're here," she whispered to them.

Her blue T-shirt was stuck to her chest, sodden with

dark ocher bloodstains. She lay on her left side, curled like a sleeping child. With the bag peeled back, Johnny could see the spreading bloodstains low on her back, above her right kidney.

The two sheriffs exchanged glances. The bullet had gone right through her, and there was bound to be serious internal hemorrhage. But there was little they could do here to help her. And, every minute they waited for a hidden sniper to make his move threatened her chances of survival.

Johnny rose and spoke clearly into his radio. "Twenty-five-eight, 25–1 . . . Jay, get that chopper in here with the stretcher. We found her and she's alive."

"Ten-four," Jay Cosgrove replied. "He's on his way."

Johnny knelt again and hovered above her, helpless, waiting like John Onstad across from him. Working delicately with his big fingers, Onstad plucked a splintered twig from Kari's tangled red hair.

"The helicopter's coming, honey," Johnny said, stroking her forehead. "We're going to have you out of here real soon."

Kari gripped his hand. Her fingers were like cold bone. "I'm all right," she said, then lost her breath and wheezed, a dry, crackling gurgle.

Once more, the two men exchanged a glance. Lung shot. They would have to be very careful when they moved her.

"They shot that man." Kari's face was smeared with tears, dried blood, and crusted sweat. She nodded to her right. "His name is Al . . . they shot . . ."

"It's okay, Kari," Onstad said gently. "Everything's okay. We'll take care of him."

Johnny unslung his rifle and strode across the clearing to a thick dead lodgepole with a naked gray snag rising from its roots like a giant's longbow.

Al Goldstein lay on his back, his arms extended, his hands open, palm up. His eyes were half closed, clouded in death. His face was swollen and black. His lower jaw jutted at a terrible angle, broken by the impact of the rifle bullet. There was a lot of dark blood. And insects.

Johnny muttered a soft curse.

At the open neck of the checked lumberjack shirt, the dead man's flesh looked young, tanned and strong. But he was not asleep. He was dead forever. Murdered.

Johnny turned and studied the clearing, noting for the first time the three stones of a campfire ring and the logs lying near it. That was where they'd chained her. He scanned the surrounding trees, searching for the probable angle of the rifle shot. After a moment, he looked back at Al's shattered face. When the old man fired, Al's head must have filled his entire scope.

Time passed. Finally, Johnny looked away from Al Goldstein. A square automatic pistol lay in the columbine stalks, about two feet from Al's right hand. A black walkie-talkie lay a similar distance from his right hand.

Johnny studied the scene a moment, then returned to Onstad. "Dead," he said softly. "About four hours maybe. Doesn't look like anybody's touched him."

Onstad was about to answer when they heard the clatter of the helicopter.

Johnny bundled the soft folds of the sleeping bag around Kari's throat. "Sweetheart," he said. "We're going to have to hurt you when we lift you into that stretcher."

Kari nodded, her eyes hot in her chill, waxy face. "Don't worry. I'm all right."

Johnny bit his lip. He could see the pain she was in. This kid had incredible guts and discipline. There were a lot of questions he should be asking her right now. How many men were there? Had they raped her? But Kari could not speak without pain, and probably without worsening the wound. He had to limit his questions to the vital minimum.

"Can you tell us how long they've been gone?" Johnny asked. "Did you see which way they went?"

"They've been gone a long time," Kari said. She tried to breathe, but again her voice became a sickly wheeze.

"That's okay, Kari," Johnny said. "We'll talk to you later, in the hospital."

Kari shook her head, her eyes shining with angry determination. "They packed their stuff . . . right after they shot Al—" Her head inclined to the left. "That's the way they went out of camp . . . down the stream there. . . ."

The chopper's rotors clattered above them. Bob Pearson was standing in the most open spot, his rifle held above his head to signal Francos. Now the rotorwash blasted up twigs and dead needles. The metalmesh casualty litter descended into the clearing, spinning slowly on its steel cable.

"Sorry, Kari," Johnny shouted above the engine whine. "This is gonna hurt."

He took her shoulders and John Onstad lifted the foot of the sleeping bag. In one long motion they had her off the ground and in the litter. Kari stared into the sky, her eyes filled with the pain. But she did not cry out.

Working quickly, Onstad and Johnny buckled the nylon straps to secure her in the basket. Johnny squinted up into the sunlit rotorblast, trying to judge the clearance among the branches. This clearing was badly overhung by trees. It was going to be dicey getting her out. Almost as an afterthought, he reached down to cover her face with the soft edge of the sleeping bag.

Kari gripped his hand with her chill fingers. "Thank you," she said, her voice suddenly strong.

The litter spun as it rose, lazy, glinting in the sun. Only ten feet short of the treetops, the foot end of the stretcher twisted into the dead limbs of the big lodgepole that stood above Al Goldstein's body. With a clatter and a shower of twigs, the litter jammed hard against the branch. Then Francos applied more throttle, and the litter slammed along the dead limbs, to strike the trunk. For an awful moment, it looked as if Kari would be crushed between the branch and the tree trunk, then the branch snapped. The litter shot up and the dead limb crashed to the forest floor, barely missing the startled deputies.

The slapping rotors faded. No birds sang around them. The five men stood in the clearing, their ears echoing with the engine blast.

After a while, the deputies who had been guarding the perimeter came forward to stare with silent anger at the body lying in the wild flowers beneath the thick lodgepole.

8

Madison Range

July 16–17, 1984

THAT AFTERNOON JOHNNY TOOK OVER JAY AND TERRY Cosgrove's log house as the command post for the manhunt. The house stood alone on a grassy hillside above the gravel road to the trailhead, the last building in Big Sky's upper village. Like many of the handsome homes in the resort community, the Cosgroves' house was custom-made, built on a large scale with picture window views of Lone Mountain from the living room and den. A wooden staircase cut down the steep slope, connecting the front porch and the double garage below.

This staircase, Johnny soon realized, would be an effective barrier to the news media, if the manhunt dragged on very long. Seated at Jay's dining room table, a jumble of radio messages held down by coffee cups before him, he could see the reporters milling around the driveway. Television remote-broadcast vans had replaced the initial station wagons. Already, there had been one dispute about a late arrival's microwave dish blocking a competitor's antenna.

The reporters had assembled below for a five o'clock

93

briefing. He was trying with limited success to keep them away from the house, sealed off by the preliminary roadblock he'd established below. But he was learning that they had ingenious, sometimes insidious ways of sneaking up here.

The layout of the property, however, offered natural lines of defense. If they made it past the roadblock, they'd have to get by the deputy at the end of the driveway, then past the men on the porch. These barriers also shielded Johnny and John Onstad from most of the distractions and noisy bustle endemic to any large police operation. Here in the dining room, the clattering choppers and squawking radios were less of an insistent presence, constantly reminding them that hours were slipping by with the suspects still at large. They'd both been in law enforcement long enough to realize that the chance of catching criminals diminished proportionally to the length of time that passed from the commission of the crime.

Johnny was tired. It was almost five, but the draft of the official announcement was only partially written. Every time he tried to complete it, one of the deputies would barge in with some authentically urgent message or request.

Beside him, Terry Cosgrove manned the police radio, acting as a relay when needed for the deputies deployed up on the trailheads and at the roadblocks in the valleys. John Onstad worked in the living room, hunched over a big map of the Gallatin National Forest, as he briefed his key deputies on the placement of roadblocks and vehicle patrols.

Johnny rose, then reluctantly sat back to his task. He had to go before the cameras and microphones with very little information, but if he didn't give the media something to chew on, they'd just spread whatever rumors they could pick up.

The phone rang, and he waited while Terry took the message; maybe it was Deaconess Hospital in Bozeman, and there'd be some news on Kari's condition. She'd been out of surgery for over an hour and in the Intensive Care Unit. John Onstad's detectives had been able to interview her briefly and had called back with a fairly detailed description of the two suspects. But Kari had been too weak for them to press her hard for a full report.

The call was just another press query, this one from Salt Lake. He was always amazed at the ability of distant reporters to track down an obscure phone number only hours after a major crime.

Before continuing with his press release, Johnny leafed through another yellow pad to make doubly sure he had covered all his bases, that he had indeed deployed his men effectively and that he'd done everything possible to assure the security of the local people. The roads were sealed by armed reserve deputies at all the trailheads and public campgrounds. John Onstad's people had spread the warning to stay out of the mountains among the residents of the Gallatin Canyon. Johnny, himself, had spoken personally to Bob Morton of the Forest Service about alerting backpackers in the Spanish Peaks trails.

Jay Cosgrove, Brad Brisban, and Merlin Ehlers had been up in the Moonlight Creek area since one, working that entire draw with Bear, Brad's German shepherd, and Merlin's Doberman, Gypsie Lady; in fact, they'd called in a few minutes earlier to announce finding a smeared Vibran bootsole print in the mud. The crime scene itself was secured. Johnny had taken his pictures and walked off the gunshot measurements before strapping Al Goldstein's body into the same metal litter that had lifted Kari out an hour earlier.

There really was not much more he could do right

now. In the morning, of course, all his and Onstad's reserves would be in place, and they could hit that country with more dog patrols, aerial searches, and ground sweeps. Now, he could only wait, hoping that they had, indeed, covered all the exit points.

But the plain truth was that the two killers had gotten a four-hour lead on them that morning, and four hours gave them plenty of time to find a hiding place deep in the woods, all to hell and gone up those drainages. He did have the area sealed, but he certainly did not have any miraculous plan on how to find those two up in that wild country.

But the press would surely ask him about his immediate plans, that and the identity of the two criminals, of course. Scowling at the meager lines on the pad, he picked up his ballpoint once more and read:

23-year-old Carrie Swenson . . .

He crossed out "Carrie" and wrote "Kari."

23-year-old Kari Swenson, a world-class Biathlete, was abducted on July 15 while on her daily run. On July 16, two persons from the Big Sky Resort Area involved with a search for Kari, came upon a camp where two men dressed in military-type fatigues were holding Kari captive.

At that time, the individuals in fatigue-type dress . . .

Johnny bent over the pad. He had to hurry, but words never came easily, much less now. He had not eaten anything since his toast in Bettie's Cafe, almost twelve hours earlier. He wiped the exhaustion from his eyes and tried to focus on the yellow pad.

The meeting that morning in the cafe seemed like

something that had happened months earlier. As he tried to summarize the terrible events of this long day, the image of Al Goldstein's grotesquely swollen face rose in his mind.

"The deceased, Alan Goldstein," Johnny read, trying to keep his voice loud enough for the microphones that they jabbed at him, "was transported to facilities in Bozeman, also by helicopter."

"What about suspects?" a reporter yelled from the crowd jammed up against the porch railing.

Johnny saw that the young man was not local; then, with a tired sag in his chest, he realized that several of the cameramen facing him were network crews. They must have chartered planes to get there so fast. He cleared his dry throat. The words he was speaking would be on the CBS Morning News and Dan Rather tomorrow night. One network minicam focused on his shoulder holster and the butt of his big .44 magnum "make-my-day" gun. Slavishly, several other cameramen took the network guy's lead.

"The suspects are described as follows: White male, early fifties, six-feet-one, slender build, long, wiry black hair and long, graying beard. Last seen wearing green shirt and black pants, and a hard-leather, cowboy-style hat."

"How about the kid, Sheriff?"

"Leather cowboy hat? What's that?"

"Green shirt? You mean fatigue shirt?"

"You just said they were wearing fatigues, Sheriff. Which one is it?"

This was Johnny's first exposure to pack journalism. For a long moment he simply gaped at the ruby "on" lights of the minicams and the whining motor-drive Nikons. Was he supposed to answer these shouted questions?

"Ah," he began, regaining his composure. "Suspect number two—"

The reporters went silent.

"—white male, about nineteen. Long blond hair, maybe over his shoulders, and a blond beard. Five-feet-ten, one sixty pounds. Last seen wearing a denim jacket, green shirt, and black pants. Also wearing a leather cowboy hat. Possible name of Dan."

"What's your source, Sheriff?"

"Are they doing an autopsy on Goldstein?"

"What about the fatigues?" the network guy persisted. "You reported a minute ago that they were dressed in quote military-type fatigues unquote. Which is it, Sheriff?"

Johnny blinked into the cameras. A hot floodlight snapped on. "The . . . ah, earlier report was from the first witness, James Schwalbe. The second description was from Kari Swenson, herself."

"Which one are you going with?" Again, the network guy cut to the core of the question.

But before Johnny could answer, one of the young women from a local station interrupted. "They've canceled the fatigue description. I heard it on my scanner."

Johnny stared at the girl, trying to recall her name. All these local reporters had police radios in their cars and were monitoring the manhunt frequencies. And they were feeding the information directly to their stations, which in turn, he'd been told, were interrupting their programs with special announcements. He also realized that if the two suspects up there were part of a larger, organized outfit, they'd be sure to have transistor radios. They might even have police scanners. He realized that whatever hard information he gave the press could easily reach the criminals a short time later.

He and Onstad were going to have to get their acts together about these press briefings, and also about who could talk to the reporters, even off the record. Earlier that afternoon, Johnny had seen that same girl from the local TV station charm her way through the lower roadblock, past the reserve deputy at the bottom of the driveway, and right up to the open front door of the house. Most of the reserves from the two counties were ranchers and miners, honest, straightforward people but not prepared to handle hungry reporters. And, from the way he'd just seen that girl cozy up to the network man, he realized that this story represented an unprecedented career opportunity for the young local reporters, and that some of them might break all the rules to take advantage of it.

"Johnny," a TV reporter cut in, "what can you tell us about this station wagon with Alaska plates?"

Earlier that afternoon, they'd gotten a report that a long-haired, "mean-looking" young guy in an "army shirt" had been parked near a Big Sky store the day before, annoying everyone with loud rock music from his radio. His car was described as a tan Japanese station wagon with Alaska license plates. Personally, Johnny did not put much stock in the report; the description of the young man did not really match Kari's details. However, it was about the only tangible lead he had, and the report might provide a smoke-screen, should the reporters run with it, and should the criminals up there hear the story on their transistor radio.

Johnny cleared his throat dramatically. "We have an all-points apprehend alert out on that vehicle right now."

The reporters bent over their narrow notebooks. The TV people leaned even closer.

"You think that they've fled the area?"

Johnny tried to look earnest, but he was too tired to play these games well right now. "Well . . . we believe the suspects know the area well, and we believe that they are still confined to a specific area, several miles from the Big Sky resort."

The reporters exchanged expressions of disbelief.

"Why look for the Alaska car, if you think they're still in the mountains?"

Tiredly, Johnny read from his prepared notes. "A search is currently being conducted in the upper region of the Jack Creek drainage for the suspects—"

"Come on, Sheriff," someone shouted from the back of the pack. "What's really going on?"

Patiently, Johnny folded his yellow pages and composed himself to answer. "We have every reason to believe that the suspects are still in the area, but we are also searching for that tan station wagon with Alaska license plates because we—"

Parry and thrust.

The voices came at him from beyond the hot glare of the minicam lights. He listened, then tried to form an answer that might further confuse the criminals when they heard an edited version of it on their radio.

If this manhunt drags on very long, he thought, I'm gonna get downright sneaky, myself.

The sun cut behind the stone shoulder of Lone Mountain. Around the command post, tired deputies dragged on long filtertip cigarettes and fiddled with the various knobs of their radios and deadly hardware. Birds of prey glided on the afternoon thermals above the draws. Tourists and curious locals bounced up the potholed road from the lower resort, only to be turned back by the deputies at the roadblocks.

Time moved silently on, and the two men who had murdered Al Goldstein remained at large.

* * *

Bill Hancock brought the news as Johnny and John Onstad bent over the big map on the dining room table, trying to decide the best route for the dawn posse sweep.

There was a local woman, Bill reported, a Mrs. Joel Beardsley, who believed she had seen the two suspects up at Ulerys Lake on Saturday morning. Merlin had assigned Bill to interview the lady in her home down on Yellow Tail Road, and he was now here to report. Hancock had been Johnny's first reserve deputy; he was the sergeant of the reserves, a steady, older guy who took his responsibilities seriously. In typical Hancock fashion, his report of the Beardsley woman interview was detailed and complete. He read from his notes.

The lady, he said, was in her forties, articulate and well dressed, obviously a solid citizen. Her story sounded true.

Mrs. Beardsley, her husband, and another couple had been up at Ulerys Lake on Saturday morning around ten, fly fishing; she'd been using an innertube float to drift across the lake.

A bearded man, "in good condition, actually rather good-looking," had called her from the far shore. "Lots of fish over here," he'd said. "Come on over." He asked if she knew the date. She had been startled.

"You must have been up here quite a while, not to know the date," she'd replied.

"Quite a long time," he had answered.

Mrs. Beardsley told him it was Saturday, July 14. She was sure, she said, because the day before had been Friday the thirteenth.

As she spoke with the man, Mrs. Beardsley had said, she suddenly became aware that they were out of sight of her husband and the other couple in the fishing party. It almost seemed to her that the bearded man

101

was trying to lure her closer to the thickly forested shore.

At that point, she saw another, younger man up the slope, standing at a large lodgepole from which he had stripped a square of bark.

"Are you surveyors?" she asked. They both wore long-barreled pistols in their belts.

"No," the man answered. "We're just carving our name on a tree."

At that moment, Mrs. Beardsley's husband called from down the lake, and she yelled back that she was there. When the two men heard her husband's voice, they grabbed their rifles, put them into dark cases and "rather hurriedly" departed, straight up the steep bank of the shore.

After a while, Mrs. Beardsley said, her group climbed the bank at this end of the lake. They found the tree the boy had been carving. Surprisingly, he had stripped the bark back very deeply, but had inscribed the actual message with a black felt pen, using a bold but graceful script. "Actually," she had reported, "it was rather beautiful."

"Bill," Johnny asked, "did she remember the names?"

Bill Hancock flipped shut his logbook. "Sorry, Johnny. I pressed her on that, but she just couldn't remember. But she thought maybe one name was Don."

Johnny went to the front porch and called Robin Shipman. He and Steve still had their horses saddled. "Get a chain saw from Merlin's Bronco," he said, speaking softly. One of the reporter girls was lingering at the end of the porch, interviewing a deputy who'd helped transport Al Goldstein's body. Johnny had authorized the interview, but he knew the girl was dragging it out to remain at the command post as long as possible.

"What we gotta cut down, Johnny?"

"There's a lodgepole up at Ulerys Lake with some names written on it. I want that section of the tree."

"You bet," Robin said, smiling at the prospect of some action.

While the massed camera crews had their predictable field day with the section of lodgepole trunk, Johnny and Onstad stood in Terry Cosgrove's kitchen, well shielded from the camera lights and microphones on the porch, speaking intently about the suspects, Don and Dan Nichols.

Obviously, these were the men who had accosted Mrs. Beardsley. They probably had tried to lure her close enough to shore to grab, but had dropped the plan when they discovered that she wasn't alone.

But they had not hesitated the next afternoon when Kari Swenson came jogging up the lakeside trail.

Nor had the old man hesitated, Johnny knew, when he raised his rifle and sighted the scope on Al Goldstein's face.

"John," Johnny said, looking up to meet Onstad's eyes. "These have to be the same guys that gave Dave Wing so much trouble the past couple of years, the hermit types who burned down the cabin at Cowboy Heaven and the Spanish Creek ranger station."

Onstad frowned. "Dave Wing's in California on that forest fire, and we're going to have to get some details on the Nicholses as soon as possible."

Johnny nodded, his mind occupied with a half-remembered event . . . something his predecessor, old Sheriff Kitson, had told him. He tried to think while John Onstad listed all the logical, methodical steps that they must now take to compile a complete file on the two suspects. First, of course, they must contact the Law Enforcement Services Division's Criminal Investigation Bureau in Helena, then the Motor Vehicle Division, next the Identification Bureau of the Department of Institutions, Probation, and Parole. . . .

John Onstad had a sheriff's department of over fifty deputies and support personnel. The city of Bozeman alone had five times the population of Madison County. By necessity, Onstad ran a modern, well-organized, impersonal operation. He was a skilled administrator, a law-enforcement executive who believed in technology.

Johnny France had considerable respect for computers and modern communications technology, but he understood one basic fact that his colleagues in the neighboring cities might have forgotten in the stampede to build hi-tech sheriffs' departments in the 1970s. There'd been plenty of federal anti-crime money and expertise available, and some people had begun to confuse fancy equipment with old-fashioned experience or even common sense. At the end of the day, criminals were just people who got themselves in trouble. A computer in Helena could probably provide a lot of facts about Don Nichols and his son, Dan, but no data bank could give Johnny what he really needed, a clear human understanding of those two strange people, a sense of them as human beings who had gotten themselves into deep trouble.

While John Onstad handled the logical channels of modern criminal investigation, Sheriff Johnny France got on the Cosgroves' phone and began calling those people whom he knew had encountered the Nicholses at one time or another.

It was after dark when Johnny completed his initial round of phone calls. Although his effort had been punctuated with unavoidable interruptions, he had learned a great deal about his suspects.

While the Criminal Investigation Bureau computers were buzzing and beeping up in Helena, Johnny was following one phone lead to another, the receiver propped under his chin, a fresh mug of coffee near his elbow, the dusty yellow pad open before him.

The picture of the Nicholses that he formed from these preliminary inquiries was both interesting and troubling. They definitely were not a couple of bums who'd gone up to the high country for a weekend of beer and target shooting, then just grabbed a pretty girl who happened to come by. If that were the case, tracking them down and talking sense to them might be a relatively straightforward job.

But Don Nichols and his son did not fit this conventional pattern. According to the people Johnny had contacted, it seemed that Don Nichols had never fit into a normal mold. Originally, he came from Norris, a small crossroads community of gold miners, just north of Ennis. His dad, Pat Nichols, had brought his family there during the Depression, like so many other displaced Dust Bowl farmers. Pat had worked as a miner, and, according to Johnny's sources, had been a friendly, generous kind of guy, who loved to hunt and fish, if he wasn't otherwise occupied down at the saloon.

When the boy, Don, was about seven, Johnny discovered, his dad had been driving home from a Saturday night party in Ennis, "drunk as a lord," missed a curve on the old Norris hill, and slammed the car into a deep ravine. Pat Nichols was killed instantly, and the other passengers were pretty banged up.

Maggie Nichols remarried pretty soon after that, another miner, named Steve Engleman. And not much later, she and Steve got saved at a revival and started having prayer meetings right in their own house.

The people who spoke with Johnny were of two opinions about Don Nichols's stepfather, Steve Engleman. Some said he was a hard, stingy kind of guy who'd take the last egg in the house off the dinner table and eat it himself, a bad-tempered perfectionist who believed in using his razor strap on his stepchildren. Others described him as a God-fearing, hard-working fellow who believed in everybody pulling his share of the load and spending his free time—if he had any—in church.

One thing that everybody who knew Steve Engleman agreed about, though, he did not like to hunt and fish. He certainly never took young Don Nichols up to North Meadow Creek or the Beartrap Canyon on fishing trips, the way the boy's real father, Pat, had done.

Not long after Don's mother married Steve Engleman, the young boy apparently began to show signs that he wasn't what you'd call well adjusted. He was bright enough; no one Johnny talked to in Norris or neighboring Harrison would dispute that, but Don had been a loner in school, quiet and intense. People told Johnny that the boy spent a lot of time alone up in the mountains, either in the Beartrap Canyon area or higher, past Cowboy Heaven, right up in the Spanish Peaks. He just didn't go on camping trips, they said, he sort of went up there to live for a few months. And hike, they all stressed. Old Don Nichols could hike damn near anywhere. While most folks would drive where they had to go, Don Nichols would walk.

He had done well in high school in Harrison, and then he had left home and joined the Navy. But that didn't last long. Don couldn't adjust to the regimentation; he just did not like authority. Perhaps it reminded him of his stepfather.

He left the Navy and ended up marrying a girl named Verdina in West Virginia. Here Johnny's sources got a little vague. But, sometime in the early sixties, apparently, Don had brought his wife back to Montana and tried to run a homestead up near Noxon, right on the edge of the Bob Marshall Wilderness. He just couldn't stay away from the mountains.

Danny, the son, was born in the mid-sixties, but nobody seemed to know where, exactly. When the homestead went bust, Don moved his family down to Jackson Hole, where he worked as a machinist. But he really could not stay away from the mountains, especially the Beartrap Canyon and the Spanish Peaks, where his dad, generous, old Pat Nichols, used to take him camping and fishing, thirty years before.

Instead of keeping a steady job, Don Nichols would work long enough to get some money together, then take off for the mountains, where he'd live a few months, picking berries and poaching game, hiking up and down the range. He got increasingly bitter about normal society, what he called the "rotten system."

Up in the mountains, he'd told everyone who'd listen, a man can be free.

His wife divorced him, remarried, and settled in Three Forks, up near Bozeman.

But Don did not give up on family life. People said that he loved that boy of his, Danny, with the same intensity that he felt for the mountains. After Danny got old enough for Don to take the boy with him, their "camping trips" started lasting all summer long.

According to people in Harrison, Don Nichols had been living up in the mountains full time, summer and winter for at least this last year.

In 1973, Sheriff Roy Kitson had to go after Don Nichols on a truancy complaint from the Three Forks schools. It was well after Labor Day and the start of school, but Don had kept his eight-year-old boy with him, way above the granite cliffs of Beartrap Canyon, in that steep, wild country above Barn Creek. That was the part of the high country that few people ever went into, even the experienced elk outfitters. But people said Don had gardens and food caches up there, that he had enough supplies to hang on twenty years.

Somehow, Roy Kitson got word up to Don Nichols to bring the boy out, and they arranged a rendezvous at the south end of the Beartrap, not far from the power plant.

Sure as hell, old Don showed up with the boy in tow, right on time. He apologized to the sheriff for keeping his son up there so long, but said that they did not follow any kind of man-made calendar in the mountains. He'd been waiting, he said, for the wild strawberries to ripen, before bringing the boy down to civilization.

I promised Danny strawberry shortcake, he told Roy, and I always try to give the boy what I promise him.

That night, Danny Nichols stayed at the Kitsons' house. After Roy's wife had gotten the boy a bath and a clean set of clothes, Roy tried to cheer him up. But the little kid with fine blond hair and surprising brown eyes sat morosely by the window, staring up at the dark mountains, like a cub separated from its mother. He had a pair of ex-Navy binoculars that his father had let him keep when the sheriff had taken custody.

"What do you look for with the binoculars, Danny?" the sheriff's wife had asked. "Grizzlies? Elk?"

The boy turned his dark, serious gaze on the sheriff. "With the what?"

"With the binoculars, Danny," Sheriff Kitson tapped the glasses. "That's what they call these here things."

"No," the boy said, angry and confused. "They're called 'people watchers.'"

Johnny drove the patrol car on the dark curves of Route 191, north along the Gallatin Canyon toward Bozeman. In a plastic trash bag beside him he had a collection of smaller Ziplocs containing the evidence that he'd recovered from the crime scene that morning. He hunched over the wheel, staring into the bright cone of the headlights, as the dark trees and rocky canyon wall flowed toward him out of the moonless night.

The Gallatin County crime lab would fingerprint Al Goldstein's pistol and the walkie-talkie, then run tests on the packs and spent shell casings they'd found in the clearing.

Once that chore was completed, Johnny was scheduled to meet a Forest Service detective named John Marsh at the airport in Belgrade. Johnny had reserved a Cessna 182 and a pilot named Larry Corbin to fly him over the Beehive Basin and Moonlight Creek area. Earlier that day, Bob Morton had suggested this tactic, but, at first, Johnny had almost rejected the idea. After what he'd been able to piece together about the Nicholses, however, he thought the dangerous flight in the middle of the night might actually be worth the risk.

John Marsh was going to lend him a piece of hi-tech hardware that would have surely pleased even John Onstad. The gadget was an infrared accumulator scope, an electronic viewer called a Probeye that could locate the "hot spots" of campfires from the air. The more Johnny thought of the plan, the more he liked it.

Don Nichols was definitely weird, but he just might not prove impossible to understand. Johnny was beginning to realize that Don had spent so much time in those mountains that he felt invulnerable up there. That would account for their camping so close to

Ulerys Lakes, after they'd grabbed Kari, and his sense of invulnerability would also explain why they'd chanced building a fire in that three-stone fire ring in their camp.

Well, tonight Don and Dan Nichols were again camping somewhere up in those draws or on the ridges. They had to eat, so they probably had a fire going. According to Bob Morton, the Probeye scope could pick up the residual heat of a campfire, even hours after it had burned down to ashes.

And, if he did find a hot spot, Johnny could be reasonably sure that it was the Nicholses' campfire; all the legitimate backpackers had been accounted for and warned off.

Johnny drove like a robot, letting the car find its own comfortable speed around the curves. He was beyond normal fatigue now, in a kind of exhaustion where there was little danger of falling asleep at the wheel. His body was functioning autonomously, and his mind was pulsing with the collective images of the strangest day of his life.

Al Goldstein's face was there, as were Kari's pain-bright eyes and the glare of the camera lights.

But the picture of the morose little boy, clutching his binoculars, rose now to eclipse the other images.

"People watchers."

What kind of a man, he thought, would convince his eight-year-old son, whom he supposedly loved so intensely, that a pair of binoculars were called "people watchers"? That surely wasn't normal, or healthy, or whatever you wanted to call it. Don was sick, he now realized, badly twisted by the events of a troubled life.

But Johnny could not muster any pity for Don Nichols. Whenever he tried, Al Goldstein's swollen features blossomed behind his eyes. Don Nichols had progressed from watching people through navy surplus glasses to sighting on a man's face with a telescopic sight and firing a bullet through his living flesh and bone.

The black canyon walls slid by. Off to the right, Johnny sensed the dark flow of the Gallatin River. In an hour, he would be up in that blacked-out plane, using a people watcher of his own.

9

Madison Range

July 17, 1984

THEY WERE FLYING AT 12,000 FEET, ON A COMPASS heading of 335, northwest from the lights of Big Sky, toward the unbroken darkness of the Spanish Peaks Wilderness.

Johnny was in the rear portside passenger seat, the chill bulk of the Probeye against his chest. For the past five minutes, Larry Corbin had been climbing, a tight spiral above the lights of Huntley Lodge. Now they were about to make their first pass above Beehive Basin.

Johnny unlatched the Plexiglas window and the cold propwash blasted into the cabin of the Cessna.

"Okay, Larry," he said into his headset. "I've got the window locked open, and I'm gonna stick this thing out now. Keep her straight and level."

The Probeye was bulky, about half the length of a wastebasket, with thick handles on each side and a nylon safety strap that John Marsh had made Johnny promise to keep looped around his neck at all times.

"If I drop her out the plane window," Johnny had joked at the airport, "this old strap'll pull me out with it."

"If you drop her," Marsh had answered in the same vein, "you'd better go after her, Johnny. I hate to tell you what that son-of-a-gun costs."

On the flight south from Belgrade Airport, Johnny had followed Marsh's checklist of operating instructions. The Probeye worked on some obscure electronics principle that involved circulating supercold liquid nitrogen across an "accumulator lens." When the circular lens was pointed toward infrared heat sources, the images of these "hot spots" appeared in an eyepiece that reminded Johnny of a small television screen.

Once the battery pack had been turned on to start the cold gas circulating and he'd adjusted the brightness of the viewing screen, there was nothing else for him to do. You didn't focus the Probeye; you simply pointed at a heat source and waited. Supposedly, this thing had worked well in Vietnam, up on the Ho Chi Minh Trail, where the Air Force could spot the heat of enemy truck engines and cooking fires right through the triple canopy rain forest.

There was, however, one special requirement of the infrared scope that had a direct impact on their flight tonight. The Probeye was only accurate within a thousand feet of low-intensity heat sources like campfires. Naturally, that meant that they must fly a course only 1,000 feet "AGL," Above Ground Level. But the Beehive Basin was exactly that, a basin, a deep glacial depression among steeply rising peaks. The FAA chart they were using stated in bold red letters:

13,000 MSL

That meant, of course, that flying below a minimum flight level of 13,000 feet was not safe, especially at night, especially on a black, moonless night like this one. But Marsh had been very clear about the thousand-foot maximum range of the Probeye, and also about the instrument operating best in the darkest, coldest hours after midnight.

So Johnny and his pilot were obliged to fly a very careful course, northwest from the bright landmarks of the Big Sky lights, five minutes at seventy knots airspeed on a True compass heading of 335. Then they would turn back on the reciprocal course of 155, throttle back for a quiet approach, and glide down to an altitude of 9,000 feet. This would give them their thousand-foot range above the black slopes and draws of the Moonlight Creek and Beehive Basin area where the Nicholses might be hidden.

And, in theory, this route would also keep them well clear of the dark stone summits of the Beehive, Blaze Mountain, and Gallatin Peak that formed an invisible rampart, directly ahead. To assist in their navigation, Johnny had positioned Jay Cosgrove in his Blazer down on the Jack Creek logging road. Jay's bright headlights gave them a triangulation point due west of Big Sky. The only problem with this system was that the north corner of the triangle, the part that could kill them in a fractured second, was hidden in the moonless dark.

Johnny thrust the bulky instrument into the cold slipstream and bent over the eyepiece. The Probeye weighed over fifteen pounds, but there was no easy way to brace it on the vibrating edge of the window. In order to get the proper angle for the accumulator lens, he had to support the full weight before his face, as if the device were a bloated Polaroid.

As Johnny gripped the handles and squinted into the eyepiece, he realized that he should have worn gloves. The outside air temperature at this altitude was around forty; the seventy-knot wind-chill factor was going to make holding this damned thing very long an unpleasant job.

In the eyepiece, the world was a pale green, watery shimmer. There were no solid lines or dimensions, just wavering, chalky ripples. Before the flight, they'd set the sensitivity controls to eliminate false readings; in principle, only valid heat sources would appear, and he couldn't reasonably expect to see anything—if see was the right term—before they dropped down to their thousand-foot AGL search altitude.

"About a minute to the turning point," Larry Corbin called.

Johnny hunched uncomfortably in the cold prop wash, squinting into the electronic ghostscape.

Then, as Corbin banked south, a dazzling, lime green blossom burst at the scope's right corner.

"Hold it," Johnny shouted. "I've got it . . . it's right there."

But Corbin could not "hold" his turn. Instead, he did the right thing by adding left rudder and skidding around in a tight three-sixty.

As the plane flattened out of the bank, the bright green pulse faded in the scope, then disappeared. Johnny swore softly. If the Nicholses were down there, it looked as though they had heard the plane and doused their campfire.

"Can you put her back in a bank over the spot we just passed?" Johnny realized that he was almost pleading. He was tired and groggy, but he certainly wanted to catch those two murderers down there.

"Okay," Corbin called, "I'll try."

Again the plane banked sharply left. Johnny scanned aft in the dark wind, then forward.

Bingo! The green neon flower blossomed, even brighter this time, once again forward of his window.

115

As he pressed his face to the soft rubber eyepiece, he felt the plane banking through its turn. The glowing hot spot in the scope remained steady. But the plane was definitely turning, so the image should also move. Gripping the handles to steady the Probeye, Johnny raised his face to see where the lens was pointing.

He sagged, embarrassed and angry at his mistake. The lens was aimed directly at the bulbous metal cowling of the port landing gear. Engine exhaust blasted back to heat the wheel cover, causing the cowling to glow brightly in the infrared spectrum.

His campfire hot spot was four feet from the window.

"False reading," Johnny muttered. "Let's head south again."

On the fourth or fifth pass above the Beehive Basin at a thousand feet AGL, Johnny got a sudden green flare in the scope. The image was bright and ragged; it lasted for maybe two seconds. But he was sure he'd gotten a good heat-source image because the afterglow took several seconds to fade from the screen.

"Swing her back around, Larry," he yelled, forgetting he had a headset on.

But there was no repeat. They orbited the dark Beehive Basin for ten minutes while Johnny fiddled with the sensitivity controls of the Probeye and angled the scope back and forth in the chill wind.

Nothing, not even a glimmer.

"Well," Johnny conceded, "must have been a glitch or something. Let's work those draws to the south there, closer to the crime scene."

As they droned south toward the headlights of Jay's Blazer, Johnny forced his mind free of that fading green afterglow. No sense thinking about that. Must have just been some kind of a false image, something wrong with the electronics.

116

The blacked-out plane flew south in the darkness, toward the shallow draws above Moonlight Creek.

A thousand feet below, under the shelter of an over-hanging pine, Don Nichols and his son stamped down the dirt and gravel they had heaped on their campfire when they first heard the low-flying airplane. It was better to risk smoke by lighting a campfire in the morning, than to have that plane spot the coals they had carefully banked before bedding down.

Traveling at night was hard, but they had no choice. And it would probably be at least a week of night marches before they got back to the Beartrap, where they belonged.

Johnny's arms were cramping badly, but every time he tried to rest the weight of the Probeye on the windowframe, the engine vibrations made the viewing screen dance with the neon worms of false images. He had no choice but to accept the pain stoically through his exhaustion, to try to separate his mind from his aching body.

They were flying low circles now above the black void of the Jack Creek drainage. From this altitude, the summits to the north were faintly outlined against the cold bands of the Milky Way. But this visibility offered a false sense of security. Down here below 9,000, they might be pushed by invisible winds to drift in-to the surrounding ridge. He guessed they'd been fly-ing for over two hours, and he knew they'd have to pack it in pretty soon. Then suddenly the screen lit up.

"Steady," he called to Corbin. "Now, bank left . . . hard."

The heat source swelled to fill the center of the scope, a wide, pulsing green flower.

"Mark your position, Larry," he said into his head set. "We've got a winner."

Corbin throttled back even more, and the plane hung in a steep, slow bank, less than a thousand feet above the headwaters of Moonlight Creek.

Johnny's face was out in the slipstream now. The frigid wind revived him, and he blinked hard, forcing his eyes to focus. As the plane spun in its tight orbit, the ghostly green hot spot seemed to breathe, to flare and puff like a bed of coals remaining from a late night campfire.

"You getting our position, Larry?"

"Pretty good," the pilot answered. "We've got Jeffers in the valley bearing . . . 285 True, and the Big Sky ski lifts at. . . ."

Larry Corbin noted the bearings to known landmarks, using his accurate gyro compass.

A few minutes later, he told Johnny that he was confident of their present position, ". . . give or take a couple hundred yards."

Johnny was still halfway out the window in the buffeting slipstream, gazing at the pale lime hot spot in his scope. There could be no doubt about this one. Without question, there was something hot down there, and he knew it had to be a campfire.

"Climb out of here slow, Larry," he called. "I don't want them to hear us."

Flying back to Belgrade, Johnny stowed the Probeye in the backseat and climbed forward over the seat top to sit beside Larry Corbin.

They were back at a safe 14,000 now, well clear of any nearby summits. Around the small plane, the night was silky black. The lights of Three Forks and Bozeman spread before them, marking the north end of the Gallatin Canyon. Johnny was excited about the mission's success; they had a positive fix on a large heat source, less than a mile due north of the crime scene itself.

He rubbed his numb hands against his numb cheeks and thought for a moment about coffee.

"Kinda cold out there," he muttered.

Larry Corbin chuckled in the faint glow of the instrument panel. "People at the airport say you kind of like hanging out of airplanes, Sheriff."

Years ago, in the sixties, when Johnny had just broken into flying, he'd been involved in a bizarre mishap that had ended up landing him with a reputation as a daredevil.

He'd been flying with Tom Westall, his original flight instructor, in a brand new Cessna 210. Tom had a contract to fly as a "bird dog" guide plane for a flight of Forest Service spray aircraft, heavy old World War II torpedo bombers assigned to dump insecticide along the western slopes of the Madison Range.

They had a young government forester with them to do the actual spotting, and Johnny had just come along for fun, and for the chance to take the controls of Tom's fancy new airplane.

But there was not much fun that afternoon. Early in the mission, one of the spray plane pilots called them on the VHF to announce that their right main landing gear had failed to retract properly, and that the wheel strut was out there "flappin' around like laundry."

This Cessna was one of the first to be equipped with retractable landing gear, and Tom muttered about damned hydraulic systems always causing problems, as he went through the emergency recycle procedures. They tried just about every trick Tom knew—and that was a considerable bag of tricks—but the gear remained where it was stuck out at an awkward angle, like a crippled limb.

Having exhausted known remedies, Tom flew up to Belgrade Airport near Bozeman and threw the light plane through a series of high-G aerobatics that seemed almost to jar the engine off its mounts.

The stuck gear remained stuck.

By this time, the FAA was in on the act, and Tom was fielding a series of exasperating questions from "groundpounders" down in the tower. Finally Tom demanded that somebody contact the Cessna factory in Wichita to see what they suggested.

"Ask 'em if I can belly land this plane all right," Tom added in disgust.

The word that came back from the Cessna people was not promising. This model had a tendency to flip over on belly landings; and there was a bad record of fatalities for such mishaps.

Johnny had been watching the way the wheel strut behaved out in the slipstream. He'd eyeballed the angle between the wheel and the wing strut. Ah, maybe, Tom, he'd offered, I can crawl out there and kind of kick it down.

Kick it down?

Yeah, well. . . .

Ten thousand feet above Belgrade Airport, Johnny France had forced open the door of the Cessna and held it there until the forester could crawl into the front seat to jam his feet against the door panel.

Johnny then linked together several seat belts to make a Rube Goldberg safety harness, crouched at the edge of the open door and finally lunged into space, throwing his body completely clear of the cockpit.

He caught the wing strut all right, but, hanging there in the blue sunlight, his body blown back parallel to the line of flight, he was unable to loop his ankles over the jammed wheel strut.

Time did strange things while he hung outside the plane. When he moved, time seemed to stop. When he rested, hours seemed to roar by.

At some point, he managed to lock his ankles around the wheel. Now he had to drag the bulky metal joint into place. But he was pulling against an eighty-knot wall of wind, and he was tired.

At that point, Johnny had realized with a rush of fear that the only way he could get back into the cockpit was to pull the wheel down, so he could use it as a step.

After a long, exhausting time, the wheel strut began to move. Slowly it turned and locked into place. He twisted back through the half-open cockpit door with his last reserves of strength.

A local TV reporter had collared Johnny after they had safely landed. "What kind of guts," he asked with breathless intensity, "did it take to climb out of that airplane without a parachute?"

Johnny was still battered by the prop wash and the strain of the ordeal. He thought a moment, then answered as honestly as he could. "A lot less guts than it takes to get killed in a belly landing."

They were entering the pattern for Belgrade Airport now. On the instrument panel, the clock read ten past three in the morning. Johnny sat heavily in the passenger seat, watching the familiar strings of lights loop up toward him. He was worn down, dull with fatigue. Less than forty miles away, Don and Dan Nichols were sleeping beside a campfire, the source of that last steady, green hot spot on the Probeye. He had a reliable map position for that fire, right here on his Forest Service map. If he could make it back to Big Sky before dawn, he'd be able to assault their camp and capture the Nicholses before they moved on.

Johnny had quit smoking several years before, but now he longed for a cigarette in a way he never had experienced during the pangs of nicotine withdrawal. He had to make it back in time. He would hit that camp at dawn. Those guys had kidnapped a girl and killed a man in his county. And they weren't just going to walk away free.

That afternoon, once they'd gotten the tree section from Ulerys Lake and had a positive I.D. on the Nicholses, Johnny had conferred with John Onstad and his detective deputy, Bob Campbell. Bob had proposed an interesting idea that Onstad clearly favored.

"Yellowstone County's got a real good, FBI-trained SWAT team based in Billings," Bob said. "We could get them over here tomorrow, and have them running grids up there by Wednesday."

Johnny had listened patiently while Onstad and Campbell outlined the advantages of calling in the SWAT team from Billings. They'd been trained for just such a search and capture operation. They had modern, lightweight radios, and they were in damn good physical condition, good enough, Bob stressed, to really get up there and cover that high country.

Johnny had stated that he thought their suggestion was a "real fine idea."

He'd called Gary Lincoln, the resident FBI agent in Butte, and Gary had forwarded Johnny's official request to the proper authorities in the Yellowstone County police hierarchy.

The last Johnny had heard before leaving the command post to meet Corbin in Belgrade was that the SWAT team, equipped with jungle fatigues and automatic rifles, was due in Tuesday afternoon by chartered plane.

"Running grids" was all well and good. Tough young

deputies in camouflaged fatigues, carrying mean-looking M-16s would please the media. Certainly, the citizens in Big Sky and down in Gallatin Canyon who felt most threatened by the two armed crazies up in the high country would feel good about the SWAT team. But Johnny was less optimistic than his colleagues from Bozeman.

First of all, a grid existed on a map, not in the real world of the timbered draws and ridges. Secondly, no matter how fit the SWAT team boys were, they'd never be able to cover all that country up there. And, third . . . maybe most importantly, the Nicholses, especially old Don, would no doubt treat the heavily armed Special Weapons and Tactics officers just as he'd treated poor Al Goldstein. Don Nichols would shoot when threatened. And he'd shoot accurately.

By accepting the SWAT team from Billings as a kind of stopgap, public relations effort, a politically acceptable move to appease the local citizens, Johnny knew that he might be condemning some dedicated young officer to death.

But, if he and Jay and maybe Brad Brisban or Merlin could get up those draws above the crime scene by dawn tomorrow, they could jump Don Nichols and his son before they had a chance to rub the sleep out of their eyes.

Unless. . . .

Larry Corbin banked the 182 over onto final. Outside the wide Plexiglas windscreen, strings of amber runway lights turned silently in the night.

Unless. . . .

The Nicholses just might be disciplined enough to set a predawn ambush, standing to at their camp, waiting for deputies to approach. Or worse, using their camp-fire as bait for an ambush.

If they were that smart and crazy, Johnny realized, tugging down on his seat belt for touchdown, then he'd be condemning himself or one of his deputies to death, not some kid from the Yellowstone SWAT team.

What kind of guts did it take to run a predawn assault on the Nicholses' camp? A lot less, his mind answered, than sending some boy from Billings in to do it for me.

10

Madison Range

July 17–19, 1984

THEY PARKED MERLIN'S BRONCO ON THE DEAD-END SPUR of the Jack Creek Logging road. For ten minutes, Johnny and the two deputies waited for enough daylight to see the yellow plastic crime scene ribbons that marked the trail into the camp where Kari had been held and Al Goldstein murdered.

It was cold. Dew clung to weeds and wild flowers along the road's edge. Their breath was steam.

"Okay . . . I guess," Johnny muttered. He chambered a round in the mini-Ruger and slipped the rifle into the crook of his arm.

Beside him Merlin Ehlers and Brad Brisban went through the same "lock and load" ritual. As they used to say in all the old war movies, This is not a drill.

The military atmosphere was heightened by their semiautomatic weapons, their loose camouflage shirts, and by the clumsy weight of the armored flak jackets they wore.

They formed a very small army. Johnny had decided against trying to put together a large, well-coordinated assault on the "hot spot camp" above Moonlight Creek. After he'd gotten back to the command post from the airport, he had sat down in the big recliner in Jay's living room with his maps and duty roster of deputies, to form his plan, then proceeded to slip into forty minutes of exhausted sleep.

When he woke, it was almost five. There was no time to form a large strike force, so he chose the two best men available, Merlin and Brad. He would have liked to include Jay Cosgrove, but Jay was already out on patrol. Besides, Brad and Merlin were good in the woods. They'd been over this same country the day before with their dogs, and they could picture the place marked as a hot spot on Johnny's map.

Driving up from the command post, Johnny had told them his theory about the heat source: The Nicholses had no doubt decided to move at night, he said, and to hole up during the day. They'd left the crime scene yesterday morning at around eight and had probably laid a false trail back down toward Jack Creek, or up over the ridge to the Beehive Basin. Then, after dark, they'd ducked back south to make a hidden camp in the thick timber, only one draw above the south branch of Moonlight Creek.

He couldn't be certain, but, "something pretty damn hot was pumping out infrared last night, right north of the crime scene."

Brad and Merlin nodded with somber agreement. There sure as hell weren't any stray backpackers up there, not so far off the trails, not after all the publicity and deputies guarding the trailheads. But there apparently had been a campfire, only six hundred yards due north of the Nicholses' first camp.

When they reached the stream at the edge of the crime scene camp, Johnny signaled them to form an open V; once more, he chose the point. Before they entered the camp itself, each man released his weapon's safety and double-checked to be sure his radio was turned off. Johnny did not want anyone's radio suddenly breaking squelch to alert a hidden sniper. And he certainly did not want anyone fumbling with his rifle's safety, if they came face-to-face with Don Nichols.

According to the ranchers and forest service people Johnny had spoken with the day before, Don Nichols was known as a man who didn't believe in using a safety on a weapon. He also had a reputation as a "head shooter" of whatever game he hunted. Johnny could attest to that part of Don's reputation.

Except for the yellow crime scene ribbons, the camp was just as they'd left it yesterday afternoon. There was dark matted blood in the pine needles where Kari had lain, and the shape of Al's body could still be seen in the damp depression among the golden rod and columbines at the base of the big dead lodgepole with the bow snag. Just to be certain, Johnny bent to touch the charcoal in the three-stone fire ring. Cold, wet, and greasy. The Nicholses had not been crazy enough to return to this same camp.

They waited silently in the camp for a few minutes, each man trying to breathe as softly as he could. Then Johnny scanned the trees up the slope to the left of camp for maybe the thirtieth time. Then they moved out.

The gray geometry of deadfalls was even more confusing in this dawn halflight than it had been at midday Monday, and the cold dampness amplified the noise they made picking their way through the crosshatch of dead branches.

Once more, Johnny realized that he had not carried a canteen. His mouth was so dry that his tongue was sticking to his teeth. But there was no way to overcome the discomfort. Few people, other than law enforcement officers, actual frontline cops, and combat soldiers realized that this kind of deal never got easy or routine. Television and war movies made it seem that way; that was probably the reason kids joined the Marines, or signed on as reserve deputies, for that matter. But, it just never got easy.

The guys who wrote police and war novels always stressed the rage of battle. No one ever said how lonely and frightening it was.

Johnny raised his open palm, and took cover behind a thick dead tree. His map was folded into a thin vertical wedge, the Jack Creek drainage. By his estimate, they'd come over five hundred yards from the crime scene, due north on Merlin's compass heading.

He swallowed and leaned around the tree. The slope here was just about the right angle. To his left, he could see the same big area of young beetle-kill fir they'd passed on the way in the day before.

"Just ahead," he whispered to Brad, then turned to pass the same message to Merlin.

Johnny moved away from the tree's cover and negotiated a tangle of dead branches. Beneath his boots, the ground was spongy needles. A towering spruce rose among the lodgepoles, twenty feet ahead. Even in this gray light, he could see there was a clearing.

But this clearing held no secret camp. The rock pile rose above the jumble of thin deadfalls, like boulders among driftwood in the Beartrap. Merlin and Brad were out of the trees, crouching to scan the perimeter. Johnny stared at the huge slab of orange granite. This was the rock pile where the choppers had landed yesterday.

Then he sat down heavily on the granite slab, the fear and tension seeping away. Beneath his fingers, the surface of the granite was warm to his touch . . . not hot, certainly, but tangibly warmer than chill soil under the trees. This rock pile faced southwest. All afternoon, the granite absorbed the full heat of the sun. All night, the granite radiated that heat back to the sky. Infrared.

Johnny unfolded his map to its full width and took a rough eyeball bearing on the summits of Blaze Mountain and the Beehive. If he hadn't been so tired, he would have laughed out loud.

He stared at the timbered ridge that ran northeast toward the Beehive Basin. There had definitely been that first, sudden green flare in his scope when they overflew that depression. His impression at the time was that the scope wasn't working well . . . a glitch.

But now, as he stroked the residual sun heat in this stone, he understood that the Probeye had functioned perfectly.

The instrument had, indeed, picked up a heat source in that draw beyond the main ridge. Someone who didn't know the country that well might have said the first hot spot had simply been another rock pile, but the green flare in the eyepiece had disappeared suddenly as the plane approached. Boulder piles did not turn themselves on and off like light bulbs.

"Well," Johnny said, getting stiffly to his feet. "Kinda looks like a washout, boys."

As Merlin called in their position to the command post, Johnny cleared his weapon.

That possible heat source in the Beehive Basin was probably two hours away by foot. He shook his head. Last night, he hadn't been able to get any kind of bearing at all, not in two seconds. Bushwhacking their way up there now, just the three of them, would be a waste of time, and potentially dangerous. But somehow he knew the Nicholses had been up there last night. And now he had an idea which way they were headed. From everything Johnny had learned about Don Nichols, the dense mountain forest above the Beartrap was his real home. Not just the place where he went to camp out but his home territory, his turf. That was where Don Nichols was now headed, and that was where Johnny would have to hunt him.

The media was milling around again, just below the porch railing. Johnny cupped his hand over his ear and pressed the phone receiver hard against his head to block the noise of the nearby radio and the deputies in the living room.

"Bill," he said, "I'm glad I caught you before you got that budget printed out."

"What's up, Johnny?" Bill Dringle asked. "How's the manhunt going?"

Bill was a county commissioner with whom Johnny worked closely on the budget and fiscal matters of the Sheriff's Department.

"Well," Johnny hedged, not eager to spring his bombshell. "Bill, I'm gonna need at least another eight thousand to cover this deal we got going up here."

In principle, Johnny's budget had been approved and divided into line items two weeks earlier. Now he was asking for "at least" a five percent increase.

"Johnny," Bill began, "I guess you've heard the old story about gettin' blood out of a turnip."

"Yeah, well, I guess I have."

"I'll have to talk to some people and see what we can do." Bill sounded more frustrated than angry. "What's going to cost so much, Johnny? Eight thousand dollars is a lot of money."

"Well," Johnny ticked his finger against his thumb. "I've got overtime for the regular deputies, and we've had to call all the reserves out, Bill. Then there's meal allowances and . . ." the list went on, mundane, unglamorous, absolutely vital. A patrol car used gasoline. A deputy was paid three dollars for lunch and five for dinner when he had to eat away from home. Some of the reserves were using their own pickups; they were all using their own horse trailers. They received reimbursement, as per an exact schedule.

In Madison County, there were five thousand citizens to support the Sheriff's Department. Five thousand citizens did not provide a large, flexible tax base. Bill's tax-reserve turnip surely did not have much extra blood to support Johnny France's expensive manhunt.

"I'll see what I can do, Johnny," Bill added. "You see if you can't catch those two pretty soon."

"I'm working on it, Bill," Johnny said.

Below the porch, a clot of reporters dashed down the gravel driveway to intercept a helicopter that thumped in for a landing. After fifty yards, they slowed, then stopped. The chopper was from a TV station, not an official part of the manhunt.

Johnny was trying to grab an hour's sleep in a darkened upstairs bedroom when they woke him. He was so exhausted that it took almost a minute for him to sit up on the bed. Jay Cosgrove had brought a report on Kari Swenson. She was still in the Intensive Care Unit, but they'd taken her off the critical list. And, almost as important, two of John Onstad's detectives had been able to interview her.

J.J. Lane, Johnny's best woman reserve deputy, was now on duty downstairs as the command post dispatcher, and Terry was relieved of that responsibility. Now all Jay's wife had to do was provide food and coffee for twenty-some men, twenty-four hours a day.

Jay offered a coffee mug, and Johnny nodded his thanks while he scanned the report. The important points were outlined in brief, emotionless priority. Don and Dan Nichols had not raped Kari Swenson, according to her statements, to her doctors, and to the detectives.

The Nicholses had explained that they were "mountain people" or perhaps "mountain men" and that they wanted her to "try out" living with them for three or four days. They had told Kari that she would then probably want to become the bride or simply the "woman" of one of them. At some point, they had said that they had hidden camps in large, comfortable underground dugouts. They also had told Kari that they would shoot anyone who tried to rescue her.

They'd said that they would not be taken alive, and that she should warn law enforcement officers not to pursue them.

"Geez," Johnny said. "They wanted to make her a bride? What's that supposed to mean, Jay?"

Cosgrove shook his head. "Damned if I know, Johnny." He flipped copies of the local newspapers onto the bed. "Ah, I think we got a little problem with the press."

Johnny was up now, buttoning his stale shirt. He glanced at the dark headlines and the detailed follow-up features. Naturally, the Swenson kidnapping and the manhunt were the main topic.

"Read this paragraph," Jay said, pointing to the bottom of the *Bozeman Chronicle*'s headline story.

"Aerial surveillance of the area last night by an airplane equipped with an infrared scope, which detects heat on the ground, located a small campfire. Onstad said deputies would try to locate the fire today."

Johnny nodded pensively. "Yeah, well. . . ."

"Kind of shoots down using that scope again," Jay said. "I mean, once the Nichols boys hear about that on the radio, they aren't likely to build another campfire . . . not at night."

Again, Johnny nodded.

"We've got a lot of reporters around, Johnny," Jay said, pointing toward the front of the house. "They're getting into a kind of feeding frenzy with this stealing a bride for the mountain man stuff coming out and all."

Johnny was on his feet, slipping on his heavy shoulder holster. "First amendment, Jay. Not much we can do to stop the reporters asking questions, and John Onstad, just like me, has got to be available to answer those questions. He runs for office, same as I do, and we both have to let our people see that we're doing something." He smiled another hard, humorless grin. "In a deal like this, we got two sets of problems . . . catching the criminals, and convincing the citizens that we're doing our best to catch the criminals."

"Well," Jay conceded, "the press is doing its best to spread the word, that's for sure."

Johnny stood tiredly at the dresser, leafing through the accumulated reports.

"Hell," he muttered, "you see this?"

The Gallatin County department had received a call, from the antiterrorism office in the Pentagon, asking whether Kari Swenson was to be a competitor in the Olympic Games, scheduled to begin in two weeks in Los Angeles. Apparently, they thought her kidnapping by men in "military fatigues" might be an act of international terrorism directed toward our Olympic athletes.

They had been assured, Johnny read, that the biathlon was a winter event.

Johnny hitched up his holster, smiling now with real amusement. "Wonder how much snow those fellows think they get every summer in Los Angeles."

He was still laughing as he went down the stairs; then he saw the size of the press mob out front. This deal was getting too big, he realized, and it'd get a lot bigger if they didn't catch those two crazies soon.

Johnny France had dealt with the press before, but never on this scale; network correspondents did not cover the race for Madison County Sheriff, traffic accidents in Virginia City, or loose stock on the Norris Hill Road. The newspaper report about the Probeye scope might be just the tip of the iceberg. For sure, he realized, he was going to have to watch what he said in front of these reporters. He certainly didn't want to be accused of holding out on them, and definitely did not want to get into a situation where he'd try to manipulate them. That could backfire on you, real fast. But he just wished he had more experience on managing the PR side of a deal like this.

Once more he stared out the window at the milling reporters. Well, he thought, there aren't any deals like this one. What we've got here is a one-time-only case, and there aren't any rules to go by.

It was stuffy in the crowded conference room. John Onstad had scheduled the meeting with the concerned citizens of the Big Sky area for three that afternoon, but people were still pouring into the community center at quarter past. By three-twenty, all the folding chairs had been taken, and it was standing room only at the back of the hall. About half the people here were summer residents, and the rest local working people.

Almost from the start of the meeting, Johnny was aware of the sensitive political issues involved. The boundary line separating Madison and Gallatin counties ran north-south, right down the middle of the Big Sky resort complex. Big Sky's Mountain Village and ski complex lay in Johnny's county, the larger Meadow Village and commercial complex was in Gallatin County.

The crime had occurred in Madison County, but the Spanish Peaks, where the Nicholses might now be hiding, were almost equally divided between the two jurisdictions. Therefore the tasks of the two sheriffs this hot afternoon presented several potential conflicts.

John Onstad's job was to assure his tax paying, and voting, citizens that every effort was being made to protect their lives and property—and, of course, their businesses that depended heavily on the short summer season.

Johnny's responsibility ultimately was to catch the men who had committed serious crimes in his county. And he certainly did not want to reveal tactical secrets that might jeopardize the success of the manhunt, just to convince a local motel owner that he wasn't going to lose any more business. As the meeting progressed, the inherent conflict in their two positions came close to surfacing.

Once the preliminaries had been waded through and everyone had been given the bare-bones facts about what crime had actually occurred, the names of the victims, and the names of the suspects, the two sheriffs took turns detailing the actions they had taken to seal off the mountain area and, eventually, to capture the criminals.

As Johnny expected, Onstad stressed that the Nicholses appeared to be bottled up, that they were surrounded by heavily armed officers, way up there in the isolated Jack Creek drainage. He assured the audience that these two criminals posed no threat to life, or to commerce in the valley.

Johnny tried to skate around the topic of just exactly where the criminals might be holed up. There were enough reporters in the conference hall, he realized, to assure that everything said here would be repeated on television and radio in a matter of hours.

Once more, TV cameramen were having a field day with his big .44 magnum in the shoulder holster. But today, they also had John Onstad's camouflage shirt to provide exciting "visuals."

One older summer resident—maybe a retired lawyer, judging by his articulate, but nagging, manner—tried to pin Johnny down as to what resources he had committed to the actual search and capture, not just to sealing off the Madison Range.

Just before the meeting, Johnny's senior deputies had brought in their initial reports of the interviews they conducted that morning among the ranchers who leased pasture in the Cowboy Heaven and Beartrap areas and several outfitters who knew that country well. Johnny now had definite leads on the most promising potential hideouts. But the old gentleman's question gave Johnny a chance to send a misleading message up to his quarry.

"Don and Dan Nichols," Johnny said, speaking loudly for the microphones, "have spent the past twelve summers up in the high country." He paused to allow the print reporters to scribble their shorthand. "They've lived up there continuously since last August . . . almost a straight year. They know this country real well, sir. Until we get some more information, it would be nearly suicidal to send my people in there after them."

People rose with more questions. It was parry and thrust again, a repeat of yesterday's press briefing.

At one point, Johnny said that Don Nichols "fashions himself a Daniel Boone type. I'm surprised his weapons are as modern as they are."

In reality, Johnny was not surprised at all, but he hoped the word would filter up to those dense pine forests that he was underestimating the Nicholses' disciplined resourcefulness.

As the inevitable drudgery of the meeting ground on, Johnny thought once more of the sudden green blossom in his Probeye scope the night before. That had to have been their campfire up high in the Beehive Basin.

Without question, they were moving north, back toward the Beartrap and the primitive elk and grizzly country above Cherry Lake.

Citizens rose in the glare of the camera lights, some to ask sincere questions, some in hopes of five seconds of taped glory on the Six O'Clock News.

Johnny listened to their words, but his mind was elsewhere, roaming back through all the years he had hunted mule deer and chased stray calves up in those high summer ranges above the Beartrap. It was about as wild and thick a piece of back country as you could find in Montana. But that's where they were headed, he knew it now, right down in his bones.

Later that afternoon at the command post Johnny got a new batch of interesting reports. There was more evidence of the Nicholses living in the general area of the Beartrap Canyon and Cowboy Heaven. A reliable outfitter had seen their gardens of turnips and carrots, growing in spongy creek bottoms that stayed wet all summer. Cowboys had reported signs that somebody had been taking pancake mix and other staples from the food reserves left behind at the cow camps in the high summer pastures leased from the Forest Service.

When we make our push, Johnny decided, it's definitely going to be up in that country.

The next report didn't help him in his immediate tactical problem, but it certainly gave him some insight into the mentality of his two suspects.

Jay had answered a complaint from Jim Allison, the foreman of the Jumping Horse Stock Ranch. At least eight head of cattle showed up missing on his weekly count, Jim said, up there in the high pastures of the

Jack Creek and Mill Creek drainages. Then his boys had found several cows and calves that morning, shot dead at close range. Not butchered or mutilated, just shot.

When Jay found the carcasses, they were pretty rank. He estimated they'd been dead five days, maybe a week. But he had been able to confirm that the cattle had all been shot with a single, small-caliber bullet, right between the eyes.

"Looked like a .22 to me," Jay said. "Same as they shot the girl with."

"Not cut up at all?" Johnny asked. "They didn't even take the liver or anything, a little slice of steak?"

"Nope," Jay said. "And something else is weird. They were all cows and heifer calves . . . every one of them was female."

Johnny had spent the first twenty-one years of his life on local ranches. He knew the value of a cow and calf better than most people. He also understood that Don Nichols fully realized the outrage such an act would cause among the ranchers in the valley.

It's a challenge, Johnny thought, a crazy kind of damned macho challenge.

By that evening, the next day's scheduled arrival of the Yellowstone County SWAT team had leaked to the press. Just before dark, a herd of impatient reporters had formed a delegation and had bullied their way right up, onto the porch. Johnny went out to talk to them.

He was slowly becoming accustomed to shouted questions and blinding minicam lights, and learning that he couldn't answer everyone who yelled at him with a full-length statement. Apparently, the reporters didn't want a detailed briefing, just a summary, some "visuals" and a few quotes.

First off, he confirmed that there was, indeed, a

Special Weapons and Tactics team in Billings. But, he said, there were SWAT teams from other areas under consideration, as well. In any event, he continued, he planned to use a "good-sized force of men" who would be ferried into the target area by helicopter and four-wheel-drive vehicle. It was, Johnny told them, to be a "military-style assault" on the Nicholses' camp.

"Can you tell us when?" someone shouted.

"Soon," Johnny replied.

"As early as tomorrow?"

Johnny paused. Full disclosure was about to cut into operational security. "Well . . . I kind of don't like to talk about that. I—"

"Could it be as early as tomorrow?"

"What about the hideout, Johnny?"

It amazed Johnny how quickly reporters put themselves on a first-name basis with cops they had never seen before.

"Well," he said, "we have their hideout pinpointed, but I just can't discuss the details."

A lopsided white moon hung above Lone Mountain. Johnny patiently warded off the reporters' probes and thrusts. Up in the high country the Nicholses would be getting ready to move about now. If they had a radio they would soon be hearing that the sheriff of Madison County had their hideout surrounded—which might not be so bad, after all. He wanted to goad them on their way, back to their familiar haunts—their gardens, supply caches, and underground dugouts, up above Beartrap Canyon.

Early the next afternoon, the media's feeding frenzy reached a new pitch when the Yellowstone County SWAT team arrived at Huntley Lodge, the main hotel of the Big Sky resort complex.

To the disappointment of the cameramen, there were

not a lot of "sexy" visuals. The Billings policemen and sheriff's deputies who made up the eleven-man team did not leap from the Big Sky minibus in camouflaged tiger suits, with their faces blackened, and their M-16s cocked and ready. In reality, they did not look like hardened professionals.

In Johnny's eye, they appeared to be a collection of perfectly normal young guys in T-shirts and jeans. A few sported Airborne tattoos and macho mustaches, but the majority looked to be exactly what they were: young family men from a small Montana city. None seemed to be anything like a hard-core old tracker who could just sniff the breeze and accurately predict that the Nicholses went thataway.

It had become clear to Johnny that Onstad thought the Billings SWAT team was a heaven-sent answer to the vexing tactical problem of catching two murderous psychopaths who just happened to know the high country far better than the men on his force, or, for that matter, far better than anybody.

The SWAT team provided a tangibly reassuring presence. Everybody knew about SWAT teams from television; these men were "trained by the FBI." They were experts in a bewildering variety of martial skills and tactics. They were heavily armed, and they could move with stealth. In short, to John Onstad the boys from Yellowstone County were a comfortably modern solution to a nasty police problem.

Johnny had never had to serve in the military, but he understood a fundamental military principle that Onstad and his subordinates seemed to be overlooking in their optimism at the SWAT team's arrival. In an assault on an entrenched, hidden enemy defending high ground he was familiar with, the clear advantage lay with the defenders, no matter how well trained and equipped the attackers might be.

The day before, Johnny had told the citizens of Big Sky that sending his people into the trailless country of the Spanish Peaks would be "suicidal." Sending these young guys from Billings up there wouldn't be much different. A flak jacket might not protect a man from Don Nichols. Johnny could not publicly admit his fears; he had to remain as visibly sanguine as Onstad. But he knew there was a good chance that one or more of these young fellows was going to be shot if they managed to flush out the Nicholses in the morning.

Earlier that day, Johnny had talked with Dan Cummings, the manager of the Windy Waters Ranch, near Indian Trail, just north of the Spanish Peaks. Dan had seen the Nicholses up there several times.

"It's funny, Johnny," Dan said on the phone. "Those boys have a way of disappearing if you happen to ride up on them. Don't ask me how they do it, but they sure can vanish."

Now Johnny stood in the entrance of the Huntley Lodge lobby, watching the SWAT guys load their gear onto a luggage cart. One lanky young fellow in a checked shirt smiled at him; another short, stocky boy with a military tattoo waved. Johnny's fame from rodeo days, and his current reputation as a gutsy cop's cop, had evidently traveled as far as Billings.

Nichols would not let these young officers just march right up in their tiger suits and put the cuffs on him and his boy. From what Johnny was learning about Don Nichols, the man's mind simply did not work that way. If threatened, he would shoot, and Johnny knew how well Don shot.

In the end, of course, the massed firepower of the SWAT team's automatic weapons would prevail.

But which one of these boys would be hit by Don's first bullet?

11

Madison Range

July 19–23, 1984

JOHNNY MANAGED TO GET IN ALMOST FOUR HOURS OF uninterrupted sleep Wednesday night. But when Jay woke him just before three Thursday morning, Johnny was still exhausted. Like a robot, he dragged his legs off the bed and reached for the inevitable mug of black coffee.

"How's the weather?" he asked.

Jay went to the window and bent his tall frame to peer outside. "Lots of stars, Johnny. Looks like the moon's set already."

"We could sure use a little rain, Jay," Johnny said. "There's just not going to be anything for those SWAT boys to track up there today."

"Well, don't bet on rain. The weather report says hot and dry."

As they drove through the chill darkness to Huntley Lodge, Jay briefed Johnny on the final schedule for the dawn SWAT operation. Murray Duffy from Central Helicopters had called to confirm the 0500 ETA to pick up the SWAT team from the road, near the bridge across Spanish Creek. Duffy's son, Mark, would fly the

142

number two helicopter. They both had high-band radios.

Merlin Ehlers and reserve deputy Steve Orr had spent the night in a hidden observation post at the TV transmitter site on the west side of Beartrap Canyon, opposite Cowboy Heaven. Their position gave them a pretty good line of sight into the country above the granite cliffs to the east. They had called in at 0250 to report no sign of a campfire.

"Yeah, well . . . I didn't really figure they'd see one," Johnny said. "I suspect the Nicholses are traveling these nights, not building campfires."

The men of the Billings SWAT team had apparently gone to bed early, Jay reported. They'd gotten up at 0230 and were just now finishing breakfast.

Finally, the press was scheduled to assemble at the Spanish Creek Campground at 0500, under the watchful eye of John Onstad. The media had been a real pain in the neck about this SWAT operation. On the one hand, they all agreed to follow any ground rule he set down about not jeopardizing the security of the assault plan, but then they'd insisted that they all have access to the landing zone up at Spanish Creek, where Johnny planned to load the team aboard the helicopters. Johnny had hedged on that one, but he'd flat refused to allow interviews of the SWAT officers.

These men certainly did not want to meet the press, and they sure as hell didn't want to discuss the routes and targets of their all-day sweep. Since the previous afternoon, when Johnny had briefed the team members, the reporters had been playing cat-and-mouse games, trying to provoke a leak which would tell them where the SWAT team was headed.

Because the team was assembling in the open range foothills, north of the Spanish Peaks, he hoped the press would speculate that the SWAT assault was planned for the Hell Roaring Creek or Indian Ridge area.

In reality, the two choppers would lift the eleven-man team due west, past Cherry Lake and into the wild country north of Cowboy Heaven. In the previous three days, Johnny had received an almost constant stream of new reports concerning the Nicholses' movements in this area during recent years.

One veteran elk outfitter, Rob Arnold, had reported that Don Nichols had a whole series of caches and gardens up those steep gorges. Once Arnold's pack horses had gotten loose and had eaten Don's turnip patch right down to the ground. In retaliation, Don Nichols had burnt Rob's carefully stacked pile of winter firewood.

Dave Wing was back from fighting the fire in California. He'd given Johnny a thorough briefing on the Nicholses' suspected routes, camps, and caches. As with the other sources, Dave's leads all pointed to forested ridges above Cowboy Heaven, and to the densely timbered gorges that dropped steeply into Beartrap Canyon.

One real old-timer from Ennis, Ben Sheffield, told them he'd seen several of Don Nichols's camps up above the Beartrap. "They're funny places," he had said, "sort of like the kind of camp a soldier in a war would make, you know, all hidden in the brush . . . just like Nichols don't want no one knowin' he's up there."

The country was a natural fortress. To the west, the massive granite cliffs of Beartrap Canyon stood like a rampart. The only access from this direction was up the nearly vertical ravines of Barn, Fall, and Beartrap Creeks, but these gorges rose almost two thousand feet in less than a mile from the Madison River rapids down in the canyon. In effect, the western wall was sealed by natural obstacles.

To the east, the open parkland of Cowboy Heaven quickly gave way to scrub forest, then thick timber. There were no trails from the summer pastures on the high plateau to the gorges dropping down to the Beartrap. The only access was through the timbered draws and small drainages of the feeder streams. But these routes could be easily blocked by a well-hidden sniper who knew the country. The Nicholses had chosen as their home turf some of the best natural ambush country in Montana.

The more Johnny learned about Don Nichols, the less surprised he was at Nichols's preoccupation with security and geographic advantage. The guy was what the psychologists called a paranoid. Over the years, Johnny had attended his share of FBI and Law Enforcement Assistance training sessions on a variety of subjects, including psychological profiling of criminals. At the time, he'd found these courses interesting, but not readily applicable to his job in Madison County. He had grown up there and knew several thousand adults in his jurisdiction by their first names. But now those training sessions had some practical advantage. It wasn't good enough to just say Don Nichols and the boy were "crazy." You had to try to understand what kind of crazy they were.

Johnny was beginning to understand that Don Nichols was afraid of the normal world, that something bad had happened to Don when he was a little kid, and that this bad event or events—what the shrinks had called severe trauma—had eventually driven the old boy back up into the mountains where he had been happy with his real dad.

Once Don had staked out his territory up there, he did not want anyone trespassing. To keep people out, Johnny speculated, Nichols might have constructed a series of hidden sniper's nests and observation posts where he could use his "people watchers." And now events had acquired a kind of inevitable momentum of their own; the SWAT team was saddled up, ready to sweep that stretch of wild high country in the hopes of finding Don Nichols and his son on their home turf.

The night before, during one more nagging encounter with the press, Johnny had been asked about the chances of a shootout, should the SWAT team "flush out the suspects." He had avoided spilling out his fears, even though the urge to voice his worry had been strong. He had to remember that he might be speaking indirectly to the Nicholses.

"We feel," Johnny intoned dramatically enough to be certain of being quoted, "that, if they are confronted with a tactical force such as we have, they will surrender."

The SWAT team, he added, was supported by an FBI-trained professional negotiator, Detective Chuck Newell. Once the team members had cornered their suspects, Chuck would be brought in to talk sense to them. In other words, the searchers had a good combination of resources and a high chance of success.

Obviously, the reporters liked the prospect of a dramatic confrontation in the forest, the wily "mountain men" cornered on a rocky ridge, the cunning, FBI-trained negotiator calling up to them through a bull horn. Such a scenario could last for hours, for days. A young reporter could make his or her career by covering such a hot event.

Johnny could not really blame the reporters. He'd never seen anything like the number of wild rumors and false leads that were mushrooming out of nowhere, often from perfectly normal local citizens. It seemed that men answering the Nicholses' descriptions had been spotted all over Madison and Gallatin counties, over in Idaho, up in Canada, down in Wyoming, even as far away as upstate New York. His police log was filling up with dozens of such calls. Each one had to be checked, of course, and that was taking a lot of Under Sheriff Gary Dedman's time.

One thing that Johnny did not want to do was to rile up the press any more than they already were. But, if officers were going to risk being shot up there, he also did not want to go on the record that the morning's assault was what young Francos would have called "a piece of cake."

"I think, however," he concluded softly, gazing full into the camera lenses, "that the possibility of a shootout still exists."

They bounced across the gray washboard. In the Big Sky minibus, there was just room for Jay, Johnny, and the eleven armed members of the Billings SWAT team. Up ahead, the dark bulk of the Spanish Peaks rose in the pale dawn. No one talked much; each man seemed preoccupied, staring out the misty windows, his automatic rifle gripped between his knees. Their dark green face paint, floppy bonnie hats, and mottled woodland camouflaged fatigues seemed to give them an unreal, television presence. They had become symbols, not people. It was as if they'd shucked off their human skins, and slipped on this standard Green Beret identity. They no longer even had names, Johnny mused, just call signs, "Fat Man" and "Striker," and the others Johnny had scribbled down, but couldn't now remember.

Johnny sipped cold coffee from a foam plastic cup as they chattered across this bad patch of road below Finnegan ridge. In half a mile, they'd turn south into National Forest land and the road would be paved again.

In the beautiful, windless dawn, the sky went slowly from mauve to faded eggshell blue. Here in the bottom land of Spanish Creek, the dew was thick on the juniper brush. Mist rose in tendrils from the cottonwoods along the creekbed. Outside, the world was silent, primitive. In the jolting bus, the men sat silently.

They bounced north across the bridge and onto the asphalt road. Abruptly the quiet was broken by the slapping rumble of helicopters. Johnny turned in his seat to see the two choppers cutting left, then angling off in a slow bank to set down directly ahead of them on the widest spot of the blacktop road. As they flared out for touchdown, their rotors blew up fine sprays of dew from the weeds.

At the back of the bus, someone began singing, "Into the air, junior birdmen. . . ." No one laughed.

Johnny stepped into the chill and stretched his legs, then ducked back into the front seat to grab his hooded hunting parka. One thing about getting so exhausted, it made a person cold, even on a relatively warm morning.

By the time he'd pulled on his parka, the SWAT boys had saddled up their web gear, loaded their weapons, and were standing by in two squads, one of five men, one of six. Johnny did not immediately realize that the men were ready, that there was certainly no reason to wait around here, wasting daylight. Then he saw the grim expressions on their painted faces.

The two choppers could carry a total of six armed men, and that meant two lifts into the jump-off point north of Cowboy Heaven. He was confident that the two squad leaders understood their assignment, and, obviously, they were not eager to sit here, diddling around while the press got wise and made it down from the Spanish Creek campground, just over the ridge ahead.

"Good luck," Johnny called, then pointed his finger at the choppers.

The first squad crouched low and trotted to the helicopters. Within a minute, they were airborne, Murray Duffy in the lead chopper, cutting due west above the brown foothills.

Johnny had his high-band radio raised, but he didn't know what to say. He'd been too busy getting the first lift off to even think about consulting John Onstad up at the campground. "Choppers away," he finally managed.

Onstad came back immediately, his voice distorted by the radio. "Johnny, where you at?"

"On the road, with the choppers," Johnny replied. "Where you at, John?"

"I'm on the road." Onstad paused, a little exasperated. "On the road where I was supposed to meet you, Johnny . . . at the campground, with the press."

"Well . . ." Johnny noted the frustration in Onstad's voice. The scene up there was easy to picture. There were seventeen reporters and cameramen, probably suspecting that Onstad had tricked them by acting as a decoy to keep them away from the SWAT team's actual take-off point. "Well, John," he repeated. "The choppers landed here. We're all down here."

The press did make it down from the campground to document the departure of the second SWAT squad. As Johnny had feared, the event threatened to degenerate into a first-class media circus, and the reporters' cars and remote vans managed to block the wide level stretch of road that Duffy wanted to use as his runway.

Jay and Johnny had to act as traffic cops for a few minutes, waving cars and vans this way and that. By the time that was sorted out, the frantic cameramen were dashing about, towing their soundmen behind them.

Johnny stood by the open passenger door of Onstad's car, talking to Murray Duffy on the high-band. He was too busy to take Onstad aside and review the details of the operation, which they had wearily plodded through the night before. And it was also unfortunate, but the reporters seemed to be blaming Onstad for the mix-up. They milled around his open car window, yelling angry questions at him.

At least this took some of the pressure off Johnny. He watched the second squad split into two and clamber aboard the two choppers for the second lift to the jump-off point, ten miles to the west. During the excitement of the press arrival, Johnny had lost some of his anxiety about a possible sniper attack on the SWAT team. Now that fear returned full-blown.

The youngest member of the team was a lanky blond kid with the unmistakable manner of a boy who'd been raised on a ranch. Johnny had managed the Ennis high school rodeo program long enough to recognize the type: an honest, open-faced kid who had plenty of heart and a lot of courage. But this boy had another quality; he was almost a spitting image of Johnny and Sue's oldest son, J.T.

As the kid strapped himself into the front seat of Duffy's chopper, he looked up at Johnny, smiled warmly, and shot him a jaunty thumbs up.

Johnny felt like he'd been kicked in the stomach. He realized it was completely irrational, but he suddenly felt that this kid would be Don Nichols's first victim this silent morning.

Ten minutes later, the premonition had grown to the point that Johnny simply could not control himself. Even though the original operational plan called for Johnny to monitor the SWAT team's sweep from the Spanish Creek campground, he had decided that he had to get closer to the action. If the team spooked the Nicholses, he wanted to be close by, so that he could be dropped in there and be the one who took the point.

Onstad and Chuck Newell, the negotiator, were keeping the press occupied on the other side of the car. Off to the left, Murray Duffy was setting down, empty again. The plan was for him to stand by here, while Mark returned to Bozeman in the second chopper.

But Johnny had other plans. No one seemed to notice while he grabbed his rifle and scooted low beneath the rotortips to clamber aboard Murray's helicopter. A moment later, they were airborne, and Johnny could see the circle of startled faces around Onstad's car.

He probably should have consulted with Onstad, but that would have meant wading through the press, and besides, something was overpowering his common sense this morning, driving him in a way he'd never known before.

The chopper rose and turned sharply right, to the west, to the Beartrap.

He realized they had a serious problem the moment Murray Duffy pointed out the landing zone (LZ) of the SWAT team's jump-off point. They had landed and formed up on a grassy ridge surrounded by wooded hills, a piece of country that fit the description of the originally intended landing zone, north of Cowboy Heaven. But this ridge was on private rangeland, at least four miles south and east of the intended jump-off point.

Johnny boiled, giving in to the anger and frustration of the long week. Then he brought his feelings under control. In the misty dawn, the mistake had no doubt been easy enough to make, and he was not sure who had made the call, the pilots or the SWAT team leaders. What mattered was that the men had started their sweep from the wrong position. Their carefully plotted coordinates would all be wrong. Instead of working down the game trails past Rob Arnold's camp and Don Nichols's gardens, then on through Cowboy Heaven, the SWAT team would probably end up bushwhacking that thick country around Red Knob.

But he had agreed not to call them except in an emergency, so that the noise of the radio message would not squawk loudly through the forest, possibly provoking a sniper attack.

They set down on a rocky clearing overlooking the hills of the Spanish Creek range. For twenty minutes Johnny monitored static and broken messages passing among Onstad's people back to the east. But there was nothing from the SWAT team. While they waited, a herd of seventeen bull elk, their antlers all in velvet, grazed out of the pine forest and across the edge of the clearing, no more than fifty yards from them. The animals did not seem disturbed by the presence of the men or their bizarre machine.

Finally, Johnny realized that he wouldn't be able to contact the men on the ground from this far north. "Murray," he said, "let's swing north here, up around the top of the canyon and back to the TV tower." Maybe, he thought, we can get a sight of them out in the open and risk a call.

Duffy had flown in Vietnam, years earlier than Francos. And Duffy knew ways of hugging the gullies and the canyon walls that would prevent them being seen and also mute the slap of the rotors.

As they dropped into the Cherry Creek draw, Johnny twisted in his seat to get one last look at the country the SWAT team was now sweeping. The sun was up now, and, just as Jay had reported, the day was going to be hot and dry.

Danny Nichols sat in the junipers, his legs open, the butt of his rifle resting easily on his right hip. He breathed slowly, but made no other movement. None.

There were a few flies, but nothing to really bother about. And the sun was hot. But Dad had always told him heat and cold were just mental perceptions, not actual facts.

"You don't hear a spruce tree or a mule deer complain it's too hot or cold, do you?" Dad would ask. "No, no, no. People come up here, and they complain. But them kind of people don't belong here, do they, Danny?"

Those kind of people did not know how to sit so still in the trees that a deer or a whole family of grouse would just walk up and you could grab them, without wasting a bullet. Those kind of people were not patient enough, Dad said. They ran their lives according to the rich man's clock. They thought sitting still for a few hours, so that the natural rhythm of the forest came back, was some kind of hardship.

The first time Danny's dad had played the sitting game with him, Danny had gotten impatient, himself. But for the last few seasons at least, he'd gotten better at it than even Dad. And now, of course, since the trouble with the girl, they weren't playing games anymore.

Danny sat in the hot brush, moving his eyes, but nothing else, letting his senses sort out the flies and the sun from the information he absorbed through his eyes. That was how the Indians lived, Dad had explained, but white folks have forgotten how.

Well, we haven't, have we, Dad?

No, Danny, but we're not like regular white folks.

His eyes now told him that the soldier in the jungle suit, carrying that Vietnam rifle, would pass about ten paces from this clump of brush. The other, taller soldier, that they'd seen earlier, had already moved up the side of the ravine and was no danger. But this one might be a problem.

The man seemed to move pretty good, for one of those people who kept watches and calendars.

The soldier was close enough now for Danny to hear the man's heavy, puffing breath. He was a big guy, with too much milkshake and french fries fat on him. Dad said all these people were drugged by the poisons the rich men made them eat. It was part of a rotten system, and you couldn't fight it down there, you had to leave, to travel.

The soldier's face was red, and all the stupid army war paint had washed away from sweat. But he wasn't even sweating now, that's how bad off he was. As the soldier passed the juniper bush, Danny could smell the heat stink. There were white circles of salt on the back of the man's camouflaged shirt. He'd traveled a long way up here, and he was just about worn out.

It would be a while before he cleared the top of the ravine and joined up with the others. Danny sat in his place, conscious of his rifle, but immune to the flies and heat.

Time doesn't really exist, Dad had explained. It's just another artificial concept. A squirrel chattered up the slope. Locusts buzzed. The forest was returning to its natural rhythm.

Danny Nichols waited in his place, fifty paces from his silent father. In the forest, outside time.

By two that afternoon, the officers at the observation post on the west side of Beartrap Canyon were worried that the SWAT team had strayed too far south of their intended search area. Months later, these same officers would note the irony that the "lost" SWAT team had almost stepped on Danny Nichols, hidden in that brushy draw. But Johnny and his deputies at the TV tower had no way of knowing this then. They did know, however, that they'd been unable to make radio contact with the team. Occasionally, they would pick up a garbled transmission that might have been the SWAT officers, but there was no way to be certain.

One sure way to reach them, of course, was to fly over there in Duffy's chopper. But Johnny had been hesitant to resort to that maneuver, for fear of tipping their hand to the Nicholses. But when he heard that they were out of the woods and that they seemed to be on the side of Red Knob, it became clear that they'd missed their main objectives by at least four miles. Rather than broadcast this disappointing news to the world via the reporters' police scanners, however, he bit the bullet and told Murray Duffy to fly him across the canyon.

The SWAT team was resting in the shade when they got to the LZ on the northern slope of Red Knob. Some of the boys looked all right, but the rest were just beat. After a brief map conference, Johnny realized that these men had already put in over twenty miles of trailless humping since they shoved off from that ridge, just after dawn. It was tough to ask more of them that day, but he knew he had to try.

If they agreed, he began, he'd have Murray ferry

them up north of Cowboy Heaven, three at a time. Then they could work their way south and west, down past Goose Creek and through the top of the wooded ramparts, in the area of known gardens where he suspected Don Nichols had established his dugout and hidden camps. A hunter named Ron Bruno had reported seeing a dugout camp two years before, hidden in a stand of quaking asps near the Goose Creek gorge. This dugout had a canvas flap across the mouth, and had been carefully camouflaged. That was a prime target that Johnny wanted the SWAT team to find.

The SWAT team leaders consulted among themselves. "Okay, Johnny," the leader said, "we're here to do the job, so let's do it."

Once more, the men boarded the waiting helicopter. But several of them were limping now from blisters and twisted ankles, and some had that pale, waxy look that meant heat exhaustion wasn't too far off.

As the first lift clattered off into the hot sky, Johnny glanced around the shady circle at the remaining men. They were somber, silent. No one had to say it, but they all understood that three noisy chopper lifts along that ridge was going to broadcast their presence and probably their intentions to the Nicholses. If there had been the danger of a sniper attack earlier, there was a menace of one now.

The SWAT team came down into Beartrap Canyon, four hours later. They had made no contact. They had found no tracks. One officer had discovered an abandoned turnip and rutabaga garden, in a small draw up on the top, a hidden garden, cut from a stand of young fir. It looked "pretty damn dry," he said, as if it hadn't been tended in a long time.

When the men broke out of the brushy ravine north of Barn Creek and found themselves on the trail above the fast-moving Madison River, several guys dropped their web gear and weapons and just flopped into the cool shallows. They lay there for a while, not moving as the chill water washed across their bodies. One man who saw the sight was reminded of dead soldiers he'd seen in an irrigation ditch, a long time before in Vietnam.

Back at the parking lot of the power plant in upper Beartrap Canyon, Johnny helped the men load their gear into the cars. They had the slack stares and slow reactions of people at the edge of their physical limits.

The press had made its way to the power plant, but even the eager young TV reporters did not seem inclined to badger the SWAT team for the details of their fruitless day's work.

To Johnny France, the next three days acquired the spastic and fractured texture of a fever dream. The standard division between day and night had been so shattered by the manhunt, that he found himself thinking an event that had occurred an hour earlier had taken place days before, or, worse, that leads his deputies had processed early in the manhunt were actually new information.

It became difficult for him to follow the true sequence of orders and the various subinvestigations proceeding around the Big Sky command post. His sleep debt had reached the point where sleep was no longer possible. For at least two days, he didn't even try to go to bed, but just took a few minutes unconscious absence where he happened to be sitting.

Early that weekend, Jay Cosgrove came off patrol and entered his living room, looking for Johnny. He found both Johnny and John Onstad, each sitting in recliners at either side of the bay window, a big relief map spread between them on the coffee table. Each man was dead asleep. Out cold, slack down to his bones with exhaustion.

Another deputy witnessed the scene. It reminded him of a command bunker at a fire base in Pleiku Province he had once entered to deliver a message to the CO during the Tet Offensive. The captain and two sergeants were slumped across the map board, as if an enemy assassin had struck. But, like the sheriffs, those men had been ambushed by physical and spiritual exhaustion, not a knife or bullet.

Certain moments of the manhunt's final days, however, made a vivid impression on Johnny. At dawn on Friday, he flew up to the Jerome Rocks. They left the Big Sky airport over near Cameron with the stars still bright, and climbed into a pastel dawn up at 12,000 feet. There'd been a report from a hiker of a camp near Marcheta Lake where the man had seen meat hanging in green canvas bags strung from a pine tree.

They throttled back and slid into a shallow glide, due east, into the pale golden eye of the sun. They skimmed the trees above Chiquita Lake and glided over the ridge to Marcheta. Below them, a cow moose stood in the shallows, weed dripping from her slow jaws as she gazed up at this strange, whistling intruder. As they passed above the smooth, grape-blue water, a large cutthroat trout splashed free of the surface and hung there for a moment, surrounded by ruby droplets.

Johnny stared tiredly at the scene. Then he closed his eyes when the pilot gunned the throttle to climb out of the basin. There had been no campfire, no humans, but Johnny was beginning to understand something of Don Nichols's attachment to these mountains.

On Saturday, a six-man FBI Regional SWAT team slipped into Big Sky, dressed in civies, unnoticed by the press. Johnny and Onstad briefed them, and they left that afternoon with Dave Wing to carry out a night sweep, all the way from the Cherry Creek Cow Camp through Cowboy Heaven.

The next morning they returned, gray with fatigue, limping and silent. They had seen nothing. They had found no signs or tracks.

Even while the FBI team was staging for their night sweep, however, Johnny was preparing the ground for a long pursuit. When he met the press that night, he projected pessimism that was only half feigned.

The Billings SWAT team, he said, "checked a lot of country and found no traces, no evidence that the Nicholses are still here." He waited until the reporters had absorbed that information, then hit them with his bombshell.

"I feel definitely that they have left the immediate area and are moving from mountain range to mountain range."

"But," he added, "I know that we will catch them. It may not be this year, and it may not be next year, but we will catch them."

Saturday afternoon, Johnny called Governor Ted Schwinden to request National Guard support.

"Sir," Johnny said, "I could sure use a big Huey helicopter, maybe two, and I could sure use about a battalion of guardsmen, with maybe a trained recon unit to relieve my deputies down here on this deal."

The phone line hissed faint static while the governor considered Johnny's request.

"I have to disappoint you on this, Johnny," Governor Schwinden finally answered. "I hope you'll understand, but I just can't go calling up the Guard every time we've got a law-enforcement problem that's tough to handle locally."

Johnny swallowed some coffee and nodded. "Yes, sir, I do understand."

On Sunday, Johnny got a call from Ron Alles, a U.S. Marshal in Billings. Mr. Alles made Johnny an offer that managed to raise his hopes to a point higher than at any time during the manhunt.

Ron Alles was a member of the U.S. Marshals Service's Special Operations Group, the SOG, an outfit which he pronounced "sog," as in "soggy."

The SOG, he explained, had been recently formed; they were very well funded and equipped, and their leaders were just looking for a worthwhile large-scale operation to test the outfit's strengths and weaknesses.

Since Madison County Attorney Loren Tucker had been astute enough to seek assistance from the U.S. Attorney in Billings, based on the possibility that the Nicholses had fled across the state line to avoid arrest, the federal SOG might be authorized to assist the local manhunt.

"Look, Johnny," Alles said, "I don't want to butt into your business up there, but we've been looking for an operation to use as a training exercise."

"Fine," Johnny said, "I'm listening, Ron."

"We've had some pretty good success, but that operation you've got going in those mountains sounds like it'd be great for us to train on."

"Yeah, well . . . we've certainly been learning a thing or two this week."

"I'd like to fly in there tonight with a couple leaders of the SOG and check out what we can do for you." Alles paused. "Johnny, if we decide that this operation is good for our purposes, we'll bring in more officers and special equipment than you've ever dreamed of."

"Call when you've got a flight number, Ron. I'll meet you myself."

Monday morning was gray, clammy. The cloud deck was well below the shoulders of Lone Mountain. Johnny hiked into the crime scene with Ron Alles, and the two SOG leaders. One of the marshals was from Louisiana, one from Chicago. Unlike Ron, the two men did not have much firsthand experience in mountains, certainly not in mountains like this.

On the way from the dead-end logging road to the crime scene, one of the SOG leaders became disoriented and wandered off.

The officers spent a lot of time in the clearing, staring at the Nicholses' three-stone fire ring and the tree where they'd chained Kari. They gazed at the gray crosshatch of deadfall lodgepoles. They studied their maps, talking quietly among themselves.

Back at the command post, the three marshals conferred for quite a while, alone on the corner of the front porch. Finally, Ron Alles came in to speak with Johnny France.

"Johnny," he began, "you've got some impossible damned country up there." He shook his head, as if stymied by visions of those gloomy tangles of deadfall. "We'd love to just saturate these mountains with officers and choppers, but . . . I think you realize that we could come up here with a thousand men, and we'd just end up getting spread too thin in this country you've got."

Johnny nodded his glum agreement. Right now, the thought of a thousand fresh, well-financed federal officers, supported by fleets of helicopters, was a gleaming fantasy.

"Johnny, we've got a good budget, but not that good. Once you've got these people better pinpointed, once you've got them sort of bottled up . . . then we'll spend the bucks and come in here like Gang Busters, but we got to take a pass right now, Johnny," Alles concluded. "Right now, it just won't work."

Outside, the clouds were even lower. Johnny had been up here exactly one week, but it felt as if he'd been born in this room and surely that he would spend the rest of his days here.

Sue France opened the front door and stood on the porch when she saw Johnny's headlights round the corner. It was after ten o'clock and the boys had been watching a M*A*S*H rerun when they heard the car.

"Well," Todd said, "Dad's home. Let's give him a hand with his gear."

"No," Sue said. "Just let me talk to him first, okay?"

He walked with an undisguised limp to the rear of the Eagle and stood, staring vacantly into the open hatchback, as if he couldn't decide which equipment stayed and which he must carry into the house with him tonight, as if the mere thought of one more decision was too much right now for him to face.

On the ten o'clock news from Bozeman, Sue had heard the report that the manhunt was officially over. She had seen Johnny's exhausted face on the videotape, patiently explaining that the pursuit would continue, but at a much lower level. Sue remembered the pain and despair in his eyes.

He climbed the front steps slowly, cradling an armful of weapons and ammunition pouches.

Sue reached out to touch his face. "The boys will help you with the rest, Johnny."

He nodded absently, acknowledging both her touch and her words. "Good . . . real good, Sue. I sure can use some help right now."

PART 3

Pursuit

12

Madison County

Late July, 1984

THE KIDNAPPING, MURDER, AND SUBSEQUENT MANHUNT
had so altered the pattern of France's daily life that he
found it difficult to return to his normal routine, once
he had come down from the Big Sky command post.

The business of the Madison County Sheriff's Department and the commercial life of the county, however, continued at their normally hectic summer pace.
This was peak season for the river guides and trout-
fishing outfitters. Ranchers worked around the clock,
irrigating the hay crops on which their annual profit
depended to a great degree. As Johnny told people,
this was, indeed, great "summer country." The obvious
corollary was that Madison County, like most of Montana, was literally obliged to make hay—and money—
while the sun shined. Few tourists drove their Winneba-
gos through the January snowdrifts to sample the
delights of chicken fried steak or cream of broccoli soup
at Bettie's Cafe. The hay that the ranchers were now
able to wrest from their parched, chalky fields would
keep their pregnant cows alive through the frigid void
of the seven-month winter.

And everyone from ranchers to motel owners to white-water guides depended to some extent on the sheriff's department to patrol the roads, help out at accidents, investigate petty crimes, round up loose stock on the highways, and generally maintain law and order, so that the tourists would have a pleasant stay in the recently subdued mountain frontier. Between July Fourth and Labor Day, the two-month tourist bonanza reached its peak. So did the rate of car crashes, drunk driving arrests, break-ins and vandalism, not to mention an increase in the year-round problem of bar fights.

To police the whole county, Johnny had himself and seven regular deputies, around the clock. In theory, there were reserve deputies to supplement his force. But many of them were ranchers and outfitters for whom prolonged extra duty would be a real financial burden. That was a moot point, however, because he'd already overspent his annual budget for the reserves during the week-long manhunt, and he couldn't get too much more blood from Bill Dringle's budgetary turnip.

The net result of this situation for Sheriff Johnny France was that he found himself in a complicated and frustrating position. The more he brooded on Don and Dan Nichols—and there were probably not ten waking minutes in his day when he didn't think of them—the more convinced he was that they were still up in the mountains, working their home country from the Beartrap east into the Spanish Peaks. But Johnny simply did not have the human or financial resources to maintain a massive law enforcement pressure on that area. If he was going to catch them, he knew, it would be through cunning and not through any kind of large, brute-force operation.

Part of Johnny's strategy of cunning was based on the assumption that Don Nichols did carry an AM transistor radio, and that news reports on the progress of the pursuit would reach him each day. There was no way to be certain, but Johnny decided to continue his deceptive use—he hated to think of what he did as manipulation—of the news media. Since he had neither unlimited numbers of men nor vast reserves of money, he had to use whatever free resources were available.

So Johnny continued to foster the idea that the Nicholses had slipped through the dragnets of mounted deputies and heavily armed SWAT teams and had fled the area. Probably, he suggested, they were now working their way north through the mountains of Idaho, en route to Canada. This strategy had several advantages, and several distinct disadvantages. Loren Tucker, the county attorney, could legally request continued federal assistance, based on the sheriff's official statements that the Nicholses had become probable interstate, maybe even international, fugitives. This meant that Johnny would have men and special equipment from the FBI available to augment his own home-town resources. And, of course, when the news that the FBI was searching for the Nicholses up on the Canada border reached Don Nichols in his dugout above the Beartrap, he might just lower his guard a notch and start doing things like building smoky fires or leaving tracks.

The disadvantage of this maneuvering was predictable. If the Nicholses had simply walked out of the mountains, crossed several miles of flats over the Tobacco Root or Beaverhead Range—right through Sheriff France's roadblocks and patrols—and were now halfway to Canada, then Johnny France would look like an incompetent fool at best, and derelict in his duty at worst.

This was a personal and political risk that Johnny was willing to take, but which John Onstad apparently

167

wanted to avoid. Now that the two sheriffs were out of the joint command post and back at their respective county seats, Onstad's statements to the press acquired a different slant from Johnny's. Onstad and France were consulting each other on a daily basis, but they clearly had begun to keep their own council as to the way they handled the press. Toward the end of the initial manhunt, Onstad said in an interview with Karen Datko of the *Bozeman Chronicle* that his department "may be able to determine in four or five days" whether the Nicholses were still in the area. Meanwhile, he said, his deputies would conduct daily mounted patrols in the Spanish Peaks and West Fork areas.

Johnny countered this by telling Ms. Datko that he would "probably" begin horse patrols on the Madison County side at a later date.

Onstad was running a smooth operation over on the Gallatin side, and he had a lot more personnel than Johnny. Because neither sheriff seemed inclined to clear the other's press statements, Johnny saw that he might be able to orchestrate the overall public assessment of the official pursuit to fit his needs. As things stood in late July, the impression Johnny was hoping to send indirectly to Don Nichols was that the heavy pursuit pressure was coming from the east, from the Gallatin side of the range. That way, the Nicholses might voluntarily keep themselves bottled up in the more confined area of the Beartrap.

One other advantage of this informal psy-war campaign was that Don Nichols might realize that the two sheriffs had discovered a great deal about his background, his habits, and his mountain haunts. From all accounts, Don Nichols was an intensely secretive person; publicly exposing the intimate details of his life might rattle him enough to lower his guard. For example, Onstad stated in his *Chronicle* interview that he'd discovered the deep attachment Don had for Danny. Relatives, he said, "continually talk about the love this guy has for his son." Comparing Don Nichols to a sow grizzly who feels her cub is endangered, he offered a rationale for Don's apparent cold-blooded murder of Al Goldstein. Don, he said, might have become irrational when he saw Danny threatened by Goldstein's pistol.

"You threaten the cub," Onstad said, "and that sow becomes unglued."

When Johnny read that rather flamboyant statement by Sheriff Onstad, he realized that his counterpart across the mountains might just be playing a clever psychological chess game with his quarry through media manipulation himself.

Johnny was not sleeping well at all after he came down from Big Sky. He took to driving his Eagle for hours, up and down the highway from Ennis to the right-angle bridge at the lower end of Beartrap Canyon, just driving with his face out the window, gazing up at those dark, timbered ramparts. He relied heavily on his under sheriff, Gary Dedman, and Deputy Sergeant Merlin Ehlers to keep up with the paper work and maintain the deputies' duty rotations. Naturally, he had to cancel the river trips that had been reserved for the month of August.

One afternoon, Sue came into his home office with a yellow pad. She'd just called the last of the clients to cancel the final reservation. "Well," she said sadly, "I figure it's just about eight thousand dollars that we're going to lose this summer, Johnny."

He was hunched over his roll-top desk, staring at a smeared Xerox mine survey chart, trying to compare the coordinates of abandoned mine shafts in the Beartrap to actual locations on his Forest Service map.

169

After a long, strained moment, he looked up. "Sue, you remember the name of that old miner who had one leg shorter than the other? Used to live up the draw toward the Boaz Mine?"

Sue France sighed and folded her neatly printed accounting sheet in half, as if closing the page might eliminate their financial problem. As sheriff, Johnny's salary was lower than his own deputies; unlike them, the sheriff of Madison County was not paid overtime. The France family needed the money from those canceled raft trips. If Sue worked seven days a week at the McAllister Inn, from now until after Labor Day, she might earn an extra thousand on wages and tips. But they had mortgages now on two properties, and a boy about to begin college.

"Johnny," she said quietly, "we've really got to sit down and talk about money . . . soon."

Johnny nodded, as if the urgency of his message had finally gotten through. "It wasn't Henderson, was it? Old Toby Henderson?"

"I can't remember," Sue said flatly. "You knew those Norris and Harrison people better than I did."

For the past several nights, Johnny had twisted and thrashed in bed, his jaws clamped tightly, mumbling radio call signs in his sleep, ordering the deployment of phantom forces. And each night he had woken yelling a futile warning, too late to prevent a nightmare ambush.

"I'll get you some more coffee," Sue said.

One afternoon Johnny drove eighty miles on gravel tracks, checking his three remaining roadblocks at the Hammond Creek campground and either end of Beartrap Canyon. These were manned by deputies, working off duty for compensatory time, rather than overtime pay, and by volunteer reserves like Billy Clark and Bill

Hancock, men who quietly came forward to fill in where they were most needed.

When he drove back through Ennis, he simply did not have the spirit to stop at home and face the bills and phone messages that he knew had accumulated on his desk. So he headed west on route 287 toward Virginia City. But, four miles up the highway, he turned left onto the dirt road to their "place," the twenty acres of range that he and J.T. had fenced, on which the France family would build their dream house.

As the Eagle jolted across the dusty washboard, Johnny tried unsuccessfully not to scan the black timbered ramparts above the Beartrap to the east. But he just couldn't stop himself from staring at those heights. Right now, at this very moment, Don Nichols and his boy were up there, hidden in a dugout or moving carefully through the brush, alive, free, no doubt feeling damn near invulnerable. This was coming on full berry season up in the back country. They'd be feasting on blueberries and gooseberries, roasting squirrel or venison steaks over smokeless coals. The streams would be low, but there were lots of permanent springs. The yearling elk calves would be fat, and one calf would provide enough sundried jerky to keep them in meat for a month.

Well, he thought with a certain grim satisfaction, at least they won't be smoking any elk ribs or hams; that was just too damned risky. Unless . . . He gripped the wheel savagely and frowned. Unless they had found a real deep abandoned gold mine shaft, a long gallery that the old-timers blasted right out of the living granite, a mine with sumps and sinks and vertical cracks enough to disperse even the dense smoke needed to preserve large chunks of game meat.

He felt the almost overpowering urge to turn back to

Ennis, to speed home and barricade himself in his little office, and to pour over those mine survey sheets just once more, in hopes of finding the Nicholses' secret bonanza. But then he sagged at the wheel, letting the tension uncoil inside his chest. There would be raids on mine shafts; there would be slow foot patrols of those ramparts and overnight ambushes laid around the suspected garden plots. Dave Wing was back from working security on the latest forest fire, and Bernie Hubley of the FBI had gotten the green light from Helena to provide all practical assistance. Merlin and Gary Dedman were fine tuning the duty roster this very afternoon, so that Johnny would have at least three experienced deputies or reserves to run his sweeps and patrols whenever he wanted.

Within three days, he would be back up there, searching for tracks, scanning the game trails with Bernie's fancy night-vision equipment. Within a week, Johnny and his men would be stalking the home turf of Don Nichols, moving silently, laying in ambush, waiting for the old man and the boy to drop their guard, to make just one mistake.

Just as Johnny was turning through the tall gate poles of the Circle Four, a herd of twelve pronghorns stood up from the brown grass across the track and bounced past the front of the car. In normal times, the presence of these beautiful antelope, living free right on his land, would have caused him to smile broadly, or even to laugh aloud. But today he only nodded, a silent acknowledgment that the animals had right of way over the car.

He drove across the front pasture and stopped at the jumble of boards and rolled roofing felt that stood beside the half-built barn. Johnny was building the structure with seasoned pine planking from the local lumberyard, and filling in with salvaged wood when he could find it. The original plan called for the roof to be raised and covered by the end of July, but the top of the barn was still just skeleton frames, without a single roof plank in place.

Johnny took off his uniform and pulled on a tattered old work shirt and a ragged pair of jeans. Leaning back on the fender of his flatbed truck, he eyeballed the open ribs of the unfinished barn roof. The longer he stood there squinting up at the glaring sky, the more the harsh lumber skeleton seemed to taunt him. During months of backbreaking work, snatched from afternoons and Sundays, he had envisioned the satisfaction of wedging into place the long pine log of the roof's main beam, the ridgepole. But Don and Danny Nichols had wiped out Johnny's construction schedule.

He squinted at the big log that lay on its chocks near the far side of the barn. Now he stared up at the waiting frame timbers at the roof's peak. Now he examined the chains and tackle arrayed beside the log.

This peeled log beam weighed well over a ton. He was alone. All he had to work with were his improvised blocks and tackle, his Rube Goldberg scaffolding, and his rattling old Ford truck for brute motive power. But he also had his cunning, and his determination.

He reached into the greasy toolbox on the truckbed and pulled on his leather work gloves. All right, he thought, I'm gonna raise that beam up to where she goes. And I'm gonna do it this afternoon.

Four hours later, Johnny France drove through the dark, back along the gravel track to the highway. Behind him in the lingering halflight of the sunset, his barn stood capped by its main roof beam.

He jolted over the ruts, the dust billowing brown in the headlights. There was something hard and knotted, a clot of hot pain low in his back. His arms felt as if he'd been heaving hay bales all day. His fingers hardly closed on the wheel.

He had raised the main beam of his barn. Alone, with his primitive resources. And his brain.

Still, he was not prepared to go home. Sue was at work; the boys were probably working, too. The house would be empty, just those bills and phone messages.

He had definitely done something bad to his back, he mused, twisted lopsided to the steering wheel as he headed down the long dark incline toward the lights of Ennis. But that was all right, too. A little physical pain went a long way to taking a person's mind off his worries.

He called Vickie on the car radio. There were no immediate crises at the office, but she mentioned that Billy Clark was working town patrol on the eight-to-midnight shift and that he had the information Johnny wanted. He thanked Vickie, and smiled into the night.

Billy's regular job was as a talc miner, but he'd spent a lot of time up in the back country, hunting and working as both a logger and an outfitter. Johnny had asked him to draw up a list of all the abandoned mining cabins Billy remembered seeing between Jack Creek and Cherry Creek, north of the Beartrap. Now, apparently, Billy had completed his list.

Main Street was typically full; a midsummer week night brought out all the tourists and trout fishermen. It was getting so that parking near the saloons and restaurants was a real problem, what with all the pickups, campers, and sundry station wagons.

He spotted Billy's patrol car parked near the post office and figured he was walking a foot patrol of Main Street. A little early, maybe, but then Johnny looked at the dash clock and realized it was after ten. He had worked right through suppertime up on the barn roof, jacking up the ends of the log, banging temporary bracing into place, his mouth full of four-penny nails and his hammer flailing.

I'll kill a couple birds here, he thought, find Billy and get myself a glass of beer at the Long Branch.

He considered standing himself to a ten-dollar ribeye in the steak house behind the barroom of the Long Branch, but then got a whiff of the sweaty work clothes he still wore. I try goin' in there like this, they'll shun me like an orphan calf.

He parked and was halfway out the car door when he realized he'd left his stetson on the front seat of the flatbed, five miles back at the place. Johnny just did not like walking around in public without a hat. So, he rummaged around his fishing gear in the back of the Eagle and came up with a battered old trucking cap that J.T. had picked up somewhere.

Decked out in his ripped jeans, threadbare work-shirt, and greasy old gimme cap, the sheriff of Madison County was ready to buy himself a well-earned beer. Almost as an afterthought, he tucked his pearl-handled .38 snub-nose into his waistband.

Billy was in neither the Silver Dollar nor the Jack Creek Saloon. Johnny figured he needed a glass of beer more than that information right now, so he ducked into the smoky gloom and juke box noise of the Long Branch.

The bar was full, and several groups of locals and fishermen crowded around the pool table and electronic poker machines. One glance told Johnny what kind of a night it was. There were a couple drunken cowboys at the bar, propped up on stools, cadging drinks off the out-of-staters, swapping tales of the Wild West for cans of Coors. The fishermen looked sunburned, half drunk, and stuffed full of Harker's rare prime beef. Cigar smoke and pseudocamaraderie between investment brokers who made a couple of hundred thousand a year and broken-down old cowboys who couldn't keep their boots in half soles.

Johnny slid into the far end of the bar, pulled down the bill of his cap and signaled Harker for a beer. Three stools down, an old drunk with a white beard was regaling a couple fishermen about the "goddamned so-called mountain men." Harker must have thought Johnny was in disguise of some kind because he didn't even say hello. Or maybe it was the gloom at this end of the bar. In any event, Johnny found himself with a can of Lite, a dark niche at the end of the bar, and a hidden ringside seat to the old fellow's diatribe.

Johnny studied the man's face a moment, and let his mental file of mug shots flip slowly ahead. All right. He couldn't remember the name, but the man himself emerged. Used to call him Gabby Hayes, back when Johnny was a deputy. The old guy was a sometimes prospector, sometimes elk outfitter. Wasn't at all as old as he looked, either. Had a cabin down near Quake Lake at the bottom of the county. Brad Brisban collared him once for a real nasty DUI down at West Yellowstone. Far as Johnny knew, old Gabby Hayes had never found any gold. Maybe he spent too much time looking for it through the snout of a beer bottle.

"Damn it," Gabby shouted. "Them two ain't mountain men. They're just a couple crazies that got some dumb idea to take that girl." He sucked on his beer can, pinky finger cocked to impress the dudes. "Whole damn thing's got blown out of control . . . SWAT teams, and helicopters. . . ." He shook his head for effect and the hovering fishermen leaned low to hear his whispered comment.

"I said," he repeated, "that I could of taken my two hounds and just walked into the woods from that there lake up there and had them two fellas up a tree in half an hour."

Again, he shook his head, muttering.

The dudes popped fresh beers and the noise seemed to revive Gabby Hayes. His washed out old eyes sparkled in the smoky light from the pool table. "Tell you one thing. . . . This here sheriff they got here . . . he's lazy, and scared and he couldn't find the side of Blaze Mountain up there, and that's no lie." He slurped some beer and wiped his billowing mustaches. "Why, hell . . . they'd of asked me, I'd of had both them Nichols boys up a tree in half an hour. Instead, that old Johnny France let 'em just stroll on out of the hills and drive their car up to Canada."

For a moment, Johnny considered upbraiding the old fool. But to what gain? Let Gabby Hayes and the dudes think what they wanted. Somehow, the afternoon's long battle with the roof beam had given him the confidence that he would win the other victory he wanted so badly.

The moon was high, cold and bright above the circling timber. Danny moved quietly through the grass, his rifle held before him, his eyes open to any sign that the tent held danger. Behind him in the trees, Dad had a good position, a boulder and tree trunk that gave him cover and a full view of the Cowboy Heaven cow camp.

They had been watching from the trees, waiting and watching, since sunset. Now it was after midnight. No soldier or deputy could stay inside that old frame tent without moving, without taking a leak, without talking on his fancy radio, for so many hours.

The tent held no danger. But there was food inside. And they needed food. Traveling so much at night, avoiding their regular gardens and caches, they had gotten kind of worn down, and they'd not been able to hunt much. Dad was right about that. A shot was too risky with the helicopters and soldiers and posses riding around. So they had traveled on berries and a few snared grouse. But now they needed real food.

For a day and a night and another day, and now since sunset, they had watched the cow camp. No cowboys, no deputies. No human beings. It was easier to watch a place at night, because you didn't really have to stare, just to listen to the night sounds, the mice and the owls, the moles and the bats. The little animals got scared first and were the last to come out when the danger was over.

And now, with the moon so high, it was plain to see the owls and bats. There was no one hiding in the tent.

He moved as quietly as he could. Then he used his rifle muzzle to pull back the tent-flap. It was lashed from the outside, secured against wind or rain.

Inside, he could smell there was no one hiding. Working carefully so he wouldn't spill in the dim light, Danny filled his plastic canisters with Krust-eze biscuit mix from the big box near the stove. He took a bottle of Karo syrup and filled a canister with white sugar. He had nothing to carry the Mazola oil in, so he took the whole plastic jug. Then he filled two more canisters with biscuit mix. There were no red beans. Too bad; Dad said you could travel a long way on red beans. But there was a bottle of whiskey. Danny held the cold glass between his fingers and swallowed the hot sweetness. Dad would smell the liquor on him. Maybe. Dad didn't really smell as good as he said he did.

Danny slung his rifle and moved slowly around the dark corners of the tent, feeling among the cots and blankets with his free hand. There was no radio. Dad had said to check the cowboys' personal gear to see if there'd be a little transistor radio. But there wasn't any personal gear up here now, just tools and some food.

Their own radio was hidden at the Fall Creek cache,

and it was too dangerous to go dig it up. Anyway, the batteries were dead, so it wouldn't do much good. Dad said a radio would help them stay away from the posses. But Danny was not so optimistic. You kill a girl and a cowboy, and people were going to keep looking for you. They just didn't forget something like that. But Dad said they would, that they'd stop caring in a while, next year, maybe after that.

But Dad wasn't right about a lot of things anymore. He opened the whiskey bottle and drank another hot sip. Dad was right about one thing, though. That cowboy had no right to come busting into their camp, waving a pistol. Dad always said, you never let anybody just come into your camp that way. You've got to keep them out. You've got to keep the advantage.

He wrapped the whiskey bottle in canvas and thrust it to the bottom of his pack, then loaded the plastic canisters.

Outside, the owls worked the darkness, searching out mice that crisscrossed the meadow. There was no danger.

13

Big Sky and the Beartrap

Late July–Early August

THE LAST THURSDAY OF THE MONTH BROUGHT JOHNNY France the first real break in the case, plus the promise of potentially vital assistance.

That morning, he got a call from Dan Cummings, the foreman of the Windy Waters Ranch. Dan and his crew leased the Cowboy Heaven cow camp from the Forest Service and ran cattle up there, using the surrounding meadows for their high summer range. Seems that Dan was moving his herd around yesterday, and the boys stopped at the cow camp for a meal. And they discovered that somebody had been in the tent and had taken off with a fair amount of food. Far as Dan could tell, the thief had taken biscuit mix, sugar, cooking oil, and maybe a bottle of liquor.

"You sure about that, Dan?" He gripped the phone so tightly that his fingernails paled.

"Course I'm sure, Johnny," Dan replied. Like most ranch men, he wasn't overly talkative, but when he did speak, he meant just what he said. "We keep a pretty good estimate on the food supply up there, and I know when something's missing."

"Well, okay," Johnny soothed. "Real good, Dan. This'll help us a lot, and I really appreciate your calling."

Neither man spoke for a moment, then Dan broke down and asked, "Johnny, you figure it's the Nichols boys?"

"Uh . . . well," Johnny stalled, "can't be certain, Dan, but you know we're gonna check her out real good."

"Yes, sir," Dan stated. "Oh, yeah . . . one thing, Johnny. Whoever went in the tent there tried to tie the flap back, just like we'd left it, but they didn't quite get the hitch right."

"I understand, Dan."

Again, silence on the phone line.

Once more, Dan's curiosity rose. "That's not the kind of thing just some hungry hiker'd do, is it? I mean try to hide the fact he'd been there."

"Yep . . . you're right about that one, Dan."

"Well," Dan concluded, "guess I'd better have my boys be a little more careful up there, huh?"

"Probably a good idea, Dan."

Johnny went straight to Dave Wing's office at the Ennis Forest Service station. Over the past twelve years, first as a deputy, later as sheriff, Johnny had worked with Dave on several cases. Dave was a rock-steady, quiet guy in his fifties. To Johnny, Dave was a thick-set bear of a cop, the kind of man you'd want around you in a shootout or a forest fire. As Forest Service Law Enforcement Officer Dave was responsible for all the federal land on this side of the range, and was the official coordinator between local jurisdictions, state fish and game officers, and other federal law officers who had business in the National Forest. His job continually took him up to the mountains and, like Johnny, Dave Wing had often been obliged to clean up the mess when tourists got in trouble in the back country. Dave Wing was everything a good Western cop should be—tough, thoughtful, and persistent. But in Dave's case, the job also required that he be an expert hunter, tracker, mountain rider, and all-around woodsman.

They sat in Dave's office, surrounded by the inevitable contour maps and coffee mugs.

"You know, Johnny," Dave began, speaking with slow deliberation, as was his way, "when I was up working security on that fire, right after the crime, fella hands me a newspaper and says, 'You kinda got yourself a problem down where you come from, Dave.' I knew the minute I read that story that it was the Nicholses who done it." He paused. "Now, sitting here, listening to you talk about this food disappearing from the cow camp, I just know it's the Nicholses done it again."

Johnny stood up and went to the map. "If they were at Cowboy Heaven, say two days ago, hitting the tent, that'd mean they had to be crossing the same country the two SWAT teams covered, more or less, when they were covering it."

Dave paused to think through his reply. "Those twenty-four hours I spent with the FBI SWAT people, Johnny, were about as tough a deal as I can remember." He raised his calloused palm. "And they had some special surveillance equipment that's so secret they wouldn't even let me get a good look at it. And, Johnny, we covered that country up there, I can guarantee you that."

"Reckon you know those woods a little better than the boys from Billings, Dave."

Dave Wing nodded. "Expect as I do."

Johnny waited for Dave to work toward his point.

Dave got to his feet and joined Johnny at the map. "Well," Dave said, "the thing is, I've been looking for Don Nichols up there off and on for years, after he burned down the Cowboy Heaven cabin and then the Spanish Creek ranger station. You know arson's a real nasty offense in the Forest Service. Well . . . like I said, years looking for that fella, and never once, not one time did I ever see him."

Dave tapped the map several places with his blunt fingertip.

"There were times, Johnny, when I knew they were right behind me in the brush. They could see me okay, but I never once saw them." He smiled now with grim respect. "And that was when little Danny was only twelve, thirteen years old, and before they went and got themselves in real trouble." He sat down tiredly in his swivel chair. "If'n I couldn't even see 'em once back then, John, what chance you figure those SWAT teams had, or that we've got now that they're really trying to hide?"

"Yeah, well," Johnny muttered, unwilling to concede the obvious logic of Dave's argument. "Thing is, Dave, we know they're up there now, after Dan Cummings and all—"

Dave raised his hand. "I knew they were up there then, too." Again, he smiled grudging respect. "But I'd hear they was up around Rob Arnold's elk camp one day, and a couple days later they'd be clear over to Jack Creek. Those two know how to travel, Johnny."

"Hell," Johnny said, shaking his head. "We can't just let them stay up there, Dave. We gotta go up and bring 'em down. That's our job."

Dave Wing slowly considered Johnny's words, then nodded. "Oh, we'll have to keep trying, John, don't get me wrong. We're gonna be trying with everything we've got. And, if we get lucky, we'll catch them before they hurt anybody else."

Now Johnny smiled. "Dave, remember when you and me and old Roy Kitson used to talk about Don Nichols being better off, living alone up there, out of harm's way?"

Dave smiled ruefully, but did not speak.

"Well," Johnny added, "we'd figure he was better off in the hills than walking the streets, or costing the state money to keep him in some institution."

"Yep," Dave Wing conceded. "I guess we were wrong."

"I guess we were."

That afternoon Johnny received the promise of potential expert aid. Apparently Al Goldstein's family back East had contacted a well-known tracking expert, a fellow who'd written a bunch of books on the art of following human and animal tracks through the most primitive wilderness. This tracker was supposed to have helped several East Coast jurisdictions locate people missing in the woods, and, according to his publicity, he was an internationally recognized expert in "the ancient art of the new survival."

He ran a tracking and survival school in an Eastern state that was better known for its toxic waste dumps and suburban sprawl than for its untrammeled back country. But he seemed to come highly recommended, and he was coming free; at least Madison County wouldn't have to pay for him. Whatever the tracker's skills and record, he had managed to convince the Goldstein family to pay for him and his two assistants to fly out here and see if they could track the Nicholses.

Johnny's first reaction was elation. He knew full well that there were some highly skilled trackers in this country, and he knew that there were also some damned good bloodhound men, who made their living hiring out to police departments in need. And now, it seemed, they were getting the services of just such an expert, at no cost.

The tracker and his two assistants were due to fly into Belgrade Airport the next day, and the Gallatin County people or Bernie Hubley would drive them up to Big Sky. The plan called for the tracker to visit the crime scene, get a good fix on Don and Danny's boot prints and on other, unspecified, "signs," then to cover the immediate Moonlight Creek area. The day after that, Johnny planned to take the tracker and a small posse up to Cowboy Heaven to see if they could find the Nicholses' fresh tracks from the cow camp tent, back into their home ground above the Beartrap.

The combination of the food theft and the unexpected arrival of an expert tracker seemed heaven sent. This might just be the break that all cops waited for in any difficult case. Johnny knew that success usually came from the application of exactly the right resource at exactly the right time and place.

Later that day, however, after he'd waded through the accumulated bureaucratic detritus on his desk, Johnny's optimism began to fade. Since the first days of the manhunt, the department had received offers of "expert" assistance from an amazing variety of sources. Bloodhound experts from the South and East had called repeatedly. Professional bounty hunters had queried about possible rewards. A number of former "Green Beret" and other less-specified "commandos" had telephoned, offering their services at supposedly bargain rates.

One man called from Texas in the middle of the night and prevailed on Vickie Hudson to write out a long biographic note to detail his prowess. He was, he stressed, a combat veteran "Marine Ranger." Now Johnny was no expert on the military, but he knew that the Rangers were a branch of the Army infantry, and that the Marines had their recon units filling the same function. They were highly competitive entities, not a hybrid special unit, as this fellow tried to suggest. Clearly, the publicity of the "Mountain Men" case was shaking a lot of bats out of the belfry.

Another crackpot volunteer who came to Johnny's attention that afternoon was a young fellow from northern Montana named Jerry. He walked right into the governor's office the week before and demanded that Governor Schwinden "appoint him to the manhunt," so that he could "kill those two guys." The governor's assistant fobbed him off, but spent enough time in the young man's presence to note that Jerry appeared distraught, "hard-looking," and "weird."

Later in the day, Johnny had Merlin Ehlers make some phone calls, trying to check up on the authenticity of the tracker whom the Goldstein family had hired. He hoped that they wouldn't have another phony nut on their hands.

Merlin's report did little to calm Johnny's mounting suspicions. According to Merlin's sources, the tracker claimed to have been brought up in the woods back East by a "displaced Apache Indian." As a boy, the tracker apparently met this old Apache through the Indian's grandson, and the three of them spent nine years of disciplined and spiritual woods lore initiation in the coastal pine barrens. But, according to the foreword of the tracker's second book, the old Indian had conveniently returned to the Southwest in 1970, where he had died, and the grandson—even more conveniently in Johnny's mind—"moved overseas" with his family, and there, the only surviving witness to the tracker's near-mystical apprenticeship in the woods, "died in Europe in a horseback riding accident."

Johnny had spent a long time in law enforcement, and he figured he could hear the creaking stage props of a phony alibi as well as anybody. Well, the more he heard about the tracker and his background, the more suspicious he became that the guy was not everything he claimed to be.

What Johnny saw the next day up at Jay Cosgrove's house did little to dispel his suspicions. The tracker and his two assistants were given rooms at Buck's T-4 down in the canyon. Once they had changed into their working clothes, they were driven up to the Big Sky command post.

Johnny shook the tracker's strong hand, and noted that the guy was pretty darn young for someone who claimed to be "an experienced woodsman whose extraordinary skill has saved many lives." He was a big guy with dark blond hair and a shaggy mustache. His camouflaged field clothes were faded from many washings, and his jungle boots looked well worn.

But there was something more remarkable about the tracker in Johnny's eyes. The guy had a definite sense of himself, a stagy kind of flamboyance, as if he were on camera. Johnny had taken a few movie stars and TV actors on the Beartrap raft trip over the years, and had noted that these people didn't so much experience the river, but showed themselves to be experiencing the white-water adventure. No matter what the time or place, these actors had a way of just soaking up everyone's attention.

To Johnny, the tracker seemed cut from the same cloth.

While they consulted the maps on Jay's dining room table, the tracker's two assistants seemed to keep a

respectable distance behind him, like well-trained aco-
lytes. One carried a canteen and a folding drinking cup
in a belt pouch; the other provided an assortment of
measuring equipment that the tracker used in analyzing
signs and footprints. Throughout the initial briefing,
the tracker seemed to keep his leonine head aloof, as if
the mundane details of compass variation and trail
numbers were beneath his consideration.

At the end of the briefing, the tracker solemnly
addressed the assembled lawmen, asking for their
sworn word to keep his presence here a secret. He
implied that it might be extremely dangerous for him,
should word reach the Nicholses that they were being
tracked by someone of his celebrated skill.

In the dedication of one of the books the tracker had
brought with him, Johnny had read such Aquarian
phrases as "all potential and manifested universes,"
and "the reincarnational players who make us a family." No doubt about it, Johnny thought, this guy comes
on like some kind of mystic, like a guru. Now let's see if
he can track.

Hiking into the crime scene, the tracker made a point
of stopping to show his assistants several obscure
animal signs at the small swamp of the Moonlight
Creek tributary near the logging road. Johnny heard
him not only identify the animals who'd left their tracks
in the mud, but also proclaim a fair amount about the
animals' condition and behavioral state.

Okay, Guru, Johnny thought, lead on.

At the crime scene camp, Johnny thought that the
tracker was actually a little reckless. The young man
appeared to be working himself into some kind of an
intense concentration, but he also seemed to be moving
too fast around the clearing to get a good mental

picture of the crime sequence, as revealed in muddled tracks and boot prints.

He was interested in the dried mud at the stream edge of the camp, where Don and Danny had first confronted Jim Schwalbe, after Kari had been shot, but before Al Goldstein made his move. Signaling his assistant, the tracker began to work on one set of boot prints, using an assortment of wooden tongue depressors and measuring tape. He was, he explained, measuring the "pressure points" of the print. Through such scrutiny, he could separate normal tracks from those made by the fleeing fugitives. At one point, the tracker called for a glass of water, and his assistant sprang forward with the folding cup.

After his detailed examination of the stream's margin, the tracker offered his concurrence that the Nicholses had, indeed, left the camp by this route, and that they had fled down the streambed.

Fine, Johnny thought, we've been telling you that all afternoon.

He was now prepared to begin his tracking, the young man stated. But he must brief the armed deputies who would accompany him on his methods. Once more, the tracker assumed his aloof manner, raising his handsome, shaggy head above the circle of lawmen. "If you see me drop to my knees," he said, staring calmly into each man's eyes, "they are within rifle range. If I drop to my belly and lie flat, be prepared for trouble because they'll be very close."

His manner was so serious, that the men around him were momentarily subdued. But after that moment, they began to exchange glances, as if to ask, "Is this guy for real?"

The tracker and his assistants were going to be guarded and maybe even guided by Jay, Brad Brisban, and Bob Morton of the Forest Service. These men had all faced dangerous, armed fugitives in these woods; they had been searching for the Nicholses for almost two weeks. Was this young man seriously suggesting that he expected to actually find them this afternoon, right here in the Moonlight Creek drainage?

Apparently that was his intention.

The party of six spread to an arrow formation, with the tracker and his men forming the shaft, and the armed escort taking the flanks.

When they marched out of the crime scene and down the streambed, the tracker bore an expression of intense, joyful concentration. Like a good hunting dog, Johnny thought, just like a damn good elk hound.

Later that day the tracking team returned to the command post at Jay Cosgrove's. According to the tracker, they had followed the Nicholses' boot prints all the way down the streambed to the bottom of the draw, near the Jack Creek logging road. There, the Nicholses had moved onto harder ground and had eventually mounted a rocky outcropping that formed a bluff above the road. He had, he said, been able to identify clear indentations that were "buttocks marks," the sign that the two fugitives had sat with their backs to the orange granite bluff, staring down at the narrow logging road below.

But, he admitted, the signs seemed old, probably from last week.

When Johnny questioned the deputies after the tracker and his men had returned to the motel in the canyon, the lawmen had to admit that they'd not been able to see the same signs, once the young man declared that the track had left the muddy streambed and crossed harder ground.

"Well," Johnny said, "either our guru's a lot better than all of us, or he's got himself a lot of brass."

That night, Johnny called a police officer back East, whom the tracker had listed as a reference.

"Has this fella really been able to find a lot of missing people for you?" Johnny asked.

"Let's see," the man hedged. "I'll just say that he's had some success, all right?"

That same night, Johnny received a report from a lawman staying with the tracker at Buck's T-4, that the young man was regaling the patrons of the bar with tales of his celebrated career. Far from keeping his presence here in Montana a secret, the tracker seemed to revel in the admiration he received from the locals in the barroom.

I wonder, Johnny thought, if his bar bill will go on the expenses he charges the Goldstein family?

The next morning, they left Gallatin Canyon early and drove around the northern end of the Spanish Peaks to approach Cowboy Heaven from the Spanish Creek road. They formed a fairly large party and drove in three vehicles, Jay Cosgrove's Blazer and Brad and Johnny's Eagles. Dave Wing had replaced Bob Morton as the Forest Service law enforcement representative.

The plan had not changed, despite Johnny's mounting reservations about the tracker's expertise. They would drive to within a mile or so of the cow camp, form a skirmish line of armed lawmen, and let the tracker search for signs. After the previous day's tracking, he claimed to have an indelible image of the two fugitives' footprints, so, if they had come out north, after stealing the food, the tracker might be able to spot their trail as the posse moved in.

191

Wherever they crossed the Nicholses' track, however, the plan called for them to have almost fifteen hours of daylight to follow the trail, and maybe even run Don Nichols and his boy to ground up there in the rocks and timber above the Beartrap.

But this plan began to unravel early in the day. Coming up from the open rangeland to the steeper country, Jay's Blazer slipped off the ruts above a big mud hole in the track and went belly-deep in the soupy muck. Then, to exacerbate the problem, his right rear tire spun into a sharp rock and broke the bead. Now he was stuck in a chest-deep rocky mud hole with a flat tire.

Grimly, the men set to work to free the Blazer. To Johnny's surprise, the tracker suddenly shifted from his role of aloof guru to become a brute-force laborer. He seemed to relish wading waist deep into the mud to force slabs of rock under the Blazer's axle. The young man struggled steadily over an hour, digging out the rear axle, adding more stone ballast to support the wheels, and finally jacking up the car, so that he could change the tire. All they had to work with was a little Handy Man jack and a one-prong lug wrench.

Johnny watched the tracker working down in that gooey pit. Son of a gun, Johnny thought, this fella's full of surprises. However, just when Johnny was about to concede that he'd been wrong about the tracker, the young man called his assistant, and again the acolyte presented his master with a ceremonial glass of water in the folding cup.

By the time they got to the high plateau and were formed up on a skirmish line to scout the approaches to the cow camp, they were three hours behind schedule.

Entering the spruce and lodgepole north of the Cowboy Heaven meadows, a tall gray timber wolf loped off through the trees. To Johnny, that was a clear sign that the Nicholses were not in the immediate area. Wolves had become so spooky about people that they rarely moved through a piece of country that a man had even crossed within twenty-four hours.

The posse worked up the approach road to the cow camp, strung out wide on each flank, with the tracker and Johnny France taking the hard ruts of the road itself.

It was Johnny, not the tracker, who found the first clear footprint. About three quarters of a mile from Cowboy Heaven, the track branched, and just past the branch, Johnny discovered a clear boot track and a print very similar to the chain-link tread tennis shoe sole print he had seen in the crime scene camp. From later interviews with Kari Swenson, Gallatin County detectives had established that Danny Nichols wore a kind of soft-upper tennis shoe the day of the crime.

Johnny called the tracker to the prints, and the young man went to work with his measuring sticks and note pad.

These tracks, the young man stated, were made by the Nicholses within the past twenty-four hours. Johnny passed the word over the radio for everyone to keep a sharp watch.

Now the tracker was in his element. With his two assistants, he moved quickly down the road, almost leaving the armed escort behind him. When the group came to the large fenced horse pasture before the cow camp itself, he stated that the tracks ran across the pasture and into the camp.

Very carefully, Johnny glassed the cow camp with his binoculars, then dispatched Jay and Brad to circle the pasture and take up perimeter positions on either side of the big tan wall tent.

The tracker, however, did not seem concerned. He

led his men right across the open grass to the camp, seemingly unaware that he could be sniped on at any moment.

In the tent, the tracker found a faint impression of the chain-link tennis shoe sole.

When he spoke, his tone was a dogmatic proclamation. "This," he said, "is the boy's track."

Up a side trail from the tent, they found more tracks near a small pipe spring that supplied water for the camp. Here they rested a few minutes, drinking the chill spring water and washing the sweat from their faces. It was after midday, and Johnny was beginning to feel that the tracks were too old for there to be a chance of contact before dark.

Unless, of course, the Nicholses were lying in one of their rocky ambush positions up ahead, scanning the lower slopes with their people watchers.

Ten minutes west of the spring, they came to an open sage brush flat. Here, the tracker stated, the Nicholses had crossed. He said he could see clear "heel marks" leading out into the open flat.

Maybe, Johnny thought, but it went against everything he knew about the Nicholses for them to go ambling across such an exposed clearing in broad daylight.

Once more, he and his men guarded the perimeters while the tracker and his crew moved straight across the open ground.

They climbed west, up the timbered backslopes of the Beartrap's ramparts, right toward the steep gorges of Barn and Fall Creeks. The tracker was leading the posse into the inner sanctum of Don Nichols's secret kingdom. Furthermore, Johnny knew, the tracker had no way of realizing where he was taking them. If the guy was a phony, he was a lucky one.

An hour later, they came to a steep, jumbled piece of country where huge boulders rose up from the thick lodgepole forest. Among the rocky outcroppings, they found a deeply hollowed depression, a kind of missing-tooth socket in this giant jawbone of a ridge. This was the only opening among the steep deadfall timber and the sheer rock formations. Obvious game trails converged on the hollow, revealing the tracks of deer, elk, and smaller animals who used the depression to cross from this slope to the other side of the ridge.

Down in the shady hollow, the sparse soil was almost as hard as the surrounding granite. Earlier in the day, the trench must have been a sun-baked oven, Johnny saw. An army could cross those rocks and not leave a clear track. But he also saw that this depression dropped off on the other side, right onto the top ridge of the Beartrap Canyon itself.

The tracker rooted around in the hole, then climbed back up and examined the dry grass that had survived on the margins of the converging game trails.

He rose to his full height and generated his presence to the law men. "This," he said, pointing into the depression, "is their gateway. This is where they cross back and forth from the Beartrap to that country down around Spanish Creek and Cherry Creek."

Johnny had to admit that the young man's argument had merit.

But then the tracker dropped his real bombshell.

He stooped to examine the grass again. From the way this grass was bent, he proclaimed, he could tell that they moved through here with great stealth, six hours ago.

"They went down that way." He pointed once more into the rocky trench. "They crossed six hours ago. They're six hours ahead of us."

Johnny and Dave Wing hunkered down to examine

the brown grass. Sure the stalks were bent and twisted. Elk and mule deer moved through here all the time. But this young guy was saying he could see from the way the grass was bent that the Nicholses crossed here "with great stealth" six hours ago.

Johnny got Dave aside for a private word. No track that he'd seen, Johnny said, looked newer than a day old. Dave concurred. Those tennis shoe tracks back at the camp, he added, were probably the boy's when the tent was robbed. But he sure hadn't seen any tracks coming up here that were only hours old.

They returned to the edge of the depression and stared down into the Beartrap. It was almost four in the afternoon. If they took off through that trench now, and tried tracking down into that terrible broken country around Fall Creek and Barn Creek, they'd get caught out by dark. Worse, they would be bushwhacking those steep slopes, right in Don's home country in the dark, making God knows how much noise, easy prey for snipers.

According to Dave Wing, Don Nichols could be invisible up here in the daylight. What would he be at night?

Johnny signaled in the deputies from their flank-guard positions. "Boys," he said, "I'm afraid we're gonna have to call it a day. I don't want to head into the Beartrap with only three hours of real daylight left."

The men came to stand on the lip of the depression, gazing down into the long blue shadows of the creek gorges. One by one, they nodded.

That afternoon on the way out, another deputy's car got hung up on the terrible gravel track that led down from Cowboy Heaven to Spanish Creek. They met FBI agent Bernie Hubley at the Spanish Creek cow camp, and he drove the tracker and his men to Belgrade Airport to catch their plane back East.

En route to the airport, the tracker told Bernie Hubley that he had tracked the Nicholses to an obvious "gateway" in the mountains.

He also told the FBI man that the sheriff had called off the search when the posse was only "two hours" behind the fugitives.

Two days later, Bernie Hubley phoned Johnny at his office.

"Johnny," he said, "I got to talk to you."

"What's up?" Johnny said, anticipating some kind of trouble.

"Well," Bernie began, "our tracking guru got back East and he told the Goldstein family that he was only twenty minutes behind the Nicholses, and that you called the search off."

Johnny groaned.

"Listen, Johnny," Bernie added. "The Goldsteins called me. They were furious. They said their money's been wasted."

"Well," Johnny managed, almost sputtering mad. "I think maybe it has been . . . but not by me."

"Johnny," Bernie soothed. "I'll tell you what we're going to do. We're going to get that guru back here and give him a chance to show his stuff. But this time, the FBI's going to pay for the trip, and, by God, he'll have to work for his money."

Two days later, the tracker returned. He traveled alone, without his cup bearer or the man who carried his "pressure point" sticks.

Dave Wing and Johnny France rendezvoused with the tracker and the FBI caravan down on Cherry

Creek, and they drove up to Spanish Creek cow camp through the old Wiley and Butler ranches. The FBI group included an unsmiling eight-man SWAT team of men who appeared to Johnny to be tough, hard-time cops. He doubted if they were intrigued by the tracker's theories of "manifested and potential universes."

Johnny and Dave Wing left the group at Cowboy Heaven, and took off on a scouting trek of their own, down Beartrap Creek, looking for abandoned mine shafts.

That night, Bernie Hubley called to report.

They'd taken the tracker back to the depression in the rocks and let him try to locate the Nicholses' trail again.

Somehow, as the armed team deployed west of the rocky "gateway," the tracker had disappeared. For a couple of hours, the FBI men had anxiously searched for him, thinking that the young man might have fallen into a silent ambush.

Then, a couple of the SWAT party had returned to the vehicles to use the more powerful car radios. They found the tracker there, looking cool and fit, waiting for them in the shade. He had, he said, taken off alone in order to move faster. While tracking alone, he continued, he had "covered" both Fall Creek and Barn Creek, all the way down the two drainages. But the only tracks he found, he said, were three days old. They have, he added, moved out of this country. We should have gone in after them three days ago. We missed our chance.

A couple of the FBI SWAT party had been in the original night sweep of the area, two weeks before. They knew what kind of country lay in the Fall and Barn Creek drainages. And they also understood the superhuman effort it would have taken to "cover" those two timbered gorges in so short a time.

The FBI's effort with the tracker was canceled before dark. There was no point in continuing under the circumstances.

The moon was rising dusty brown above the shoulder of Lone Mountain.

Don Nichols stood in the trees, trying to sniff the breeze that flowed down the draw from the black stone of Blaze Mountain behind him. His legs were bad tonight, crampy and sore.

This climbing in the dark was hard.

For a moment, he regretted leaving the Beartrap after Danny got the food from the cowboys' tent. But now, they were almost back on the Jack Creek side, and he knew they'd make their cache there before dawn. The gooseberries were ripe on these southern slopes. And they had raspberry jam in the cache. Tomorrow, they could eat biscuits with raspberry jam, then start harvesting gooseberries to dry for the winter.

This country was thick and steep, too difficult for mounted posses but good country for him and Danny. However, he wished they didn't have to travel at night like this. Soon, he knew, the weather would start closing down, and they wouldn't see any more posses.

14

The Beartrap

August

JOHNNY FRANCE'S OBSESSION WITH THE NICHOLSES slipped beneath the surface of his life. Like a jagged rock in a set of rapids when the river rises with the spring melt, Don Nichols and his son were there, just under the smooth skin of his daily routine.

After the tracker's second trip to the Beartrap, Johnny had several long, serious conversations with Dave Wing, Bernie Hubley, and certain other lawmen who were as deeply involved in the case as Johnny himself. One grizzled old officer who'd observed the tracker at close quarters gave Johnny what he considered a fair assessment of the whole tracker-guru fiasco.

"If we could have gotten him alone, so he couldn't show off to those two flunkies of his, Johnny . . . maybe we'd have had some better results."

"Maybe," Johnny agreed, thinking that Bernie Hubley hadn't had much success with the guy alone.

"Well," the officer added, "he might have been a dope-smokin' son of a bitch, but that guy sure could track. If'n we'd have kinda got a bridle on him and kept him moving."

"Yeah, well . . . " Johnny shook his head in frustration. He was sure now that the tracker actually had followed the Nicholses' tracks from the cow camp to the "gateway," not across the sage flats as he claimed, but somehow up to that jawbone ridge, maybe on instinct, maybe using some of the mystical powers he implied he possessed. The tracker had shown Dave Wing a tennis shoe print up there that could have been the boy's. But Dave had felt the track was at least a full day old, not six hours.

"You know," Johnny concluded, "they're still in the Beartrap, and if we're gonna find them, we've got to start thinking like they do."

The old officer rubbed his face and nodded sourly. "Hell, Johnny, I don't like the sound of that."

One afternoon, Johnny drove down Highway 84, along Warm Springs Creek canyon, across the right-angle bridge over the Madison, and back up the old truck track on the east side of Beartrap Canyon.

He knew this country well. Just north of here on the other side of the river lay his Uncle Joe's old place, and, a couple miles west of that was the Cold Springs Ranch, where he'd spent all those years as a foster child of Forrest and Betsy Shirley. If there was any part of the state that Johnny could really call his roots, it was in these dry rimrock canyons and timbered ridges.

He parked the Eagle in the shade of an overhanging spruce that was being undercut by the current at the edge of the bank. This was about as far as you could drive in from the north. The trail crossed Beartrap Creek ahead, and snaked up and down the granite spurs of canyon above the big sets of rapids, toward the hydroelectric plant.

From where he stood, he could study the high ridgeline that walked away south, cut by the deep side canyons of Goose, Fall, Barn, and Trail creeks. Those gorges rose almost three thousand feet in less than two miles from the river. Yet, three miles west of Barn Creek, the high plateau and broken timber began around Cowboy Heaven.

This was what the elk outfitters called "broken country," steep rock bluffs, savagely bisected by near-vertical drainages. The whole top of the Beartrap was that way, a string of timbered islands, each with its resident population of big horn sheep, deer, elk and grizzly, hanging up there between the Madison River's main gorge and the more open rangeland around Cowboy Heaven and Red Knob.

When Johnny was a kid, he'd seen a wonderful John Wayne flying movie about a World War II transport crew surviving on a frozen Labrador lake after their plane was forced down. The name of that movie was Island in the Sky, a haunting, evocative title that stayed with him, long after the details and images of the film had vanished.

Well, there was a whole chain of islands up there in the sky, an archipelago fifteen miles long and three wide, isolated from Madison County and the laws of Montana.

The outfitters didn't like it for obvious reasons. You couldn't easily move pack or saddle horses up there because of the timber and the steep slopes; it was damn near impossible to track on that rocky ground, and the gorges were so deep that it might take all day for a string of pack mules to cross one drainage.

That was the country the tracker guru told the FBI he had "covered" in a few hours.

Johnny leaned back against the warm metal of the car's hood and slowly scanned his binoculars down the canyon walls. Months later, he remembered that another childhood image came to mind at that moment, again the product of the war that had shaped the young consciousness of his generation. He saw vivid pictures of Tarawa and Saipan, Okinawa and Iwo Jima . . . fortified islands, where fanatical Japanese soldiers fought so stubbornly that the American Marines had to root them out of their caves, one by one, with dynamite charges and flame throwers. They did not surrender; instead they chose to die and to take with them large numbers of Americans.

The fact was that nobody so far had come up with any kind of logical explanation of why Don Nichols had started all this business in the first place. Lots of people had pretty convincing stories about why Don had shot Al Goldstein. The most commonly accepted line concerned Don's unusually strong love and attachment for the boy. Just like John Onstad had told the newspaper, Don Nichols had reacted like an enraged animal when he found his son threatened.

So far, however, nobody had really addressed the central problem of just what the hell old Don Nichols had been doing up there all these years. Just after the crime, there'd been this local anthropologist who stepped right up to give press interviews all about how the Nicholses were "throwbacks" to an earlier period, who had chosen a simpler form of life over more conventional patterns of living. That kind of stuff kept the reporters happy, for at least a couple of days. But so far, in the several weeks since the bizarre crime, no one had brought forth a convincing analysis of what made Don Nichols tick.

During anxious nights awake at his rolltop desk, a mug of cold coffee at his elbow, and on long, solitary drives, he'd been digesting the known facts of Don Nichols's life, trying to form his own analysis.

Such an analysis might seem alien to Johnny's normally open, direct manner. In fact his background did not provide the traditional education normally associated with such psychological assessment. But, in many ways, Johnny France was a mix of the traditional and the unorthodox. Early in his career as a lawman, he had learned that a good cop had to understand human nature. Moreover, he'd learned in violent encounters with emotionally disturbed criminals that a smart cop had to become a bit of a headshrinker, if he was going to stay alive. And, as a county sheriff, he had become the de facto hostage negotiator, a title of dubious value which he'd had to exercise several times.

Within the past year, he had put his amateur psychologist experience to a good test, during one of the most dangerous confrontations of his career. Not three blocks from his house in Ennis, Johnny had been faced with a violently psychotic young man who had barricaded himself in his basement bedroom, armed with a .357 magnum pistol, determined to kill his mother, then to take his own life. When Johnny arrived on the scene, he made the decision to face the boy alone, unarmed, to try to negotiate.

Once Johnny was in the room, under the wavering muzzle of the big pistol, the boy announced that he would add Johnny to his list of execution victims. Johnny had to draw on all his persuasive powers to cajole and flatter the kid, to sidetrack his death obsession, to give him some tangible reason to live.

The boy was in deep, unnatural mourning for his father, who had recently died after a horrible battle with cancer. In his anger and grief, the young man seemed to be using this murderous and suicidal confrontation as a means of abolishing life itself and of somehow transcending death to join his father in the afterlife, the family whole again, complete in death in a way that was now impossible.

Slowly, with as much soft-spoken calm as he could muster, Johnny had reasoned with the kid, not about the central core of his obsession, but about small things, minor concessions.

After an hour, he was able to convince the disturbed boy to begin unloading the pistol. Johnny achieved this coup by suggesting that the dead father had taught the boy to be such a good marksman, that he really wouldn't need all six bullets, just to execute two people, then to kill himself.

"Your dad," Johnny said, "was so proud of the way you can handle a gun, that I'm sure he'd want you to give me some of those bullets."

By the end of that terrible night, Johnny had convinced the boy to surrender his bullets, one by one. In the process of the negotiation, Johnny had reaffirmed for himself that he had to learn as much as he could about the background and psychological roots of any dangerous criminal he had to face.

And now, for a month, he'd been thinking about Don Nichols and his boy, Danny.

The conclusions that were slowly taking shape might not agree with standard psychological theory, but Johnny wasn't interested in pleasing the headshrinkers, only in catching the Nicholses with no more bloodshed. In fact, Johnny had only read one or two college textbooks on human behavior, and had retained little of that. But he did know from his own life that people were usually the products of the love—and the hate—of the good things and the bad things that happened to them as children. What the psychiatrist called nurturing and trauma.

So, armed with this simple analytical thesis, Johnny had sifted through the known facts of Don Nichols's childhood, to see if he could discover what had gone wrong when he was a boy, to have set him so badly off the normal track later in life.

In his analysis, Johnny could draw upon a wide and

diverse body of information, ranging from psychological profiles produced after the FBI entered the case, to third-hand out-of-date gossip dating back forty years or more when the Nichols family first moved to Montana.

Sorting through this jumble of fact, rumor, and downright lies, Johnny eventually came up with conclusions that seemed to explain most of Don Nichols's bizarre personality and behavior.

First, from all accounts of the old-timers in Norris, Don had been a happy, well-adjusted little boy. At least he was until his father, Pat, had driven that car off the curve, coming back from the party in Ennis, drunk.

Don was just six when his father died, and not much more than eight when his mother, Maggie, married Steve Engleman.

In the Catholic Church, Johnny knew, they called seven the age of reason. But the traumas of Don Nichols's young life had happened before that age. What he was discovering was that, in a weird kind of way, Don Nichols was stuck back there in his unreasonable childhood. Part of him, at least, was frozen in time, trying to re-create the happy summer days when old Pat Nichols would take his boy up to North Meadow Creek or the Beartrap. By all accounts, Pat was a cheerful, easygoing kind of a man. He drank, and he played the guitar, and sang. Pat was a tolerable artist, something you wouldn't expect in a displaced Oakie gold miner. And he loved to take his son into the mountains, to teach him about the woods, about fishing and hunting.

On the other hand, it was said that Steve Engleman was a stingy, humorless, religious fanatic who believed in discipline, and wasn't beyond using his razor strap to enforce that discipline. Don Nichols did not take to his stepfather. Nor did he accept the harsh life on the small spread of dryland ranch near Harrison where Steve Engleman established his new family.

According to information from Don's brother-in-law, Wally Schneiter, Don and Steve Engleman "didn't agree on anything. Even when he was a kid, Don would argue." And there were reports that those arguments often ended with beatings. But, Schneiter stated that Don "idolized his real father. They used to hunt and fish together. That's when he started going up into the Spanish Peaks."

Johnny tossed a granite chip into the river and watched the smooth band of current twirl the stone down. He'd come to realize that Don Nichols never really had accepted any authority after his father was killed. It wasn't just Steve Engleman, the harsh, inflexible stepfather, that Don could never agree with. It was all authority.

He was smart, so he got along in school fine because the teachers didn't challenge him.

But he didn't last too long in the Navy. "He didn't like the service," Wally Schneiter explained. "He got out early. Too many orders."

When he did marry, he was just unable to settle down in any kind of a conventional way. Something kept drawing him back to these mountains. He tried to homestead up around Noxon, near the unspoiled Bob Marshall Wilderness. But then the logging and strip mining started up there, and Don quit in disgust. Johnny was beginning to see that the encroachment of civilization was just an excuse for Don to quit farming. He really didn't want to live on a farm; that was playing Steve Engleman's game. Later, when he burnt cow camp cabins and shot heifers, he would make a stronger statement of his feelings about ranchers. Don Nichols wasn't sure what he wanted when he quit the homestead, but he knew it wasn't living down on the flats, being part of the "rich man's rotten system."

By now, he had a son, a little boy named Dan. Don's father had named him Donald Boone Nichols. Don Nichols had named his own boy Dan. No middle name, just Dan Nichols.

Daniel Boone.

People who were badly hurt as kids—traumatized— people like Don Nichols, did things out of crazy, almost unexplainable motives. They just didn't think like the rest of us. Fact was, they did not think about their actions very much at all. But they sure as hell did act. That's what the psychologist called compulsion. These people were compelled to act that way; they had no choice.

Pat Nichols got himself killed when Don was six. When Dan Nichols turned six, Don Nichols started acting so weird that his wife Verdina finally divorced him.

Then all the custody hassles started, and Don and Dan began their long summer "camping trips" up there on those ridges. Hidden camps. People watchers. Stalking old Dave Wing in the brush. Teaching the boy to move and hide like an animal.

By then, Don Nichols was working winters in a machine shop down in Jackson Hole. There were plenty of fine Wyoming mountains for him to camp in, but he always came back right here, to these granite ramparts.

When Don Nichols took his little boy up to those ridges, and cuddled him through the chill mountain nights and sudden, drenching thunderstorms, it was himself he was holding in his arms; somehow, the scared little boy was Daniel Boone Nichols, frozen in time. Don became Pat Nichols. Danny became the little boy who, this time, never lost his father. They were isolated, separated from the terrible calamities of death and cruelty.

Summers passed. And each year as Danny grew, Don Nichols tried to maintain him as a little boy, under the age of reason.

The people who ran the small stores near Ennis Lake and Jack Creek used to marvel at Don's strange devotion when he'd bring little Danny down on one of their rare provisioning trips. Don never bought anything personal for himself. He didn't drink or smoke. He didn't chase women. But whatever the boy wanted, he always got . . . ice cream, Hershey bars; he could choose as much as he wanted.

There came years when Danny wanted other things than Butterfingers and Dr. Pepper. Danny got in trouble in high school: truancy, fights, and once he chased some girls with a knife. Otherwise, he was an intelligent kid. He painted. He sang and played the guitar, country music, old songs, just like his grandfather, people said. His real grandfather, Pat Nichols.

His junior year in high school, Danny got hooked up with an older woman, a divorced lady named Sue. She liked his long blond hair, his moody, artistic ways. His lean body. He no longer wanted to spend time in the mountains, not when he had Sue.

Don Nichols was sick at the thought. He blustered. He cried, he bullied and cajoled. Danny dropped out of high school and went down to Jackson to join his father. They worked hard that summer, saving their money. Maybe they were going to build a cabin up above the Beartrap; they didn't share their plans, even with close friends.

They slept in a car parked in a trailer court. They seemed relaxed and happy together.

Then Don discovered that Danny was spending his money on long-distance calls to Sue, talking to her in

Montana for hours on the phone. Something bad happened between them in that trailer court. Some said, Don had a breakdown. Others reported that he beat the boy. Still others said he made Danny swear an oath to abandon Sue and return with him to the mountains.

Whatever really happened, Johnny knew, the result was clear. They moved up to the Madison Range last August and lived right through the winter, through spring and half of summer.

Then they kidnapped Kari Swenson. Kari reported that Don Nichols had hoped they could find an "older woman for my son." A weird desire. Why an older woman for a nineteen-year-old boy? Unless, of course, Don planned to share that woman with his son. Maybe he was having trouble separating just exactly who was the boy and who was the adult about then.

A mountain family.

Don Nichols, Johnny suddenly saw, can't let the boy go. In Don's mind, he and the boy are the same person. If Danny leaves him, Don's life is ripped apart. In a sense, he dies. Rather than die himself, he will kill again.

Johnny sat down heavily behind the wheel of his car. There was only one place they would hide. Don Nichols's perfect mountain family could only survive on those timbered mountain islands.

The horse patrols continued. When volunteers and deputies were free from other obligations, they would call Johnny, or meet him at Bettie's Cafe. There'd be a few minutes of soft-spoken conversation, and they'd set a time and place to meet with their horse trailers.

Although Sue hated the idea, Johnny often rode up there alone on Bambino, checking leads, tracing reports of hidden mining shacks. Johnny was using Bambino so much that the pace was beginning to show even on a strong, deep-chested horse like him. Johnny did not really trust other mounts in the steep, rocky country above the Beartrap.

One day he and the district ranger, Virgil Lindsay, went all the way up Trail Creek, across the Barn Creek drainage to the rim overlooking Fall Creek. They could look down on the river, on soaring hawks. Below them to the west, the irrigated hay fields and the highway looked tiny, distant in time and space. Johnny was beginning to understand why Don Nichols felt superior and invulnerable up here. But they found no signs, no tracks or gardens.

Another day Johnny rode alone up Hammond Creek, right up high to a rocky ridge where he'd been told he might find a mining cabin similar to the one Danny had once drawn for his mother. The cabin was collapsed, obviously abandoned for years, if not decades. In the brushy draw where the cabin's ruins stood, Johnny found a large mound of fresh bear droppings. Grizzly, a big old bear, judging by the tracks.

A few days later, Johnny led an organized horse posse up Trail Creek and over the ridge into the Barn Creek drainage. They had some more specific information about Don's garden plots and caches, and he knew it would be foolish to scout these locations alone.

This was the route Don Nichols reportedly used last year when he and Danny had entered the mountains to live here "permanently." Don was supposed to have pushed a heavily laden bicycle up the game trails here, as high as he could, then cached waterproof sacks of red beans, flour, and other staples.

If they'd been traveling hard since the crime, Johnny knew, they would have to resupply sooner or later. And, if he could get a handle on their main food cache,

211

then he'd be able to plan organized stakeouts and maybe an ambush.

Around noon, the party broke in two, with Dave Wing and John Onstad riding up the faint deer trail to cross over to Cowboy Heaven. They planned to install two "intruder alarms" that Bernie Hubley had obtained from the FBI's bag of electronic tricks. These devices worked on an electric-eye principle. If anyone entered the cow camp tent again, an invisible beam would be broken and a silent alarm would be broadcast by radio. Dave would have the alarms monitored twenty-four hours a day down at the Forest Service headquarters in Ennis.

Johnny's party continued searching the steep sides of Barn Creek, looking for signs of a cache or garden. Around two, they were near the top of the drainage, in thick, steep country, with visibility severely restricted by dense timber. The deputies had been picking their way up the gorge in a spread formation, their horses finding footing as best they could.

Now Bob Morton, Merlin Ehlers, and Johnny were waiting for Brad Brisban to work the last slopes of the south side before they climbed out at the top and searched their way north along the ridge.

After waiting maybe twenty minutes, Johnny eased his horse down the steep draw, among the deadfall and blowdowns, trying to get a line of sight on Brad across the gorge. Johnny was riding a borrowed horse today, a big clay-colored gelding about sixteen hands, strong-winded enough, but a little heavy on the rein.

Johnny came out of the thickest timber and found himself in a grassy clearing, cut by the main feeder stream of Barn Creek. The ground was less steep here, but soft from the streambed and brambly. For some reason the horse hunched, and sidestepped fast, as if shying from bear scent. Johnny stood in the left stirrup and worked the gelding's butt back up slope. There was real danger of a horse spooking on loose ground like this, dancing sideways, then losing his stance where the draw dropped off again.

After a few moments careful work with the reins and nudging with heels, the animal seemed to calm. But then he raised his face, scented deeply with flared nostrils and gave a scared snort. Johnny held him still, but the horse's ears were forward and alert now, he had a skittish roll to his eyes. There was something out ahead there in those brambles, something close enough to spook this horse.

Johnny was carrying a lever-action deer rifle today. He cocked the hammer and gazed in the direction his mount indicated.

As Johnny moved, the brambles exploded with a slapping rustle. Johnny turned just in time to see a large Franklin grouse bound out of the brush, ten feet from the horse's nose, a blur of blue-gray feathers. He dug in his heels and hauled down on the reins.

Soothing the nervous horse with murmured praise and a solid neck pat, Johnny found himself smiling at his own fright.

A moment later he caught sight of Brad Brisban, high up to the right, a big, solid figure on a paint horse, working his assigned grid with patient determination.

Johnny put his rifle back to half-cock and scanned the brambles ahead. For some reason, the horse was still a little spooked from that grouse. The tall gelding's ears were twitching and his eye bad. Well, Johnny thought, he's probably not used to seeing grouse so tame.

The strawberry bushes were just tall enough to conceal Danny, but not if he rose to brush away the flies. The posse had come out of nowhere, down the sides of the draw, two riders with rifles. But he knew there'd be

213

more. If he turned, he could see both riders. And he could raise his rifle. But he stayed still. He would not make a move for his rifle unless the rider on the big gray horse crossed that last bit of soft ground and actually started into the bramble patch.

Danny waited, his heart thudding in his ears, the flies feasting. How could this posse have gotten so close without Dad seeing them? It was real trouble. Armed deputies right up here at the top of Barn Creek, without Dad even guessing they were coming.

A grouse popped through the brambles behind him, and Danny grabbed for his rifle.

He heard the deputy's horse spook sideways, and the soft commands the man spoke to control the horse.

After a while, Danny heard the horseman move off. But Danny did not move. He waited in the berry patch, worrying about his Dad.

They searched the top of the Beartrap three times in the next week. No signs, no tracks. The intruder alarm at Cowboy Heaven never sounded.

Later in the month, Johnny got a call from a psychic in California. The man said he hated to bother the busy sheriff, but he was having a "recurrent vision." The Nicholses were underground, he said, in a cave, or a mine shaft.

"Do you have mines around there, Sheriff?"

"Yessir," Johnny answered, "we sure do."

"Well," the man continued, "in my vision, I see them and I hear three words . . . yellow, medicine, and thief."

Johnny repeated the words. "I'll look into it," he said.

Johnny was a good enough cop to understand that psychics—just like the tracking guru—can sometimes be helpful.

A mine shaft or cave. Yellow. Medicine. Thief.

He searched the Courthouse records for mining claims. For several days, other duties interrupted. Then he went back to the records.

He found what he wanted late that afternoon. Claim number 3834 in the section that covered the north side of Beartrap Creek near Cherry Creek, was an old gold mine called the Sulphurt.

Sulphurt? Sulphur . . . yellow.

The next mine over was called the Modesto and the owner of the Sulphur was called Jesse Wood.

Yellow. Medicine . . . sulphur and molasses . . . medicine. Jesse . . . James.

Thief.

They checked that mine late one afternoon, when the Nicholses wouldn't be expecting a posse.

And they kept their group small; Loren Tucker, the county attorney, joined the party, so did Bernie Hubley. But the rest were the hard core, Dave Wing, Jerry Mason, and Johnny France.

When they made their careful assault on the mine, they found no tracks in the dust and scree around the splintered timber entrance.

Johnny went in alone. He wasn't grandstanding; in a closed dark space, it was better not to have two people firing from the same direction. That was a good way to get shot in the back.

An hour later he was out, sweaty, plastered with dust, scratched from broken-down old shoring timber.

Nothing. The mine, he said, had not been entered for years. But the men guarding the entrance could see beneath the dust smears and scratches that Johnny France was shaken by his experience down that black, narrow shaft. It creaked and shifted in there, Johnny explained. A little bit, uh, scary.

When he got home that night, Sue told him there'd been an earthquake in the area.

"Did you feel it?" she asked, while he scrubbed in the shower.

Johnny turned off the water. "An earthquake?"

"Yes," she said. "They said on the radio a strong one. But nobody was hurt, I guess. Otherwise you'd hear about it."

"I expect so."

15

Madison Range

October–November, 1984

SOME YEARS IN THE HIGH COUNTRY, JUNE PASSES FOR spring, July and August are all the summer you get, and September has to make do for fall. The other eight months are winter. Some years, the autumn will linger on in a long blaze of golden aspens, and the real snow won't come until Christmas. That's called an "open winter" in Madison County, an exception to the normal pattern.

The fall of 1984 showed early signs of a long, harsh freeze, relented, then hunkered down again for a real cattle killer.

Johnny France watched the weather closely. He knew that, if he had any valuable allies in this case, winter had to rank right up near the top of the list. Blizzards and long stretches of below-zero weather would probably force the Nicholses down from the highest, coldest, and most inaccessible parts of the range.

An early onset of a bad winter would thin the game up there, driving the herds of deer and elk to lower country. Deep snow would slow the two fugitives down, and snow would mean that they would finally

217

start leaving tracks. Long, unrelenting cold would force them to rely on fires, both day and night—not just little squaw-wood cook fires, either, but actual campfires, banked pine logs that would burn through the night.

Johnny watched the season change. Water foul moved south through the intermountain flyway. The duck and goose hunters came and went. All along the high peaks, the naked stone was now plastered white with fresh snow. As he rode the Beartrap, searching for dugouts and tracks, alone or with his deputies, Johnny saw the elk herds forming up for the mating; their coats acquired shaggy substance as they instinctively prepared for the first real blast of Montana cold.

Unlike elk or mule deer, however, Don Nichols and his boy couldn't just grow thicker coats and scratch beneath the snow for frozen grass when winter struck. They would have to survive by killing game and by returning to their caches for warm clothes and staples. And that left them two choices, either come down from the high country and risk capture in the valleys or return to their caches in the Beartrap and risk being seen by elk and deer hunters, then tracked by the posses the hunters alerted. In any event, if the winter closed in fast and hard, the Nicholses would be obliged to follow the game down to the lower elevations.

As September sped by, with the usual display of fine autumn foilage and the endless, frustrating searches in the mountains, Johnny began to stake his hopes on a winter capture. Dave Wing and other veterans of the manhunt agreed. Snow would make tracking easier, if the snow stayed on the ground long enough for a posse to follow a fresh track back to a hidden camp or dugout. Montana snow often blew away from the high ridges and exposed draws soon after falling, to drift deep in the lower gorges and coulees. A good outfitter —or someone as good at evasion as Don Nichols—

learned that you could make fast time traveling the exposed ridges after a blizzard because the cold north wind that usually followed a deep snowfall scoured any treeless country bare of snow within hours.

But Don and Danny couldn't survive up there on the high ridges for the whole winter, so, sooner or later, they would leave tracks down lower.

Winter and the hunting season gave the law enforcement officers another advantage, which they made plans to exploit. Both hunters and snowmobilers frequented the high country after the first snows. Therefore, armed men on horseback or riding "snow machines," as they were called out here, would not necessarily alarm the Nicholses. Hunters often spent the entire day away from their tents, stalking deer and elk. The Nicholses would certainly know that hunters' camps would be a source of food, including both staples like flour and sugar, and also the sweets that Don Nichols seemed to crave.

What Don Nichols would have no way of knowing was that a good many of the "hunters" working the edges of the Beartrap this fall would be armed lawmen. Some planned to stay behind in ambush, hidden in their bait tents, while the rest of the party patrolled.

Officers would make a show of provisioning certain camps, then an equally obvious show of lashing down the tent flaps and generally securing things, as if they planned to return a little later in the season. Don would have no way of guessing that these officers had hidden high-tech tracking "bugs" in the sacks of pancake flour and brown sugar.

These electronic bugs were furnished by the FBI; they were tiny, but they could broadcast a powerful radio beacon that would lead a posse directly to the source, if the Nicholses made the mistake of raiding the baited camps.

219

Johnny worked intensely with Dave Wing, Bob Morton, and Bernie Hubley. Their planning took on the precision and detail of a modern commando operation.

More and more, Johnny France became convinced that cunning and luck were going to count, once the snow started falling. Luck would have to take care of itself. He worked on cunning.

Early in October, Johnny got a call from Kari Swenson's parents, Bob and Jan. They asked if they and Bob Schaap could come over to Ennis to talk about the details of the initial search-and-rescue operation. Fine, Johnny said, we can talk over a cup of coffee at Bettie's Cafe.

He was looking forward to the meeting because he'd been too busy to ever tell the Swensons about how brave he thought Kari had been the day she was shot. Johnny had seen his fair share of crime victims, and he knew that a person's true character often emerged in the aftermath of violence.

What he had seen of Kari Swenson that morning in the camp clearing told him that she was a kid who combined both mental and physical toughness with an unusual degree of personal courage. Kari had not panicked. She had remained coherent, despite the hemorrhage, the pain, and the encroaching shock. She had even smiled when he lifted her to the stretcher and said "thank you." Johnny had thought that Kari was one tough, classy kid. Now he welcomed the chance to tell her parents.

But the meeting did not stay friendly very long.

When he shook hands with Jan Swenson, Johnny said, "You have a remarkable daughter. You have a girl who's a real tribute to the American athlete. She's a tough kid."

The Swensons were an attractive couple. Jan was a

neat, fit woman in her forties, with obvious good taste in clothes and a sense of presence. Bob Swenson reminded Johnny of Clark Kent in the old Superman series on TV: a tall, well-built guy who seemed to wear his glasses as a disguise. It was easy to see where Kari got her beauty and physical endurance.

Jan Swenson smiled, and they took their chairs at a side table in a small alcove past the cash register, away from the ranchers and miners in the booths. Outside, it was a bright, windy fall afternoon with chunks of dead sage blowing in the half-deserted street.

Almost as soon as the coffee cups were filled, the Swensons and Bob Schaap began picking at him. They clearly weren't here on a social call, and they just as clearly did not intend to listen to his version of the story.

Why, they wanted to know, hadn't the Madison County Sheriff's Department started a night search for Kari as soon as she'd been reported missing?

Johnny began to explain that the department had not received word of the missing person until well after dark. But they insisted that he should have "saturated the mountain" with searchers, working "grid" patterns. If he had conducted a proper search-and-rescue effort, they implied, Al Goldstein would be alive and Kari unwounded.

Again, Johnny tried in his slow, soft-spoken way to explain his reasons for not deploying men at night, in rough country, when there'd been a bear scare and when he knew there already were armed men from the other side of the valley out on patrol.

Schaap and the Swensons did not seem to want to listen. The thrust of their argument was that Madison County in general and Sheriff Johnny France in particular ran an archaic, badly organized search-and-rescue team.

221

Johnny stared bitterly at Bob Schaap's well-groomed beard. This was pretty ironic, he thought, because in the first days of the manhunt, Gallatin County Sheriff John Onstad had been the most critical of Bob Schaap's original amateur search-and-rescue effort. It had been Bob Schaap who had dispatched armed men to the hills to search, before calling the Gallatin County sheriff's office. Schaap seemed to have called Jay Cosgrove, the resident deputy with proper authority, only as an afterthought.

As to "saturating" the mountain with skilled searchers who could follow a "grid," Johnny tried to point out that the thick country up there did not allow easy map reference or compass orientation, even in daylight and certainly not at night. This was steep, thickly timbered mountainside, not cleared ski slopes.

Finally, Bob Swenson, in his cool, professorial hauteur, summarized their collective feelings. Johnny's search-and-rescue attempt, he said, had been "badly bungled."

Johnny almost lost what little remained of his composure. He was tempted to remind them that it had been him, the bungling sheriff of Madison County, who had arranged the helicopter with the cable litter that had saved their daughter's life. It was Johnny France who'd had the foresight to realize a lost jogger in the woods might be badly injured and need vertical medevac. And, he knew, if they had tried carrying Kari out of that thick country, her internal hemorrhage might have worsened, and if so, she might be dead today.

But he didn't have it in him, mad as he was, to lay that one on Kari's parents. Instead, he let his anger flow coldly in his words. "You people," he began, "come into Madison County and expect all these wonderful services from us . . . hundreds of volunteers to saturate the mountain . . . and you expect magical results. Well, perhaps you should concentrate all that leisure time you've got for jogging and skiing over in Gallatin County, so they'll be responsible for you, not us."

Bob Swenson leaned across the table. "That," he said, "sounds like a threat."

Johnny realized that he might be skating on thin legal ice here. Don't let them rattle me so bad, he thought. "Well," he replied for the legal record, "I didn't consider it a threat, just some good advice."

Now Jan Swenson intervened with a calming, rational tone. She had names of local avalanche experts, people from the Big Sky ski patrol who could train Johnny's people. But the more she went on, the more Johnny's anger got stoked up again.

Johnny stared out the window at the dusty street. Apples and oranges, he thought. Madison County and Gallatin County were two different worlds. The people from Bozeman go up there to play, for recreation. People over here use the mountains to make their living. My rescue team are ranchers and outfitters, every one of them a skilled horseman who's grown up in this valley and who knows those steep drainages. Their people are well-meaning amateurs, young guys like Al Goldstein who had a romantic picture of what Western life was all about. The poor guy never should have been sent up there that way, not armed with a .380 pistol.

The meeting broke up with a chill. There were no smiles or handshakes on departure.

Back in the booths, Johnny's friends stared down at their coffee cups, not eager to share his foul mood, or to embarrass him by letting on they'd heard it all. Johnny refilled his coffee cup and stood in the alcove, watching the wind trash tumble down the street. His gut was pulsing with frustrated anger. He felt like smashing something. Those people come over here from the Gallatin side and try to . . .

The anger began to thin. He sighed and released a clenched, stale breath. These were the girl's parents, after all. They had a reason to be angry. Grief, he realized, grief and guilt do strange things to otherwise normal people. The Swensons were grieving for their daughter, for all the pain and sorrow that Kari has had to suffer, for her ruined career, for her nightmares and fears. Bob Schaap was probably wound up tight with guilt about Al Goldstein, but was too stubborn a Dutchman to admit it.

Johnny drained the last of his coffee, nodded to his puzzled friends, and stepped outside into the bright, chill wind. Instinctively, he gazed up at the high country, at the new snow around Fan Mountain.

The insight came fast with the cold sunshine. Don Nichols, Johnny realized, was a Madison County problem; Don was the product of this land, of the harsh imperatives that drove old Pat Nichols out of the Dust Bowl and up here to hack out a living for his family in the deep rock shafts of the Boaz Mine. If Don had been raised beneath the cottonwoods in the quiet old neighborhoods of Bozeman, there would have been social workers and headshrinkers to counsel the troubled boy after his father's death. That was the kind of rational, organized world the Swensons came from. But Don Nichols did not. Instead of social workers, he got a dryland ranch, the Bible, and liberal doses of his stepfather's razor strap. Country and city. Old West and New.

Don Nichols, Johnny knew, came from this land; he was cut from the same cloth as the people whose job it was to hunt him down and bring him to justice.

In the eyes of the Swensons, maybe, the Nicholses

were just trash. And maybe they saw Johnny that way, too, a "bungler."

Johnny walked sadly through the fall wind toward his dusty car. He would have preferred winning that little shouting match with Schaap and the Swensons. He would have liked to explain to them what Ron Alles, a leader of the most-elite federal law enforcement agency's best field team, the U.S. Marshal's SOG, had told him about the futility of "saturating" the mountainside with searchers. He would have liked to take Schaap and the Swensons down to Dave Wing's office to show them the bank of electronic listening devices that were monitoring the equipment they'd installed up above the Beartrap; he would have enjoyed sitting them down to read the details of the classified search and patrol operations about to begin. He did not need to be lectured to about "modern" methods.

He crossed the street, then stopped in midstride, almost physically beaten down by a sense of angry despair. Being a small-town cop, a rural county sheriff, hardly seemed worth the aggravation.

Johnny looked up at the snowy ridges, suddenly, irrationally certain that the Nicholses were gone, that they'd just walked off and were now living far away, in some anonymous Sunbelt city, never to be caught and judged by a jury of their Madison County peers.

He had not experienced such hopeless despair since that terrible time in Dillon, almost fifteen years before. Now, like then, he had come very close to just taking off his badge and handing the aggravation to someone else.

He'd been in college, working nights as a city patrolman. Money was tight, what with the two babies at home, and there was little time to study, or to sleep, or to enjoy his family. He was cowboying out in the county, breaking horses and working fence, going to classes, and working six nights a week as a small-town cop. He was not even thirty years old yet, but he felt like a broken-down old man.

That was dope and hippie time, confrontation time between the counterculture and the "pigs." The young hippie had money; his daddy provided him a bright red Mustang. Johnny had to make do with a rusted-out Dodge pickup, about to throw a rod. The hippie ran a red light; Johnny pursued in the patrol car and wrote the kid up.

But the kid got nasty, refused to accept the ticket, claimed "police harassment," called Johnny a "pig."

Johnny put the cuffs on him and drove him back to the station to be booked. All the way there, the long-haired kid mocked him, calling him a yokel "rent-a-cop" and, of course, a "pig." "If you didn't have on that uniform," the hippie screamed, "I'd whomp your ass for you."

That night after duty, Johnny couldn't sleep. He'd worked something like sixteen straight nights, accepting every chance for overtime. But now he was burnt out.

Back at the empty trailer—Susie was visiting her mother with the kids—he changed into jeans and a shirt, then went downtown and had a couple of drinks. The mocking hippie remained in his brain. "Rent-a-cop." "Pig." Johnny went to the jail; a deputy foolishly gave him the keys.

"Well," he said to the startled kid who rose from the concrete bunk with alarm in his eyes, "I don't have my uniform on now, fella, and I'm giving you your chance to whomp my ass."

The hippie was loud, but no fighter. Johnny hurt him a little bit, in the teeth and face. Then he got a pair of scissors and cut off the young man's long, carefully styled hair. Ten days later, after the newspaper scandal and the department investigation, Johnny resigned.

He quit college and drove a logging truck; he unloaded watermelons; he cowboyed and rodeoed for money. A small-town cop, he had learned, had to eat a lot of aggravation if he wanted to earn his pay.

Later, the Beaverhead County sheriff convinced Johnny to move over to Ennis, where they needed a resident deputy.

"You're a good cop, Johnny," the old man said. "And that's what you ought to be doing with your life."

For almost fifteen years, now, he'd worn one kind of a badge or another. And, of course, a gun. But now, by God, the sour spillover of the confrontation with the Swensons was so strong, that he was sorely tempted to call Bill Dringle and hand the county back its badge.

As the Nicholses later recounted, the cold was constant. On the high ridges, the snow had come early and was now chest deep in the draws and gullies. Game was scarce. On the slopes around Alder and Camp Creek, there was less snow, and the game was herding up. But the lower slopes were wide open to the north wind.

For a while, Don Nichols and his son made do with a new dugout camp on a south-facing ridge above the Mill Creek drainage. They hacked away the frozen earth, but kept the overhanging pine boughs as cover. Then they carefully rigged their clear plastic tarp across the cave's mouth and scraped out their sleeping platform. With plenty of pine boughs on the ground for insulation, and with the plastic tarp acting as a greenhouse, they were able to heat the cave with just a small squaw-wood fire. Some days they could lounge around in shirtsleeves inside their primitive greenhouse. They had solved the problem of the cold, at least for now, but their food was almost gone. For days they had hunted, but saw no large game, only squirrels and mice. And high above, the hawks and eagles.

Don knew better than to return to their caches above the Beartrap. That's where the law would be waiting. But he had his winter clothes in those caches, his sacks of red beans, his whole wheat flour, coffee, and sugar.

As close as Don could figure, it was only mid-October, but the winter had set in to stay. They needed staple food, and they needed clothes. Danny still was wearing his Levi jacket as a coat, and he only had canvas-sided hiking shoes. Twice he'd frosted his toes and heels.

Don Nichols had not brought his boy to these mountains to have him die of frostbite. He made his decision.

To the east, down the long slope of Indian Ridge, Gallatin Canyon widened into a wooded meadow called Beckman's Flats. City people had built cabins there, and they used them summers and for weekend snowmobiling. Don Nichols hated the dudes on snow machines. They were destructive; they ran the deer to death, then left the meat for the ravens. They were rich men who considered the mountains as playgrounds and the animals who lived in them as toys. But they stocked their cabins well, with food and clothing. Warm winter clothes for Danny.

They moved in stages, downslope, east. Toward Gallatin Canyon. The snow was deep.

One day they got a yearling mule deer, but they couldn't risk a big fire to smoke the haunches.

On the way down, they broke into the deserted Spanish Creek Ranger Station. There was some stale bread and some coffee, but no other food. Rummaging through the cupboard, Don found a pair of good sorrel pack boots, with warm felt liners. They fit Danny, like they'd been custom made for some rich man.

They waited all day in the thick spruce, watching the cabins on the flats below. Across the highway, they saw people in a big log house. They would not cross the road. But on this side, well screened by pine, stood two cabins and a kind of bunkhouse. At night, they would not be seen from the occupied log house or the highway.

They waited in the cold of the trees, watching. The lights of the log house had been out for hours when they moved down through the trees. It had been almost two days since they'd eaten. Don broke the bathroom window with his rifle butt, raised the sash and crawled inside.

It was warm in the cabin. The refrigerator hummed softly. He went to the back door and let Danny in. He knew the danger of staying too long. Together, they worked quickly through the kitchen cabinets. There was more food than Don could have hoped for, certainly as much as they could carry back up with them tonight.

They sorted the supplies and loaded their packs carefully. A large can of Crisco. A five-pound sack of pancake mix. Ten pounds of flour. A three-pound box of powdered milk. Hot chocolate. From the cabinet above the stove, Danny took six cans of chili, enough to keep them a week. Don found a large box of Bisquick and a package of lasagna noodles. They needed starch to supplement the squirrel and deer meat.

In the freezer they found TV dinners, dozens of frozen hamburger patties, and a whole frozen pork roast, wrapped nicely in foil.

Their packs were almost full.

Don searched the living room and the den, using the light from the open refrigerator. He found a thick sheepskin coat. That would keep Danny warm when

229

they traveled. He also found a pair of good snow shoes, but no boots for himself.

While they loaded their backpacks, they drank two cans of Sprite from the refrigerator. The heat inside had made them thirsty after all that time in the cold.

They moved on to the dark house next door. Once more, Don broke a window and crawled inside, right into the kitchen. There they found more pancake mix and flour, bacon, potatoes, and an unopened can of Maxwell House coffee. In the hall closet, Don found a pair of knee-high rubber dairyman's boots that fit him well. Now he and Danny both had waterproof boots.

Don knelt by the bookcase, searching for something interesting.

Louis L'Amour novels. He threw the paperbacks onto the floor, disgusted. He hated novels, and these hokey Westerns were the worst of all. But now he found some interesting books, history, an information yearbook. That was more like it.

They hefted their heavy packs and left by the kitchen door.

As they climbed the dark trail toward Indian Ridge, the snow began to fall heavily. That was good. By morning, there would be no tracks.

They must have taken over one hundred pounds of food, enough to last them a long time, and Danny had his coat and overshoes.

Gallatin County Detective Ron Cutting took the burglary complaint on October 20. The couple who owned the cabin up in the canyon were named Neil and Charlotte Lynch. They reckoned the break-in happened sometime between October 8 and 15. In their complaint, they stated that what had been stolen included a large amount of food, a pair of snow shoes, and a thick sheepskin coat. Lynch said that he found it strange that the burglars had not taken a .22 rifle that was standing in plain view, the snow machine that was stored outside, power tools, a color TV, or an expensive stereo set.

When the deputies investigated the scene, Bill Pronovost found tracks leading west, toward the Indian Ridge Trail and the Spanish Peaks, but after a short distance they disappeared.

But it had snowed recently, and the tracks were impossible to read.

Lynch expressed his surprise that the burglars had concentrated on food, and had left behind the real valuables. However, the Gallatin County deputies were not surprised at all. They had a pretty fair idea who the burglars were.

Johnny got the call at home on Sunday night. Three cabins burglarized. Mainly food, but staples, not a lot of heavy canned goods. A sheepskin coat, a pair of snow shoes, books.

"What kind of books?" Johnny asked Ron Cutting.

"Hard to tell, Johnny," Cutting answered. "But looks like they left behind a whole bunch of Louis L'Amour novels . . . you know, those paperback westerns."

"Yep," Johnny said, "I know."

Don Nichols had often said how much he hated fiction, especially the romantic western novels of Louis L'Amour.

Johnny called Dave Wing, and they met in Dave's office late that evening.

"They're moving back up high, Dave. They've got their food, and they're gonna build one of their dugouts up there and just try to wait us out."

"Maybe," Dave Wing said, "but they can't go too high, not the way the weather's shapin' up."

Johnny gazed at the confusing blur of contour lines and boundary markers on the map. In his mind he saw Don and Dan Nichols, trekking through the deep drifts, seeking the cover of the high timbered ridges.

"Well," Johnny concluded, "they didn't take those snow shoes so Danny could earn himself a merit badge. I think they're planning to travel."

Dave Wing scowled at the map. "Yessir," he finally said. "I expect you're right."

The twenty-fourth of October was one of the most miserable days Tom Heintz had ever experienced in the mountains. Tom was an outfitter who'd worked the north slope of the Spanish Peaks for over ten years, but he'd never had such a terrible October. The night before, the blizzard wind must have topped eighty miles an hour, howling through his spike camp near the north fork of Spanish Creek. That morning the storm continued, but the wind backed south and the temperature rose above freezing. Now drenching sleet had replaced the buckshot snow.

The bad weather had driven the elk down low, into the timbered alluvial fans of the creek drainages. Tom had a total of twelve client elk hunters—guests, he preferred calling them—sleeping in three spike camps along Camp, Placer, and Cherry creeks. He had four hands and a camp cook. Two of the hands worked a pack string, bringing in supplies and packing out meat and trophy heads. Medicine Lake Outfitters was a well-organized, successful operation.

Tom knew that this weather was putting a real crimp on the final week of the season. The elk were bunched up in the thick timber, spooky from the blizzard. Now the sleet was crusting the snow, and when the wind went north again, the ice layer was going to make tracking a real problem.

That day Tom was working with two young hunters from Billings, Matt Tudor and Doug Keller, experienced hunters, but admittedly novice horsemen. They rode three sure-footed saddle horses, the two guests with rifles across their saddles, Tom in the lead, trying to read the snow for game signs. All three wore Day-Glo orange safety vests over their parkas. They were cold, wet, and miserable. The horses weren't going to be good for very long today.

They ate their lunch sandwiches in the shelter of some timber on the north fork, then headed south in a slow loop of the canyon floor, checking for signs of a big herd that Tom guessed might be holed up near Willow Swamp.

Around two-thirty, the sun broke through for a few moments, dazzling the riders with its sudden warmth. Across the canyon floor, sunlight played on a weird, pulsing bauble that hung above a stand of timber. Tom felt the shivers dance up his backbone. It reminded him of the special effects in a Steven Spielberg movie. Sun dog, he thought.

A fifth-generation Montana native, Tom had been raised near an Indian reservation; he had undergone certain initiation ceremonies as a kid, fasting up on lonely buttes. He understood medicine, and that sun dog evoked the spiritual power of these ancient mountains.

Without explaining his plan, he led Matt and Doug across the stream and toward the timbered slope where he'd seen the image. Now he realized that the sun dog had actually been sunlight catching a puff of smoke, just above the icy latticework of a big spruce tree.

Using his binoculars, Tom glassed the tree and saw two hunters, hunkered under a makeshift rain tarp, sheltering beside a warming fire.

As he rode up to their camp, Tom's first impression was that these guys were really living rough. They looked like old-time prospectors, bearded, sooty, with thin, tattered clothing and greasy cowboy hats. Tom did not see any down vests or Gortex parkas in that scrawny little camp. In fact, the only piece of winter clothing he observed was the sheepskin jacket the younger man wore. That scrap of green tarp was all they had for a tent, and it looked like one battered skillet was the extent of their cooking gear.

Tom's second impression was that these two guys were about as dirty as anybody he'd ever seen. They must have been up here quite a while, living in the woods. Suddenly he understood. Jesus, it's Don and Dan Nichols.

Tom Heintz had already worked this country for several months that fall, what with the gun and archery seasons on both deer and elk. He'd understood that one day he might run into the Nicholses, and he'd made plans. The Gallatin County deputies and Bob Morton of the Forest Service had advised him to treat the Nicholses casually, in a nonthreatening manner, should he encounter them. Then to get to the nearest phone and call in the law.

Now he was staring down into Don Nichols's lean, scowling face, and all the carefully constructed contingencies went right out the window.

"Howdy," Tom called, his voice almost sticking in his dry throat. "You fellas seen any game?"

Danny Nichols had his right hand inside the sheepskin jacket. He'd have a pistol in there, Tom thought, probably the gun he shot Kari with.

234

"Ain't seen any game at all," Don answered. He stepped near his rifle that was leaning against the tree trunk. "Nothing," he added with rude finality.

"Right," Tom answered, wheeling his horse around. "Thanks. See you."

Tom led his guests down the slope. If they were going to get shot, it'd be right about now.

Matt and Doug had heavy-caliber rifles, but Tom's only weapon, a long-barreled .357 revolver, was in his saddle bag.

Just then, Doug snared his stocking cap on a snag and the cap fell to the snow. Tom slipped from his saddle and retrieved the cap. "Look," he whispered, "you just ride on down across the creek and wait in the thick timber there. I'm going to have to go back and talk to them a little."

The two young hunters nodded acceptance. Their expressions were a mix of fear, excitement, and intense curiosity.

Tom rode slowly up the slope, keeping his hands high on the reins to show he carried no weapon. Don and Danny were right where they'd been when he'd first seen them, glaring at him from under the dripping shelter of the spruce.

He climbed down from the horse real slow, then crunched to the edge of the camp with his gloved hands open before him. "Fellas," he began. "Listen. I know who you are. I'm just paying a little visit. I'm not armed and I sure don't mean you any harm."

Don Nichols edged even nearer his rifle. It was a heavy, full-barreled foreign job with an expensive scope, a real hunter's weapon. The boy's rifle that stood beside it was a cheap .22 with a dime-store scope. On a tattered ground cloth lay two dog-eared paperback books, a biography of Sitting Bull and the history of the Bozeman Trail.

"Think maybe you're mistaking us for someone else," Don finally answered.

Tom smiled nervously. "No, I do know who you are. But I just want to talk a little bit, that's all."

"That your outfit down by the trailhead?" Don asked. His eyes were jumpy and he was clearly unhappy about this social visit.

Tom replied that the horse trailers and pickup down at the Spanish Creek campground were his.

Don said that he'd seen Tom's camps on the creeks, and that Tom obviously knew how to pick a good site for a hunting camp.

Tom thanked him for the compliment.

Sleet dripped down off the wet boughs. The fire hissed and crackled.

Slowly, Don Nichols's angry tension began to seep away. Finally, he turned to Danny and said that Tom was all right because "he lives up here, too."

Don asked the news; obviously he meant the manhunt and pursuit.

Trying to phrase his answers carefully to avoid offense, Tom explained that the initial kidnapping and shooting had provoked national media attention, but that interest had kind of tapered off. Kari Swenson, Tom said, seemed to have made a pretty fair recovery.

Danny literally jumped forward. "She's not dead? She's not dead?" His face showed excitement for the first time. "She didn't die up there?"

Tom patiently answered his questions, but Danny persisted. At least five times he repeated the same question about Kari Swenson, as if the news was too impossibly good to be true. The boy's stiff aggression that had met Tom on his return to the camp evaporated, and Danny became a happily excited kid, eager to chat and gossip.

But the old man did not seem pleased to hear about

Kari Swenson. He interrupted Danny's banter to tell Tom that there was a lot of hunting pressure over in the Cherry Creek country. He wanted to know which of Tom's camps were going to be used, so that he and Danny could avoid those areas.

Taking his father's lead, Danny tried unsuccessfully to dampen his own effusiveness, but his surprise and relief at learning he was not a murderer showed clearly on his face.

Tom said he was surprised to find them camping so close to a trail.

Don said sourly that the storm had caught them out in the open, and they'd had to settle for what shelter they could find.

Once Danny's excitement tamped down a bit, he asked Tom if he had any food. Danny nodded to the sooty skillet. "All we got is this squirrel stew." He could not explain their caches of stolen food.

Sorry, Tom replied, his food was in the spike camps.

The old man began to question Tom in great detail about the trails and ridges leading west and southwest. He wanted to know the best route for them to take in order to avoid other hunters.

Tom answered each question in equal detail.

Once more, Danny asked about food. "We can trade you some elk ivory for food," he said.

Tom could see the desperate, cold hunger in the boy's eyes.

"You ain't got any whiskey in that flask of yours, do you?" Don asked.

Tom was surprised; he carried cold tea in a plastic hip flask. They must have seen him drinking from it on the trail that fall. Amazingly, they'd been watching him for months.

Danny asked Tom for a cigar, but Tom carried no tobacco.

Tom turned to Danny. "Don't you ever miss people up here?"

Danny's answer was immediate. "We don't miss people," he said flatly. "We don't miss parties."

Tom Heintz nodded. The boy had said "We don't miss" as if they were two people with a single mind.

Tom cleared his throat. "Listen," he began, "I got a camp cook working for me, and she's armed, got herself a .357, and she does know how to use it. She's going to shoot first and ask questions later if you show up."

Don stared into Tom's eyes, weighing the message.

But Danny broke the tension of the moment. "Well," he said, grinning broadly, "I kind of lost interest in girls."

All three laughed loudly under the lonely, dripping branches.

Don wanted to know exactly what had been reported about the shooting in July. Tom tried to reconstruct the press reports as clearly as he could. He stressed the speculation that Don had shot Al Goldstein because Don had felt Danny was threatened.

Don leaned close to Tom's face and spoke with a sorrowful intensity. "Tom," he said, "don't you think only professionals should point guns at people?"

Tom did not fully understand Don's meaning, but he assumed the old man was implying that amateurs like Al Goldstein had no right to threaten somebody with a gun. Tom saw that Don was in no mood for an argument, so he nodded somber agreement.

After some neutral banter, Tom decided it was time for him to leave. "Fellas," he said, "good luck."

He strode out of camp, down the snowy slope to where he'd tied his horse. Surprisingly, Danny marched right along with him, chatting happily, asking more questions, clearly pleased to have someone other than his father to talk to.

Don Nichols's voice boomed from under the shelter tree. "Danny, what are doing down there? Get back up here right now."

Tom turned to see Don holding his rifle. The boy stopped in the crusty snow and reluctantly faced his father. Then Danny trudged back up the slope to join the old man who was half hidden beneath the icy spruce boughs.

As Tom Heintz rode down the trail to find Matt and Doug, he pondered the meeting and the decisions he now must make about alerting the law. It was after three; on a day like this, darkness would come in two hours, well before a large posse could be organized and ride in here. That meant there'd be a lot of confusion in the darkness . . . snow machines, tracking dogs, dozens of armed deputies, maybe even the famous SWAT team again. In any event, lots of guns, lots of nervous cops. But with this wind gusting to sixty miles an hour, tracking would be impossible; already his earlier horse-track had vanished.

In the morning, the law would be all over these slopes. Very possibly Don and Danny would be chased into one of Tom's camps and they'd hold up there, taking Tom's guests as hostage.

Tom had three camps and twelve clients spread across a wide, difficult piece of back country. If the law came in here like mechanized Gang Busters, there was a real chance his people might get hurt.

Medicine Lake Outfitters was Tom's whole life. If he lost a hunter to a police crossfire or to a bullet from Don Nichols during a hostage stand-off, his business would be ruined.

Tom stopped his horse and looked up at the lowering cloud deck. He had reached his decision. In the next two days, he would pull out his hunters and the camps, then he would report his meeting with Don and Dan Nichols.

Tom and his hands rode twenty-five miles a day for the next three days. They pulled back their clients and loaded up the spike camps. The weather was terrible, but no one complained much.

By five-thirty Sunday morning, Tom was back at his place near Three Forks. He called Bob Morton of the Forest Service and made his report. Early Sunday morning, Dave Wing called Johnny France. An outfitter named Tom Heintz, Dave said, had seen the Nicholses up near Willow Swamp; he'd talked to them. It was the first positive sighting since July.

Dave Wing continued his report. "Heintz says they're headed west, Johnny, toward the Beartrap."

"Well, all right," Johnny finally answered. "I guess that's good news."

"Heintz also says that they're hungry, Johnny, real hungry."

"That's good, Dave," Johnny answered. "That means that they've gone through all that food they stole. I kind of figured they would. It looked like a lot of provisions on the burglary report, but we forget how many calories a person needs to survive up there in this weather. I think they're gonna start getting sloppy now."

Johnny realized that the Nicholses had gone through almost sixty pounds of stolen food between the first and the third week of October. Obviously, the harsh weather increased their daily calorie requirement. Living out in the open, they needed more food. The game up there was scarce. That meant they'd have to hunt in the lower country, then hole up in their cave or dugout back up high.

With this early winter, there'd be chances for tracking that hadn't existed in the summer. Now, he knew, the Nicholses were trapped in a vice; one jaw was the weather, the other was the law.

The pursuit was redoubled from both the Madison and the Gallatin sides. Deputies on snow machines and on horseback scoured the country around Willow Swamp. They found no tracks because the squally snow continued through the whole next week.

That Wednesday, Dave Wing and Bernie Hubley returned to the Cowboy Heaven cow camp and planted brand new beeper bugs in sacks of pancake mix and flour. These bugs were a new, experimental model that represented, they'd been told, "the state of the art." If the Nicholses disturbed those food supplies, alarms would ring down at the Forest Service office in Ennis.

November dragged along, cold, snowy. Johnny picked up some frostbite on his face, up in the Beartrap, searching alone one gray afternoon.

On November 11, Detective Bill Pronovost received a letter from the FBI fingerprint section in Washington. They'd developed five fingerprints from the books and soda cans found at the burglarized cabins in Beckman's Flats. None of the prints matched those of Don Nichols.

On November 15th, Johnny and Sue's twenty-fifth wedding anniversary, Johnny joined a night patrol to the steep, wind-blasted slopes of Blaze Mountain. The snow had pretty well been blown off these ridges, and the lawmen wore forest-pattern camies, not white snow suits.

They were acting on a report of a suspected cave camp on a rocky spur side-ridge of Blaze Mountain.

This camp, the report stated, would be an ideal winter hideout for the Nicholses. The plan called for about half a dozen lawmen to drive in as far as they could after dark, then trek the rest of the way up the slope. Once more, the FBI had furnished its high-tech support, this time in the form of night-vision goggles.

They met in the gym of the Law and Justice center in Bozeman, and Gary Lincoln of the FBI passed out the night goggles and instructed the men on their use. The party included John Onstad, Jim DeBoer, the game warden; Deputy Wally Schumaker; and Dave Wing.

Then they departed Bozeman in three all-terrain vehicles, hoping to reach the slopes of Blaze Mountain by 0200. Driving in on the Spanish Creek road, they doused their headlights, and all three drivers steered by the weird lime green images in their night goggles. The green patterns reminded Johnny of his night flight with the Probeye. That seemed like a thousand years ago.

Near the trailhead, they spotted a big herd of elk, browsing in some timber. Evidently, the blacked-out vehicles were effective because the elk didn't spook until the last minute, when the sound of the tires on the frozen mud hit the trees.

The hike in was nasty, cold, and dangerous. When they finally staked out the suspect ridge, it was almost daylight.

Johnny's fancy night-vision goggles started breaking down as he and Dave climbed out to their position on a steep, rocky spur. One of the side brackets had come loose, and he could not focus on close objects, only on the distant ridges. They waited in the dark; when they had enough daylight, they'd assault the cave—if they could find it.

Just before dawn, Johnny slipped on the smooth rock, fell backwards, and tumbled down the slope into the dark brush. His right hand jammed in a crevice and dislocated his thumb. Hanging upside down in the tangled brush, his night goggles off his head, he cradled his mini-Ruger with his elbow and used his left hand to yank his right thumb back into place. The pain almost made him pass out.

Just after dawn, Brad Brisban and his German shepherd, Bear, found a small cave on the side of the ridge. But the hole only went back about five feet and showed no signs that it had ever served as a shelter for man or animal.

Johnny stared at the chill gray slopes. His hand throbbed like a drilled tooth.

The mountains were empty.

Toward the end of November, the lawmen on the Madison side met in Dave Wing's office to devise a new operational plan. In the event the Nicholses were sighted again, Johnny and Dave wanted to have a fast-reaction capture plan that would involve a small group of experienced officers.

They were tired of big, elaborate productions like the Blaze Mountain high-tech fiasco. And they wanted local boys who knew this country and would be ready to move on a phone call. Each man would prepare a small backpack with some rations and water, and each man would keep his radio and weapons ready. The alert code had to be kept clear and simple. Once a man was contacted by phone and was given the code word, he would know what was happening.

"Well," Johnny said, leaning across Dave's conference table, "what should we call the code word?"

They all looked at Dave. He sat stolidly at his place, then looked up at the big map of the Beartrap. His eye fell on Barn Creek. "Yeah . . . well, let's call her Barnstorm."

* * *

In November, a reporter from the *Washington Times* who called himself W.J. Elvin III came out to Montana to interview Johnny. Toward the end of the long taped interview session, Mr. Elvin asked Johnny how long he planned to continue the pursuit of the two fugitives.

Johnny pondered the question a moment, then gave his answer. "Well," he said, "I've got about twelve years until I retire." He paused and considered his words. "There's another chapter to the story; it just hasn't been written yet."

PART 4

Barnstorm

16

The Beartrap

December 11–12, 1984

WINTER NOW DOMINATED THE HIGH COUNTRY. COLD AND snow were a constant presence. At night, the temperature fell to thirty degrees below zero. Some days when the north wind scoured the rock ridges, crippling frostbite hid in the deceptive sunshine.

The last of the big game moved down from the tree line and deep blue timber of the Spanish Peaks to bunch up in the wooded gullies and foothills of the Cherry and Spanish Creek drainages. Now that hunting season was over, mule deer and elk congregated in huge herds below Cowboy Heaven and the trailhead ranger stations. Every day when the cowboys of the Flying D Ranch rode out to spread feed among their scattered herds of yearling heifers and cows, they saw large bunches of shaggy elk, browsing in the lodgepoles, just above the snowy ranges. The deer and elk left the timber at night and grazed among the standing cattle.

For a month, Don Nichols and his son were able to hole up in dugout camps hidden high in the Beartrap. They came down to shoot a deer or young elk when they needed meat, traveling at night to avoid hunters *and the game wardens who patrolled the slopes. But now the game was too far below their camps for them to replenish their meat without risk of leaving tracks that might be seen by cowboys or deputies. Snowmobilers and cross-country skiers had replaced the elk hunters on the lower ranges. With every hunting trip below the frozen sanctuary of the Beartrap, they faced the danger of ambush or, at the least, sighting by some zealous skier.*

And, Don soon realized, there were more than amateur sportsmen on the northern slopes. Almost every clear day brought the frightening intrusion of low-flying airplanes, shiny, high-winged Cessnas, quartering the snowbound meadows and gullies, searching for tracks. Some men on snow machines rode higher than the others; they wore white suits, not red hunters' vests, and they carried rifles across their handle bars long after the elk hunters had disappeared.

If he and Danny had a good supply of staples, Don knew, they could survive the winter on squirrels and grouse as their only source of meat. But they had almost exhausted their flour and beans, their stolen Crisco and Bisquick. They needed fats and carbohydrates; they needed calories to endure the killing pressure of the wind.

Another burglary raid on the cabins of the Gallatin Canyon would be suicide. Hitting the camp at Cowboy Heaven was equally risky. Judging from the snowmobile and foot tracks, the law had staked the camp out for ambush several times during the hunting season.

And there was another, less obvious, but equally compelling force that drove Don Nichols and his son down from the icy safety of the Beartrap. Ever since their meeting with the elk outfitter, Tom Heintz, Danny had been acting strange. Distant, moody, stubborn.

Now Danny bitterly complained about the cold hardship, about the hunger and the isolation they had to endure. He believed what Tom had said about the girl, that she had lived, that people all felt her shooting had been an accident. Danny now realized that he had not killed her, that he did not face a murder charge. The boy knew enough about the law from his juvenile troubles down in Three Forks to see that he could probably bargain a guilty plea of some kind for a light sentence if it ever came to that. But Danny also understood that his father had no such option.

Before Tom Heintz, they had been united by their common guilt. Two murderers could not expect mercy from the law. For all they knew, they'd killed a man and a woman. Down in the valley, they faced ambush and death. Up here, their survival was a matter of daily pain and vigilance, but surrender was unthinkable.

After Tom Heintz, they were no longer united by blood guilt. Now Danny was less willing to accept the dead white cold, the hunger, the sour fear that came with the whine of a distant snow machine or the drone of an airplane.

For the first time in their life together, Danny began to openly challenge Don's authority. They argued at first about small matters . . . an easy source of dry wood, the best way to stalk a deer . . . the domestic fabric of their daily lives. Then Danny's mood darkened. He grew sarcastic, mocking. For the first time, he laughed at his father.

Now, when Don hit the boy, Danny hit back. They screamed in rage beneath the silent, snowy lodgepoles.

At night, they were forced to huddle together in their double sleeping bag in rancid, smoky union, waiting out the long darkness.

* * *

Finally, Don proposed a plan, and Danny accepted it.

They would cache their sidearms, their heavier tools, their plastic tarps and extra ammunition. Traveling light and fast, they would descend the Beartrap Canyon, then cross the Madison River highway bridge at night and strike out across the hills, northwest toward Harrison. Don knew that country well; as a boy, he'd trapped and hunted there. The willows around Harrison Lake were dense, good cover, full of game in the winter. They could build a hidden camp that no lawman would ever find. And Don argued that the law would never think of looking for them there, down on the flats.

They had twenty-five dollars in cash. Once they'd made their camp, Danny could get cleaned up and walk into the store in Harrison. No one knew the boy in town. With his hair cut and his beard off, he'd be impossible to recognize.

Twenty-five dollars would buy an awful lot of red beans, flour, vegetable oil and sugar. The white tail deer and rabbits in the willows were almost tame, Don said. There was good shelter from the wind. There they could live out the worst of the winter in relative safety and comfort.

In the spring, they'd hit some outlying ranches and cabins for more staples, then climb back to the Beartrap to build new secret camps and plant their gardens, high in the steep draws where the deputies never went. By next winter, they'd be better prepared, with two or three crops of turnips and rutabagas, with smoked deer haunches and sacks of sun-dried berries.

Another winter, another spring and summer. The law would forget them. Don and his boy would have their life together in the high freedom of the mountains, away from the system and the vengeance of the law. Danny agreed. He seemed to like the idea of a hidden camp, sheltered from the wind, the searching airplanes and ambushes.

They shot a deer above Beartrap Creek. Here they had good cover, and they carefully butchered the deer, cutting the quarters into thick steaks. In a rocky cleft, they built a hot, smokeless fire of squaw wood and fried up a dozen steaks, the heart and liver. When they'd eaten their fill, they packed the remaining meat in two plastic sacks, one of cooked steaks, one of raw. Then they rested, waiting for night.

The clear, windy afternoon grew still. An overcast crept across the sky from the west, and the shadowy canyon grew even darker. Below them, the gray water of the Madison rapids churned between twisted shores of sugary spume ice.

The river was their obstacle. It was too deep and cold to wade. There were only two bridges within twenty miles, the wooden bridge below Ennis Lake, and the "silver" right-angle highway bridge at the north end of the Beartrap. Men from the power station crossed the wooden bridge at all hours of the day and night, and the road out from Ennis Lake to McAllister led past ranches and a busy crossroad. Their only safe route was the highway bridge.

Once across, they would be in the lonely scrub timber and rangeland, laced with abandoned mine drifts, that led all the way to Harrison Lake. It was only eight or ten miles from the bridge to the lake, a distance they could easily travel in darkness. There'd been no snow for several days, and the north wind that blew each day had cleaned the ridges down to brown, frozen range grass. The traveling would not be hard, and—most important—they would leave no tracks for the airplanes to spot. If, for any reason, they got caught out by daylight, there were stands of cedar and spruce at the tops of most draws where they could hole up, living off their cooked meat without risking a fire.

They waited in their gully, the last rocky highground above the canyon floor. In a few hours they would leave the wilderness, their first trip into civilization since raiding the cabins in Gallatin Canyon in October.

The snow began to fall after they were across Beartrap Creek, marching through the darkness, north along the gravel Forest Service road. Because it was already night, and because they were sheltered by the steep walls of the gorge, they could not immediately judge the intensity of the storm. If they had been able to feel the blizzard's force, they might have turned back to seek shelter in one of the side canyons. But, with the river roaring among the icy boulders and frozen snags, and the overcast hunkered right down on the ridgetops, they had no way of gauging the savage force of the storm.

As they trudged along the gravel track the snow began to drift, ankle-deep at first, then up to their knees. The river widened and the canyon walls dropped away. And the blizzard hit them with full force. They hunched beneath their packs and plodded on.

For a long time the snow blasted them from across the dark water of the upper Madison. Then the wind stopped as if some gigantic vent had been closed. The snow spiraled straight down with silent intensity. Already, there was a foot of dense powder on the ground, level on the flat surface of the track, drifted into soft curves on the dark slopes to their right. Pines and junipers stood like white domes in the nearby darkness.

Sometime around midnight, they reached the north end of the Beartrap road. Ahead of them in the snowy *night, they could distinguish the dark angles of the steel highway bridge. Don called a halt, and they took cover behind an icy boulder to watch for passing cars, or maybe a deputy's patrol vehicle staking out the bridge.*

The snow was less intense now, but thick enough to prevent a decent view of the draws and ridges across the river to the west.

While they waited, numb and winded in the snow, several pickups passed, moving slowly on the icy pavement of Route 84. Danny grumbled about the cold, and about their exposed position out here in a snowy field on the edge of the main highway between Ennis and Bozeman. Still, Don waited.

It would take them, he knew, at least ten minutes to move from this cover, cross the bridge, walk down the highway a few hundred yards and up a draw to the hilltops above. In the snowy night he thought he could see a dark band of timber climbing the opposite slope, but he couldn't be certain. They might need that timber, he now realized. The wind had died away completely, leaving a deep, uniform snow cover across those hills. Without a wind, they would leave obvious tracks, right out of the Beartrap, across the bridge, and up into the draws across the river. In the morning, some patrolling lawman would find their tracks and call in another airplane. The plane would then spot their trail, leading across the snow hills, right to Harrison Lake.

Off to their right, the brown cube of the Trapper Springs Store stood dark and isolated in the night. Once, Don had considered this store as a source of food, but he then realized that a burglary on this side of the range would alert the law to search for them over here. They would bypass this lonely store for the security of Harrison Lake.

An hour later, when no car had passed for a long time, they rose stiffly and scurried out of their cover, dogtrotting tiredly toward the looming shape of the bridge. When they were on the plowed highway, crunching through the crusty slabs at the roadside, a yellow glow cut the night from behind them, and they dove for cover in the deeply drifted ditch. A ranch truck rattled past, throwing up a buckshot spray of ice. Again they waited.

Then they climbed out of the ditch and trotted across the icy bridge, their boot treads pinging on the exposed metal bridge joints.

They were over the river, on the west slope of the Beartrap for the first time in a year. Moving fast down the highway, they tried to judge the country that rose ahead of them. Here the road swung back south, following the river toward the Beartrap. They had completed a hairpin loop; now the western slope was on their right. A few hundred yards down the road, the hillside was a steep scrub-forest of juniper and Christmas tree fir. But Don could feel a draw opening ahead.

Half a mile from the bridge, they found their draw. But instead of plunging right into the snowy mouth of the gully, Don backtracked to a rocky outcropping. The climb would be more difficult, but they would leave fewer tracks.

He was right about the difficulty of the climb. Exhausted from the long trek against the blizzard wind, they were in poor condition to pick their way up icy shelves of crumbling quartz. Don fell and wrenched his knee. Danny tumbled off a sharp, snow-covered angle. They swore in the cold darkness, cursing the rocky slope, and each other.

Now the snow had stopped altogether. Chunks of chill-black, starry sky opened above them. The snowy dome of the ridgetop hung over them, white, silent.

By the time they reached the top of the draw, they were battered, numb and winded.

Danny sat on the snow, staring dully at his outstretched legs.

Don dumped his pack and staggered around the slope, searching for a decent, overhanging tree where they could make camp. They needed rest, and, more importantly, they needed cover from airplanes. There was open rangeland ahead of them, and they couldn't cross it until the wind had blown the ridges clean of snow.

Don found a tall, bushy limber pine standing alone on the edge of the drop-off to the steepest part of the draw. He couldn't judge the country above, but it looked pretty open. Here the rock shelves around the tree dipped to provide natural cover and shelter from the wind. When he squatted beneath the tree's lower boughs, he couldn't see the white curve of the highway, five hundred yards to the east and eight hundred feet below him.

There was plenty of squaw wood in the low branches, and nearby junipers and firs would provide even more. And the level rock offered an excellent sleeping platform. Once the shelf was padded well with insulating pine boughs, he and Danny could curl up and wait for the wind to blow the ridges above clean of snow.

Don rose to his full, stooped height and whistled in the cold darkness. In a minute, he knew, Danny would come with the packs, and they could prepare their camp.

He was sore and thirsty; his face was both numb and burned from the blizzard snow. But they were out of the Beartrap now, across the river, on their way to safety. They had escaped almost five months of manhunt.

Now they simply had to wait for wind, and they would be free of pursuit.

Daylight came, cold, gray. Windless. Camp robber jays sounded down in the brushy draw. Up here on the shoulder of the gully, the snow was almost knee deep.

Don could see the twisting snake of their tracks leading up the rocky side of the draw, right to this lonely tree. Their camp beneath the limber pine was in the last of the scrub timber that climbed the sides of the draw.

Above them, the expanse of snow rose in an unbroken dome to the wide summit of the ridge. There was almost no timber to be seen up there, just wide-open, snow-bound rangeland.

And the snow was deep, undisturbed by wind. Traveling through that country would be like a skywriter leaving a track across a cloudless blue sky.

As Don stood in the cover of their camp tree, a vehicle whined below him on the highway. Carefully, he edged around the tree and stared down, frowning. In the darkness, under the weight of their fatigue, the road had seemed much further away. Now, in the overcast morning, he could see how exposed they were.

They had no choice. The wind had to blow soon. This was Montana in December. And they could only wait for the wind to clear the white dome and ridges above them.

Even from this low on the hillside, Don could see the geometry of the fence-lines quartering the snowy ridges above. In the darkness, they had climbed the draw onto a working ranch, its pastures divided by barbed wire fences and gates. Where there were pastures, Don knew, there would be cowboys, and cowboys paid a lot of attention to man tracks on their land. There was only one route open to him and Danny—up that slope, *across the exposure of that snowy dome of rangeland, and out into the flats to the northwest below. But they would have to wait for the wind before crossing those pastures.*

They had meat, some flour, and some cracked horse oats they'd stolen from a cow camp manger. For a day or two, they could live on the cooked deer steaks. But water would be a problem. In the dry cold, thirst was constant, and they'd have to build a fire to melt snow. As far as Don could see, there was no live water in this draw, and he wasn't about to risk leaving more tracks by scouting around for a spring.

Danny lay bundled in the sleeping bags beneath the snow-heavy boughs of the limber pine. In a while, Don would wake him, so that they could gather more wood and cut some better sleeping boughs.

But now he let the boy sleep. Danny looked so small and peaceful when he slept.

All day, the gray overcast hung low on the distant ridgetops. Gray, chill. Windless. They waited under their tree, and around them, the snow stood deep.

Below the draw, pickups and cars droned along the snowy highway.

They ate their cold cooked deer meat, chewing slowly, rubbing the creamy fat from their whiskers.

Afternoon came, then dusk.

They waited, cold and thirsty, huddled in the thin cover of their tree.

17

Cold Springs Ranch

December 13, 1984

BY MID-MORNING, ROLAND MOORE REALIZED HE'D HAVE to ride up to the top and chop water for the cattle. It would be the first time for the tedious chore this winter. The blizzard of Tuesday had been followed by a skiff of light snow Wednesday and some real cold weather overnight. Now, on this windless Thursday morning, the sky was clearing to a bright, frigid day. The noon temperature probably wouldn't get up much above ten or so, not enough to melt the ice in his high stock tank.

Cattle needed plenty of water in this dry cold. It took a lot of energy to move around in the deep snow and graze on the frozen range grass. Some people didn't realize that about cows. But then, some people weren't as careful about ranching as Roland Moore.

The care he took with the Cold Springs Ranch was the product of several factors. Most importantly, he and his wife, Elaine, had acquired ownership of the property ten years earlier. Elaine's parents, Forrest and Betsy Shirley, had spent twenty-eight years working this land into a profitable ranch. They'd raised four kids here and several foster children, including Madison County Sheriff Johnny France. When the Shirleys decided to take it easier, they'd entrusted Roland and Elaine with the future of the land.

Roland Moore understood the responsibility of that trust. And he also understood the complexity of turning a profit—or, conversely, not going bankrupt—that underlay family ranching in the 1980s. Making a go of a place these days meant more than dedicated hard work; a rancher also had to be tough and smart and flexible. In that regard, Roland was the ideal candidate to carry on the tradition of the Shirleys.

He was in his middle thirties, a tall, wiry man with sandy hair and mustache. If they'd been photographing Marlboro Country ads in Madison County, they'd have probably offered Roland a contract. But he was more than a traditional cowboy. He had a degree in range management from MSU, and he'd spent six seasons working as a smoke jumper for the Forest Service, a grueling, dangerous, but high-paying job that had bolstered his quiet self-confidence.

Now he and Elaine owned this land; they were raising their two kids in the handsome log home that they'd built on the grassy rise, just above the Shirleys' original lodgepole ranch house in the creek bottom cottonwoods.

To supplement the unpredictable income from their cattle sales, Roland broke and raised saddle horses, mules, and big draft horses. There wasn't much he didn't know about raising stock or the rolling rangeland on which they grazed.

So, with the first deep, windless freeze of the winter following the first big December blizzard, Roland mounted a little blue saddle horse named Toby that he was training for ranch work and set off to chop water. He planned to ride along the road leading to the Madison, cut up the slope to the snowy dome of treeless rangeland they called the Poison Pasture—it contained larkspur, fatal to cattle—and break the ice on the stock tank that overlooked the Beartrap above Red Bluff.

Normally, the prospect of this chore would not have bothered Roland; he enjoyed riding across his land in all seasons, and it always interested him to see how the birds and game adapted to the first deep snow. But Toby was a clumsy little horse. He'd fallen with Roland a couple of days earlier, and there was a danger he might fall again in the deep powder snow. However, Roland was determined to work the horse this winter, so he saddled him for the ride up to the high stock tank. Toby was a well-behaved animal in every other way, and Roland felt he could work him around this clumsy streak, if he were just patient enough.

As a caution, however, he stopped by the house to speak to Elaine before he started through the bare cottonwoods to the road.

"If I'm not down by noon, Honey," he said, "have Crock come looking for me up there. I might get bunged up if this little horse falls on me."

Elaine took the news without undue alarm. She was ranch raised and had married a rancher; she knew all about the dangers of cattle ranching in Montana. Elaine didn't say anything, but she'd decided that she wouldn't just send Crockett, their hired man, to look for Roland if he wasn't back by lunchtime. She would lead the search herself.

Climbing through the drifts to the first fenceline, Roland saw that there'd been no wind on the ridge during the night. The light dusting of snow barely filled the tracks of birds and jack rabbits that criss-crossed the slope above.

Like most ranchers, Roland was intensely conscious of the land around him. He instinctively scanned the skyline, searching the ridges above for signs of stray cattle or broken fence. Hunting season had just ended, but there might be some gutshot deer that had staggered onto the land to die that could attract coyotes or mountain lions.

There was always the possibility of poachers and cattle thieves, too. All during the deer season, Roland patrolled the place with a .308 scabbard rifle on his saddle. He didn't have much use for the city boys in their little red suits who roared their Broncos and Blazers right up to the door of his house and practically demanded the God-given right to kill large mammals on his land. Now that the official season was over, there were hundreds of mule deer holed up on the ranch, a tempting target for poachers. And there was always the risk of losing a cow to some laid-off copper miner from Butte with a hungry family to feed and no more unemployment checks coming in.

However, Roland had not carried a saddle rifle with him this morning. He really didn't expect that anyone would be out in this fresh snow, either poaching or looking to shoot a heifer.

He unlocked the first gates and carefully locked them behind him. The herd was in a pretty good set of pastures over on the southern ranges, and he didn't want to have to go hunting down strays if the weather closed in again. He let Toby get his wind on top of the rise and sat back in the saddle to study the country revealed above the horse's steaming breath. From up on top here he got a good view of the Beartrap and the Spanish Peaks, further east. It looked like the blizzard had really plastered that high country.

For a moment, he thought about the Nichols boys. It must be pretty tough going up in that high blue timber after a storm like this, in the biting cold and chest-deep drifts. Johnny and Sue had been out at the place for Thanksgiving, and Johnny had talked a lot about the

Nicholses. They were bound to come down, Johnny'd predicted, as soon as the real cold and snow set in up there in the high Beartrap. And when they did, Johnny added, brooding over his coffee cup, there were only two places for them to come out . . . either the wood bridge up above the power station, or down the Beartrap road and across the right-angle highway bridge.

"When do you think they might make their move, Johnny?" Roland had asked.

Johnny squinted out the kitchen window at the distant snow of the mountains. "When the weather finally gets to 'em," he'd answered. "When there's no more game left up there and they need food." He thought a moment, as if consulting some invisible calendar. "I imagine the end of January, sometime in there."

Johnny told them that he and the Forest Service had a regular capture plan worked out by which they'd marshal all their best people on the spot, as soon as the Nicholses came down and were sighted.

"If they're sighted," Johnny had said somberly.

Roland chopped the ice out of the stock tank, and watched the milling Herefords crowd in for their water. The herd looked in fine condition for this time of the year, their ocher coats thick and shaggy, their eyes and nostrils clear of mucus. He carefully examined the surrounding snow for blood signs that might mean hoof disease or barbed wire wounds. Finding no problems, he turned Toby gingerly around with a soft rein and left the steamy lowing of the cattle.

Riding back along his inbound track, he let Toby find his own pace. So far the little blue had seemed just as sure-footed as could be, even on that rocky stretch near the last fenceline before the tank. Roland saw that this snowy climb was good for the horse and decided to ride him every day for a week or so, when he came up here to chop water. Such a regular schedule might do a lot to give the horse confidence.

He was musing on the strange quirks of horse temperaments, and beginning to think about a hot cup of coffee and Elaine's lunch, when Toby gave a shiver in his neck. Roland was immediately alert; something had caught the horse's attention. Swinging in his saddle, Roland scanned the snowfield that sloped left to the ridge above. Then he saw the smoke from the side of his eye, below him to the right, about five hundred yards down the pasture, in the scrub timber at the edge of the draw.

There was just that one puff. A billow of creamy gray that rose like an Indian signal in the still air. He reined Toby in and stared hard down the snowy slope to the edge of the draw. Somebody was on his land.

Roland instinctively reined the horse right and set off at a steady walk, downslope, away from his track, to investigate the trespasser.

Then his glove tightened on the reins and the little horse stopped.

Maybe, Roland thought, I'd better not be too hasty here. He peeled back the earflaps of his wool cap and leaned forward in the saddle, gazing down the white void of the slope. No more smoke rose. There was no sound, other than the horse's quiet breathing.

Roland had survived several close calls as a smoke jumper, relying on his ability to quickly analyze a dangerous situation, then take the most prudent, effective course of action. Now he tried to analyze the problem before him and to act accordingly.

Someone was definitely on his land; smoke came from fires, and fires did not just happen, not this time of year. Roland's best course of action depended on who'd built that fire down there in the scrub timber at the edge of the draw.

It could just be coyote hunters. But, even if it was, they had no right to hunt his land without permission. It could also be poachers, and that was nastier.

Then again, it could be a cattle thief who'd come up here on a snow machine, shot a cow, and was butchering her down on the lip of the draw.

In any of these cases, Roland would feel better if he had his scabbard rifle. He breathed deeply in the cold, dry air. There was the other possibility, of course. Johnny had said that the Nicholses might come out of the Beartrap across the highway bridge. And the Cold Springs Ranch was the closest piece of hill country to that bridge, a natural place for them to hole up, waiting for darkness before crossing the open rangeland to the west.

Roland nodded toward the draw and wheeled Toby quietly back to the left. Before he did anything else, he planned to ride down to the highway and see if he could spot a parked car or pickup along the side of the road. If that smoke had come from some coyote hunter boiling water for coffee, there'd likely be an outfit pulled off the shoulder, right below the draw. Lots of people mistook that draw for public land; it wasn't fenced, and you really couldn't see it was private ranchland from down on the road.

Roland began to feel a little better. Probably just coyote hunters.

But, as he walked the horse through the soft snow toward the distant fenceline, Roland felt a sudden tingle of vulnerability. His back was fully exposed to the east, the direction from which the gray ball of smoke had risen.

Once down on the main ranch road, Roland urged

Toby into a steady trot. The road followed the valley of
Cold Springs Creek between rolling dome-shaped hills
of open range land. Off to the right, some pink rim rock
outcropped, and the scrub timber was thicker on the
steep slopes. That was where Johnny and the Shirley
boys had set their trap lines when they were kids. The
bounty on bobcat pelts was about the only hard cash
those boys had seen growing up.

Toby's shoes clacked across an icy patch on the road,
and Roland reined him in as they entered the flat near
the highway bridge. There were no vehicles parked on
the flat, or on either side of the road. He trotted the
half mile down to the mouth of the draw. No car tracks
cut the crusty slabs the snow plow had thrown up on the
highway shoulder.

Roland climbed down from the saddle and walked
back along the roadside. He saw no human tracks in the
snow, either on the roadside or leading up the draw.
Holding Toby on a short rein, he stared up through the
scrub timber that rose above him. Whoever it was up
there had been on that ridge for at least two days,
otherwise they'd have left tracks in the deep powder
snow blanketing the draw and hillsides.

Once more, Roland forced himself to be analytical,
not impulsive. Someone was camping on his land, and
whoever it was had not arrived here by car. If they'd
hiked in from the south end of the ranch after the snow
fell, he'd have cut their tracks up at the top of the
Poison Pasture on his way to chop water. But the snow
had been undisturbed up there.

Again, Roland gazed at the dark timber. Coyote
hunters and poachers drove cars and pickups. High
school kids camping out wouldn't have walked all the
way from Ennis or Bozeman. Besides, the Christmas
school vacation hadn't started yet.

Roland swung back into the saddle and prodded

Toby into a fast canter, disregarding the danger of a fall on the icy roadside. It was time to call Johnny and let him know what was going on here.

Roland placed his first call to the sheriff's office in Virginia City at 11:25 that morning. He reached Mike Mitchell, the dispatcher, and asked to speak to Johnny France.

"Sorry, sir," Mike replied, "but the sheriff's on his way over to Bozeman, delivering a prisoner. We expect him back soon. Can anybody else help you?"

Roland carefully explained the details of what he had discovered. There was a campfire on his land, but there'd been no parked car or boot tracks on the roadside leading into the draw. He didn't think it was school kids on a winter camping trip because school was still in session. It might be survivalists, but they usually played their games on weekends. It might be poachers, but they usually drove pickups.

"Or," Roland said evenly, "it might be the Nicholses. Have Johnny call me as soon as he gets back from Bozeman. I'll drive up toward Red Bluff and see if I can spot any tracks or a parked outfit."

"Okay, sir," Mike said calmly. "I'll have the sheriff call as soon as he gets in."

Roland hung up the phone and stood brooding over the desk in his pine-paneled study. He was churning inside with conflicting emotions. On the one hand, he didn't want to be an alarmist, setting into motion that whole capture-plan deal that Johnny had mentioned—just because a couple of high school kids had skipped the last days before Christmas vacation to go shooting coyotes.

But, on the other hand, if that was the Nicholses' campfire up there and they'd spotted him riding by on the ridge above the draw, they might be moving right now. By the time Johnny got back from Bozeman, it might be too late to catch them before dark.

Roland turned abruptly and stalked out of the room, his rubber boot treads heavy on the hardwood floor. He planned to drive down past Red Bluff and check the roadside closely, then use his binoculars to glass that draw from a safe vantage point across the river. If he got sight of anybody that looked even remotely like the Nicholses, he'd raise enough hell with the sheriff's department that they'd call in the Marines, whether or not Johnny made it back from Bozeman in time.

Roland drove his yellow Toyota pickup slowly along Route 84, carefully searching for tracks. By the time he'd passed Red Bluff, he had almost completed a 360-degree circle around the draw where he'd seen the smoke. As he suspected, there were no parked vehicles, no tire tracks in the deep snow, and no signs of anyone hiking in from the road.

On the drive back to the highway bridge, Roland again searched the west side of the road. Nothing. Whoever was up in that draw had been there since Tuesday night when the blizzard hit.

His pickup hummed under the gray steel girders of the bridge and crunched over the frozen crust at the entrance to the Trapper Springs store. Up in the driveway, he wheeled around to face the ridges across the river. The store had been closed for months; people said the owner'd gone bankrupt, trying to run a river raft and fishing concession on the wrong stretch of the river.

Roland scanned the level snow of the drive. No tracks.

He climbed down from the cab of the pickup and removed his gloves to focus his binoculars. Half a mile across the river, the snowy curve of his high pastures rose above the brushy draw. It took him a moment to pick out the upper righthand edge of the draw, the probable site of the campfire. When he raised his binoculars to scan the ridge, he merely intended to get the proper focus, not to begin a thorough search.

But the first object he saw when he twirled the focus wheel of the eight-power glasses was a man. A man standing alone in the snow, about forty feet from a bushy, snow-laden limber pine. The man was tall, dressed in dark clothes and a brown sheepskin jacket. He wore a wide-brimmed hat. He was staring back at Roland.

Roland stooped and steadied his elbows on the hood of the truck. When he tracked the glasses left, he saw another man, crouching at the edge of the trees.

Roland licked his dry lips, suddenly aware of who he was watching through his glasses.

The man in the open suddenly broke left and dashed for the cover of the pines, kicking showers of powder snow as he ran.

A moment later both men had disappeared into the shadows of the low timber.

Roland waited, his binoculars steady on the ridge. He saw trees and snow, no movement, no more smoke.

When he stood up, he realized that he had only seen the two men for a few seconds. And now they had vanished, but he had seen enough. Those men up there were not high school kids or coyote hunters.

He jumped into his truck and jammed the gear lever into first. The law had better get down here fast. It was after noon, and it would be good and dark up there in less than five hours.

It was 12:26 when Roland Moore made his second call to the sheriff's department in Virginia City.

No, Mike replied, Johnny France had not gotten

back yet from Bozeman. Somebody thought he might have stopped off to pick up some parts for a snow machine.

"Well," Roland said, trying to keep his voice even, "let me tell you exactly what I saw. . . ."

He carefully explained the situation, speaking slowly so that Mitchell could copy his words on the dispatcher's computer console.

"Look," Roland concluded, "you might want to blow the whistle a little harder because there are two men up on that hill, and they've been camping out in this weather for two days." Again, he searched for the proper balance between concern and alarmism. "Whoever it is up there, they got no right to be on my land. Now I've got to go up to my stock tank again tomorrow to chop water, even if it's Al Capone up there with his whole gang, so I want Johnny France or somebody in authority to come out here and check this situation out."

"I understand, Mr. Moore," Mitchell said with exasperating calmness.

"Is Gary Dedman, the undersheriff, there?" Roland asked, letting his frustration break through.

"He's at lunch, sir."

"Look," Roland said, "if you can't reach Dedman, get a hold of Merlin Ehlers. I want him to call me immediately, okay? We got a deal going on here that just can't wait."

"Yes, sir," Mike Mitchell replied. "I do understand, and I'll get right on it."

Roland was too keyed up to sit at his desk. He paced his small study, a mug of coffee cupped close to his chest.

He had seen them, both of them, not even a mile off the road, right up that first draw below the bridge. For five months the law had been busting its hump with

269

SWAT teams and out-of-state trackers and helicopters
. . . and God knows what, trying to find the Nicholses.
And now they were hiding in the pines right here on the
Cold Springs Ranch where Johnny France was raised,
and no one seemed able to locate anybody in authority.
It was damn frustrating.

The phone rang.

It was Merlin Ehlers. He listened carefully as Roland
repeated the details.

"Roland," Ehlers said, "you just stand by there.
We've contacted Bozeman, and they're trying to trace
Johnny. And I'm about to call Gary Lincoln, the FBI
man in Butte. When things start happening, they're
probably going to start real fast."

Ten minutes later Gary Lincoln called from Butte.
Once more, Roland patiently laid out the detailed
sequence of the situation.

"Mr. Lincoln," Roland concluded, "I hate to have
you guys come all the way out here with your dogs and
SWAT teams just because I saw some smoke in a draw
and a couple guys up on the ridge. It could just be
school kids playing hookey, I suppose."

Gary Lincoln spoke with the steady tone of a veteran
cop. "No," he said, "this is the break we've been
waiting for. I can feel it in my bones."

"Well," Roland replied, "right now we've got a
hundred percent snow cover, which is real unusual for
this country. When the wind starts blowing tonight,
you won't have a good set of tracks to follow."

Lincoln considered Roland's warning. "Is there
someplace close by where we can set up a surveillance
point? I doubt that we'll be able to get our ducks lined
up to go in after them today. It's after one o'clock, and
it'll be dark in a few hours. We'll probably go in after
them tomorrow when this snow stops."

"It's not snowing here, Mr. Lincoln."

"Well it sure is in Butte, and I think the weather's headed your way."

Roland thought about possible observation points. "The only surveillance spot I can picture is on the hill across the river, above the Trapper Springs store. But that doesn't really give you a clear view of the top of that draw."

"Doesn't sound too promising," Lincoln conceded.

Roland felt obliged to renew his warning. "If it doesn't snow here tonight, and that wind starts up, they'll have clear country to travel in. And, from what I hear, they can cover a lot of country overnight."

"That's right," Lincoln said. "Headquarters in Washington did a profile of the case. They say we'll never catch them if they break out of those mountains and get mobile."

"How dangerous you reckon they are right now?" Roland stared at the double-barreled shotgun hanging above the kitchen door.

"Are you armed?" Lincoln asked.

"Sure," Roland answered. Every rancher had weapons on his place, they were a tool, just like shovels and fence stretchers.

"You meet Don Nichols in his home country up in the Beartrap, out in the open . . . probably nothing would happen." Lincoln paused to consider the rest of his statement. "But you surprise him down here in the valley, just come up on him when he's stealing supplies or something, he could get real dangerous."

"Well," Roland said quietly, "I'm not leaving. This is my home. But if you think the man is much of a threat to my family, could you send some armed officers up here?"

"Don't worry about that," Lincoln said, "we've got the operation already started."

"Good," Roland muttered, not really convinced.

"Say, Roland," Gary Lincoln said, "don't tell anybody about this. If a neighbor drives up for a visit, just keep it quiet. We're getting this operation cranked up right now."

Roland replaced the receiver in the cradle and stared out through the steamy thermopane at the snow. Already the shadows of the cottonwoods were long across the frozen creekbed. If they didn't get their operation moving soon, he knew, it would be too late.

Don Nichols rolled up his gear and shouldered his backpack. Danny was already loaded, impatient to be traveling. But Don took his time. If you didn't stow your equipment right, you'd lose time later on, messing around with your pack.

Don stepped out from under the snowy overhang of the limber pine and wriggled beneath the straps, adjusting the weight on his back. The clouds were rolling in again from the west, but there was still a lot of clear sky. It was a cold, windless afternoon. Down in the towns, people would be talking about this cold, probably only five degrees or so at noon. But he and Danny didn't go by any thermometer. On the slope above, the snow curved in an untouched blanket. No doubt about it, they were going to leave a good set of tracks.

That was why Danny was so jumpy. And that guy down on the highway in the yellow truck had the boy worried, too. But Don had tried to reassure him. That man would just think they were coyote hunters. He was curious, that's all. If he'd have been the law, the highway would be crawling with patrol cars by now.

As they moved away from the camp, Don turned to make sure once again that the fire was dead. If those pine boughs they laid out for their bed caught fire, there would be a lot of smoke, and that might be a problem.

But the fire was dead cold. As he turned back, he noted the small pile of squaw wood, still stacked beside the ashes on the rock shelf. This had been a fine little camp, good shelter from the wind and snow and cover from the highway. Too bad there was no live water in the draw.

They trudged straight up the snowy hillside toward the top of the ridge, Danny making the pace. The boy seemed in a hurry. He didn't like crossing this open country in daylight, even though Don had tried to convince him that they weren't likely to find anybody out here so soon after the big snow. But the boy wasn't in a mood to be convinced. Better let it be.

At the top of the naked hill Danny stopped. This whole ridgetop was open country, a big series of wide, snowy pastures, cut up by dark fencelines. The only decent timber cover in sight was a couple miles to the west. But that was just a fringe of low pine around a rock outcropping. In the far distance, there was some thicker timber, but they'd have to cross a fair stretch of wide-open country to get there. The boy looked at him, his expression a mix of fear and resentment.

Don shrugged, but didn't speak. This open country didn't bother him much. They'd be off this ranchland in a couple hours, down on the flats where there were old mine drifts and plenty of brushy draws for cover.

Now Don took the lead, slowing the pace, so they wouldn't get all worn down again. They had a long way to travel. And with any luck, the wind and snow would start up by dark, blowing out their tracks. He strode up the snowy hillside, bent under his pack frame.

It was Don who called the next halt. They stood side by side, staring at the fresh horse tracks in the deep powder. One rider had come in from the right, from the open valley that probably led to the ranch house. By the look of the track, the same rider had come back out.

But, twenty paces to the left, he'd stopped his horse, led it downslope from the track, then turned again. As if he'd changed his mind.

Danny gazed at the tracks, his wind-burned cheeks slack, his eyes wary.

"Just some cowboy looking for strays," Don muttered. "Don't mean nothing, one way or the other."

They marched on, their boot tracks cutting the horse tracks at a right angle. For a while, Don tried to make small talk, but the boy was not talkative. So they moved silently across the dead white landscape.

At the first fenceline, Don indicated that they should slip through the barbed wire and begin to zigzag up the long incline, using the geometry of the fencelines as a barrier to slow down anyone on a snow machine or horseback who might decide to track them.

He didn't have to explain who those trackers might be.

They moved carefully now, trying hard to keep their track close to the wire, so that their trail would not be easily visible from the air.

When they stopped to take a rest, they assumed a natural, back to back position, so they could guard their flanks. Overhead, the sun drifted slowly through cold rolls of cloud. Still there was no wind.

18

Madison Valley

December 13, 1984

JOHNNY FRANCE DROVE HIS EAGLE UP THE LONG INCLINE toward Virginia City. In deference to the snow, he eased off on the gas pedal and let the car slow to below seventy. He was in no hurry today; all he had on his docket this afternoon was lunch and a dull slog through the accumulated paperwork, so there was no sense taking these icy curves too fast. Loren Tucker, the county attorney, always kidded Johnny about the way he drove. "Johnny," he'd say, "it's a good thing the daytime speeding fine's only five dollars."

You had to drive fast, though, if you were going to cover all the territory in Madison County. Even in winter, with the tourist season long over, the daily business of the sheriff took Johnny more than a hundred miles each day. Each year, he averaged over fifty thousand highway miles in his official Eagle. One of the reasons for this daily marathon was the notoriously bad radio propagation in the county. High mountain ranges, the Madison, Tobacco Roots, Gravellys, and Rubys divided the county's valleys. And these mountains often chopped up effective radio communication between the sheriff's officers and the dispatcher in Virginia City. Some days were worse than others. And today was a bad one. Coming back from Bozeman, Johnny had tried unsuccessfully three times to raise Mike Mitchell in the office. For some obscure reason, the windless cold air mass over the valley was blocking his signal.

Johnny looked out at the empty rangeland to the left. The snow was deep and unbroken out across the valley. Up in the high country, the drifts would be deep. Coming back from Bozeman on Route 84, Johnny had slowed through Warm Springs Creek and the entrance to the Beartrap, driving with one hand as he hunched over to stare at the high ridges. It had become a ritual. As if he would one day just get lucky and somehow see them up there.

As he passed through Ennis, he had considered stopping home for lunch, but decided not to. There was too much paper work facing him today. And tomorrow, he was scheduled to begin a week's vacation, driving down to Kansas for some "chicken shootin'" with his good friend Ron Pederson. It would be Johnny's first time off since the Nichols case began, five months before.

And Lord knew he needed that vacation. He was burned out on this case. His tormented insomnia and agonizing bouts of gastritis had reached a point where Sue and his close friends had become genuinely alarmed for his health. If this case didn't break soon, they told him, there was a good chance Johnny's health would. Despite the stoic acceptance of personal hardship that he had nurtured since childhood on the old Six Bar Nine Ranch, he knew they were right. His Uncle Joe had taught him that men did not complain about their health out here, or use physical pain as an excuse to shirk their chores. And Johnny had lived by that stern code for over forty years.

Now, however, he had agreed to take a short vacation, a week's break from the case, to clear his head, to purge the ghosts, to let himself get physically worn out stalking the stubble of the Kansas corn fields for quail and prairie chicken, so he could sleep a whole night through.

But this new snow had him thinking. Maybe it would be better to get some men together and run a snow-machine patrol tomorrow, up above Cowboy Heaven to check for tracks. He was reasonably confident that the Nicholses had enough of that stolen food cached to last them through the month of January, holed up in a camouflaged dugout camp up there—providing there was adequate game available. They probably wouldn't make their move until late in January, maybe even the end of February. At least that's what he and Dave Wing had decided in their last meeting. Dave had been so confident about their estimate that he'd taken off on a trip himself, driving his mother down to her winter home in Arizona.

Still . . . this latest storm had really whacked the high country. Johnny made a mental note to give Jim DeBoer, the game warden, a call that afternoon to check on the movements of the elk and mule deer.

As he pondered these questions, he heard Mike Mitchell on the radio, asking Dick Noorlander if he'd copied Johnny calling in his location yet. Johnny grabbed the microphone and broke in, telling Mike Mitchell he was "10–85 back OTH"—en route to the office, back over the hill.

The dispatcher advised Johnny that he'd been trying to reach him, but that radio propagation was bad that afternoon. Mike said that he had some important

"10–35 from Roland Moore"—confidential information—for Johnny from his foster brother-in-law.

Instinctively, Johnny's boot toe sank on the gas pedal. He caught himself breathing hard. On a dull Thursday afternoon in December, there were very few subjects so important and confidential Roland could raise that could not be discussed on the open radio channel. Unless, of course, it concerned the Nicholses.

Johnny gripped the wheel with both hands and leaned forward in his seat, as if to speed the car up the hill, just as he had that long ago morning in July, when he first heard the report of the Big Sky shooting.

It was 1:37 when Johnny called Roland at the ranch. They did not talk very long. Johnny listened, hunched across his cluttered desk, his ballpoint jumping diagonally across the yellow legal pad as he scribbled notes.

Roland spoke with his usual meticulous calm. And Johnny listened carefully, so that Roland did not have to repeat the details. As Roland described the scene, Johnny could clearly picture two men camped at the head of the draw below the Poison Pasture. He could see the tall figure in the sheepskin coat running back to the shelter of the pines as Roland glassed him from down at the Trapper Springs store.

Johnny made a few notes about Gary Lincoln's comments to Roland, then spoke at length for the first time.

"Roland, I agree with Lincoln. It's gotta be the Nicholses. You just hang in at the house. We'll get deputies there right away." He closed his eyes and tried to think clearly, but his pulse was thumping loudly in his throat. He took a slow, even breath. "In a little while, your place is gonna be crawling with lawmen . . . probably helicopters and planes, too. We'll make our command post down at your cattle guard, on the flat by the bridge. You just stand by at the house."

As he hung up the phone, Mike Mitchell handed him a pink message slip. John Onstad had called a few minutes before; Lincoln had alerted Bozeman about Barnstorm, and Onstad wanted Johnny to call, ASAP.

Before he did, however, Johnny snatched the Barnstorm alert sheet from the center of his bulletin board, tearing the corner off the page in his haste. "Mike," he began, his voice hoarse with excitement. "It's Barnstorm, and we've got ourselves a lot to do here real fast."

The cramped basement offices were almost empty on this quiet winter afternoon; the deputies on duty were dispersed across the county. But Mike was going to have to get them moving toward the Cold Springs Ranch in a big hurry.

"First," Johnny said, striding to the county map on the wall, "I want you to contact Lee Edmisten, Merlin, and Dick Noorlander. Dick's to patrol Route 84 from the College Ag station to California Point. I don't want those two guys cutting down from the top and taking cover in the cottonwoods along the creek there." Johnny tapped the map for emphasis.

Mitchell was writing fast, neat notes on his steno pad.

"Get Lee down from Sheridan to the right-angle bridge below the Beartrap. That's going to be the command post. I want Merlin suited up in his white gear with a scope rifle in his Bronco to meet me there in—" He glared at his watch. It was so damned late already. "—in half an hour. Tell him to make sure he's got plenty of gas."

Johnny strode away from the map, then spun back. "Oh, yeah. Call Billy Clark's wife. He'll be coming home from work. Tell her 'Barnstorm at the right-angle bridge below the Beartrap.' Billy'll understand."

Johnny dove behind his desk and swept the piled papers roughly aside. Then he dialed Onstad's private line in Bozeman.

Their conversation was a fast, nervous exchange. Lincoln had briefed Onstad, and Onstad was trying to get a hold of Murray Duffy, so that he could come in a chopper.

Johnny would rendezvous with Onstad and the helicopter at the command post near the bridge. Together, they would fly over the high pastures of the Cold Springs Ranch until they cut the Nicholses' tracks. Then they would follow the tracks to cover, hover low and menacing, and try to talk them out with a bull horn. Meanwhile, deputies would seal off the highway and flank the back of the ranch in four-wheel drive vehicles. Once Don Nichols realized he was surrounded in such open country, they agreed, there was a good chance he'd surrender.

The operational plan they quickly hammered out sounded okay to Johnny. Relatively simple, within their combined resources. And, best of all, fairly fast to implement. It was almost twenty past two. In only two hours, it would be dark. And, with darkness, he knew, Don Nichols would not be likely to surrender without a fight.

Johnny drove now with a speed and abandon that he had never before attempted. He left his office— clutching a flopping armful of heavy flak jackets—at 2:20. With his siren and pursuit lights on, he simply floored the accelerator and ignored the brakes, taking each icy curve on the road down to Ennis in a wild four-wheel drift.

Twelve minutes later, at 2:32, he called in from the Charging Bear Trading Post, fourteen miles down in the valley on the edge of Ennis. Down the icy mountainside he had averaged over seventy miles per hour.

Bill Hancock was waiting for him. Once more, Johnny needed to borrow an assault rifle. But this time, he knew his quarry and he knew where to find them.

"It's Barnstorm, Bill," he shouted, dashing across the porch of the log building. "Right on the Cold Springs Ranch. Can you believe that?"

For months, Johnny France and his men, and John Onstad and his deputies, had fruitlessly stalked Don Nichols in his home country, the Beartrap. Now, Don and Danny Nichols had come down from their island in the sky, to the single piece of property in the county that Johnny knew best, the Cold Springs Ranch. For years, Johnny had hunted that land, set his traplines in the draws and coulees, punched cattle and searched for strays on the high pastures. He'd walked every inch of fenceline, cut juniper posts and dug ditches on that land. If any piece of Montana could qualify as Johnny France's home turf, it was the Cold Springs Ranch.

Bill Hancock handed the rifle across the counter. Again, it was a Ruger Mini-14. But, unlike the GB model Johnny had carried in July, this one had a handsomely varnished hardwood stock. The rifle in July had evoked the failure and frustration of Vietnam. This gun felt solid, a Western weapon. It gave Johnny confidence as he hefted the weight of the shining stock.

Bill passed him a magazine of twenty steel-tipped rounds and waited while Johnny completed the ritual of lock and load. Then Bill shoved across four more heavy black magazines. If there was going to be a shootout, Johnny would need plenty of ammunition.

"Good luck," Bill said, taking Johnny's hand. "I'll be standing by my radio."

Johnny was halfway out the door, the rifle slung over

his shoulder, the spare magazines clutched in his left hand. "Oh, yeah," he called. "Thanks, Bill."

Sue was on the glassed-in back porch, which served as a sunroom-cum-warehouse for the France family. Here Johnny and the boys stored their hunting and fishing gear, their riverboat equipment, and their oddments of riding and rodeo clothes. She drew the line at saddle blankets and bridles, but practically anything else could be found back here, if you looked hard enough.

This afternoon Sue was carefully wrapping the bright Christmas presents and cartons of decorations they would take with them to Oregon, as soon as Johnny got back from his hunting trip with Ron. This would be their daughter Kathy's first Christmas away from home, and they planned a quick trip out to spend the holiday with her and her husband. The visit, she hoped, would combine with the relaxation of the hunting trip to Kansas to give Johnny the time away from the case that he so desperately needed.

As she sorted through the packages of Christmas tree lights and the rectangular boxes of salvaged tinsel from last year's tree, Sue heard the first warbling tones of the siren. Sue France unconsciously stiffened at the sound.

When the noise rose to a howl, she knew it was Johnny, and that he was coming home at high speed. Her first rush of fear gave way to the premonition that one of the boys had been hurt, that Johnny was coming to take her to the hospital before it was too late. She didn't have time to dwell long on this possibility. Johnny's car slid to a stop outside and his boots pounded up the front steps.

"It's Barnstorm, Sue," he called, clomping into the bedroom. "Roland spotted them up on the ranch."

Sue France stood dead still on the chilly porch,

surrounded by the bright decorations, trying to make sense of this incredible news. For months, she had thought of the Nicholses as distant, shadowy adversaries. Now they were real.

Only moments later, Johnny appeared in the back hall, tugging up his thick wool hunting trousers. He wore a dark wool shirt; his rubberized shoepack boots flapped open at the ankles. As she watched, immobile with anxiety, he finished dressing with grim speed.

"Where's my Barnstorm pack?"

"It's—" But Sue suddenly could not remember where he'd stored the small brown daypack in which he had so carefully assembled his Sterno stove, extra socks, hunting knife, flashlight, and emergency rations.

Johnny flung himself around the porch, tossing aside life jackets and Day-Glo orange hunting vests.

The pack lay beneath Kathy's Christmas presents. Johnny hefted the light sack in one hand and seized his long winter hunting parka that lay folded on the Ping-Pong table. This was a flapping, knee-length tent of a coat, faded green on one side, white on the reverse. The hood hung like a bulbous kettle, wide enough to accommodate a soldier's steel helmet.

When Johnny had bought the parka years before at the war surplus store in Bozeman, Sue had disparagingly christened it his "survival coat." But he was attached to it, ratty as it was. When he wore the white side out, he said, he was practically invisible in the snow. The pockets were wide and deep, with plenty of room for ammunition.

Now, as he pulled on the dirty white shroud of the coat, covering his dark wool shirt and trousers, she had no ready quip of friendly sarcasm. She could only pray with mute intensity that this old parka would, indeed, help him survive the day.

She followed him out to the car, which stood with its

door wide open, blue exhaust rising in the cold. She noted the evil-looking rifle jammed across the front seat, the stack of ammunition clips, the jumble of green bullet-proof vests.

Johnny saw her staring at the gear.

"Don't worry, Susie," he said, nodding toward the flak jackets. "I'll wear one, and we'll take the extras and . . . uh, spread 'em on the floor of the helicopter."

She dipped her chin in somber acknowledgment. Then he was gone, fast down the snowy street, his siren beginning its shriek.

Johnny sped up the Norris hill at over eighty, lights and siren clearing the talc trucks and pickups from his path. He heard Dick Noorlander call in that he and Merlin were at the bridge. They had established a command post and were checking for tracks in the surrounding country. It was five past three.

Maybe they had an hour and forty minutes of decent daylight left.

When Johnny turned right onto Route 84 out of Norris and entered the steep confines of Warm Springs Creek, he killed the lights and siren. The heights of the Beartrap rose to the right, and the snowy shoulders of Red Bluff and the Cold Springs Ranch began to show on the left. If the Nicholses were up there, watching the road, there was no sense giving them a lights-and-siren show.

He sped past the old homesteaders' cemetery. As a kid, he used to sometimes ride his pony up here and put alpine asters and columbines on the graves. There were so many children buried there, whole families of them, wiped out by cholera or typhoid in the late 1800s. Between his Uncle Joe's stern expectations and the silent testimony of that poor old cemetery, Johnny had learned real young that this could be a hard country to grow up in.

Now, all these years later, Johnny found himself wondering if Don Nichols had ever come over to this cemetery as a kid, on his way from Harrison to the Beartrap. Strange, but Johnny began feeling an uncontrollable, certainly unexpected, rush of pity for young Don Nichols, a little boy of seven who just couldn't accept the fact that his daddy had driven the Model-T off the Norris hill and was dead forever.

His musing was interrupted by a burst of static and garbled words on the radio. The dispatcher was trying to raise him, but the bad atmospherics and the canyon wall were breaking up the signal. Johnny gunned the car around a curve of blue ice, fishtailed toward the shoulder, and instinctively corrected the skid. He had to get out onto the flat by the bridge before he could expect decent radio communications.

As Johnny roared down the narrow, twisting road past Red Bluff, he received a strong signal from Bozeman, relaying a message to him from "6–42"— Sheriff John Onstad.

The helicopter was still delayed, and Onstad was not sure when he could get a hold of it. Apparently Murray Duffy was out of town, working another job. Onstad had to make a decision about waiting for Duffy, or trying to bring in another chopper from Billings, almost a hundred and fifty miles to the east.

Johnny made a mental calculation. At about a hundred knots maximum cruising speed, the Billings chopper would arrive after dark.

Onstad had already dispatched two ground units with officers, and a fixed-wing aircraft with an experienced deputy on board as a spotter. He would advise as soon as he had an ETA for the chopper.

Johnny thrust back the parka cuff and grabbed a quick look at his watch. Nineteen minutes past three. They had about an hour and a half of daylight. Maximum.

If they were lucky.

The Eagle skidded on a hard snow pack as it slammed around the last curve before the river. Up ahead, he saw rotating red lights; he quietly cursed. Someone had not gotten the message about the "10–49"—Use all safe speed, but do not use lights or siren.

First the bad news on the helicopter, now the snafu with the lights. Johnny sagged in his seat and shook his head. He simply would not allow this operation to degenerate into another screw-up like the SWAT team sweep or that fiasco up on Blaze Mountain.

Not with the Nicholses so close.

Ahead, the scrub pines and junipers of the draws came right down to the edge of the road. He was almost at the ranch.

At the command post, there was a certain amount of milling confusion, reminiscent of the scene up on the Big Sky logging road five months before. One of the Bozeman units was pulling in, and Dave Schenk of the Highway Patrol had just arrived.

Johnny took charge as soon as he jumped from the car. He dispatched Lee Edmisten back down the road to cover the draws leading toward California Point. Roland was there, standing beside his yellow pickup in a thick parka. Taking him aside, Johnny listened once more to a brief run-down of the important details. More than ever, Johnny was convinced the men Roland had seen up there had to be Don and Danny Nichols. He told Roland to head back to the house, lock the doors and stay inside with a loaded rifle.

Then Johnny told Merlin to collect a Bozeman officer

and drive his Bronco up the ranch road to make sure that Roland, Elaine, and the Shirleys were all right. Merlin was to check in from the ranch house for further orders.

One thing Johnny sure did not want to see was a deal where the Nicholses got spooked down out of the high pastures and decided to start a little hostage situation with the Moore and Shirley families. For a moment, as Johnny stood on the frozen roadside, spouting brief orders, he had a sudden bizarre sensation that this was all a game, that he was a little kid again, playing Japs and Nazis in the cottonwoods.

Never in his wildest sleepless speculations had he envisioned the showdown with Don Nichols happening right here on the ranch.

When the first officers were assigned specific duties, Johnny called Bozeman to check on the ETA of Onstad and the helicopter. No word yet, the frustrated dispatcher replied. But, when Sheriff Onstad does get it, he'll be at your command post in twenty minutes. Once more Johnny jerked back the cuff of his flapping parka to see his watch. Twenty minutes to four.

They had maybe an hour and ten minutes of daylight. Already, the sky had acquired that frozen lilac tinge that signaled the onset of brief winter dusk and sudden darkness. Such telltale colors in the sky usually meant snow in the night. Johnny knew the sky signs well. For years as a boy on these hills he had seen that weak rose tint appear above the Beartrap and he'd realize he had maybe an hour to get his horse back to the barn before it was too dark to see the snowy trail.

Johnny glared up at the white ridges above the road, and at the chill pastel sky. Don and Danny Nichols would also recognize the signs of early darkness and possible snow later in the night. More snow would cover their tracks. All they'd have to do now was head north or west from the ranch, take cover in some brushy draw, and wait for darkness.

Stamping his shoepacks on the snow in frustration, Johnny reached through the open window of his patrol car and grabbed the radio mike. Then he dropped it in disgust, realizing that he'd spoken to the Bozeman dispatcher less than two minutes before.

He was getting wound up so tight inside that he was absolutely compelled to physical action. Without a clear plan in mind, he strode down the edge of the road, his rifle in one hand, a radio set in the other. There was a clot of anxious expectation in his chest, just as when he tracked a wounded deer or elk in thick country. The optimism of the first hit was mixed with black worry that the wounded animal would escape to die in futile agony.

A hundred yards from the command post, he understood that he was unconsciously searching for the Nicholses' tracks. Without question, they had come across the bridge two or three nights before, and had climbed one of these draws to the ridge above, probably in the dark. But Roland hadn't seen any tracks when he'd searched earlier. And Roland was an experienced hunter.

Johnny hunched low over the ground, his eyes tracking like a radar dish.

There! A line of soft, undulating ovals, just past the cracked slabs of crust from the snow plow. There, ten feet from the pavement, were the tracks of two people, faint and so badly filled by new powder snow that they seemed to disappear when he stared at them. The only reason they were visible at all was because the low angle of the sun gave maximum contrast to the valley floor. At noon on a sunny winter day, when Roland had searched, the tracks—if that was what they really were—would have been invisible.

Johnny trotted back to the command post. He'd seen enough. For the first time since that terrible morning in the clearing, when he'd bent above Al Goldstein's shattered face, he was positive that he had seen the Nicholses' tracks.

The Bozeman dispatcher was brief and apologetic. Still no definite word on the chopper, but it was expected back in Bozeman any minute. Eight minutes until four.

Johnny knew he could not wait any longer for the helicopter. He understood with harsh acceptance, that the seemingly safe and simple assault plan that relied on the high-tech convenience of the chopper was no longer possible. If he was going to cut the Nicholses' track up there and trail them to their cover, he'd have to do it on the ground.

At the end of the line of patrol cars and Blazers, he saw a big brown Ford pickup. Bob Morton, the law enforcement officer from the Gallatin National Forest, had just arrived to join the operation. And Johnny also saw that Bob had clearly had the foresight to come well equipped for a snow pursuit. In the back of the pickup stood a shiny new Arctic Cat snow machine.

Johnny stood for a moment reaching his decision. Then he shucked off his parka, pulled on a heavy flak jacket, and shouldered his way back inside the flapping white tent of the coat. The snow machine would carry him up to the top. From there, he knew, he'd be on his own.

They bounced along the frozen ruts of the ranch road in Bob Morton's pickup. Johnny sat at the passenger window, Bozeman Sergeant Bill Slaughter beside him and Bob at the wheel. Morton had just had some minor surgery, and the rough surface was causing him considerable pain. But he didn't complain; like the rest of the lawmen assembled here this afternoon, he seemed able to taste victory after all those months of frustrating pursuit.

The snowmobile rattled in the open pickup box behind them. Once more, Johnny praised Bob Morton's cool professionalism. He was the only one of them all who'd thought far enough ahead to realize they might well need fast transport across the snowy hills.

They were through the first cattle guard and coming up on the cottonwoods that marked the narrowest point in the Cold Springs Creek Canyon. Off to the right, thick scrub pine stood dark against the drifted snow, hiding the rocky ledges where Johnny used to place his bobcat traplines. He gazed at the slopes. Almost thirty years had passed since those winter afternoons when he'd jump down from the school bus, fetch his tethered horse, and trot off to check his traps.

A bobcat pelt brought thirteen dollars in the early fifties, a lot of money for a teenage foster child on a struggling ranch. Once, a large predator—either a grizzly or a cougar—had taken his jack rabbit bait and stolen his trap, making off with the eighty-pound log drag in tow. Now, on this same ranch, he was obliged to track prey infinitely more dangerous than a mountain lion or grizzly.

"That'll about do her, Bob," Johnny said, nodding toward the gate that stood open at the second cattle guard.

Off to the left, the slope was clear of trees and rock. Johnny could see Roland's horse track clearly in the deep powder. Bob slipped into four-wheel drive and backed the pickup off the road into the drifts.

Working quickly, they lowered the tailgate and Bill Slaughter jumped up to push the snow machine down. Once they had it level in the snow, Johnny called the command post again on his hand-held radio.

Still no word from Bozeman on the chopper.

Johnny started the Arctic Cat motor to let it warm up. "Look," he said to Morton and Slaughter, "I don't know if they're gonna get that chopper in here or not. But I'm sure those two guys are moving up there, and it's gonna be dark here before too long, so—" he cocked the rifle and tested the safety, "—I'm going to just run up there and see if I can cut their track, coming out of the draw. If they have moved out of there, somebody better know which direction they went, so that we can get right on this thing at first light. It's fixing to snow later and maybe blow some, too." He looked anxiously at the white ridgetop. "We don't want to lose them before we do have a helicopter here."

Bobby Morton seemed half inclined to come with him, but Johnny didn't want to be slowed down by the weight of an extra person. Besides, Johnny simply knew this country better than any man out here today, and he was not eager to bring along someone who did not know those high pastures and timbered ridges. If he cut their track, he wanted freedom to maneuver as an independent stalker.

As soon as he hit the steepest section of the hillside, he was glad that he'd come alone. The snow machine yawed and fishtailed under the strain, and he needed every bit of guts this new engine had to climb the incline. The slipstream cut into his bare cheeks, searing cold, but his peaked wool hunting cap and the hood of the white parka protected his head.

With a rush of speed and a shower of powdered snow, he cleared the top of the hill, cut left past the fenceline, and roared along Roland's horsetrack toward the top of the draw.

The Nicholses' tracks appeared much sooner than he'd expected. Right before him was the obviously fresh, undisturbed track of two men, marching Indian file, straight up from the left side of the draw where Roland had seen the smoke. Johnny backed off the throttle and drifted to a halt beside the tracks. The line of deep boot prints cut Roland's horse track at a right angle and continued up the open slope toward the first snowy rise.

Johnny breathed hard in the biting chill, then lifted his radio.

"Twenty-five-seven." He called Sparky Noorlander at the command post. "What's the status on that chopper?"

"Nothing yet, Johnny."

He nodded, again staring at the line of boot tracks that marched due north.

"I've cut their track, Sparky. And I gotta see what's over that next rise. The tracks go right up there, and I just gotta see where they head."

"Ten-four," Noorlander acknowledged. "Watch yourself up there, Johnny."

At the top of the rise, Johnny could see the tracks heading off now on an angle through the open rangeland to the northwest.

"I can still see the tracks, Sparky," Johnny said into his chill radio mouthpiece, ignoring formal radio procedure. "I'm just going to check this out a little more."

From the top of the second rise, the tracks led straight west to a fenceline, then disappeared. Johnny squinted in the dull light, trying to focus on the snow beyond the barbed wire. They seemed to be using the fenceline to conceal their tracks.

All right, that wouldn't be hard to follow. He twisted open the throttle.

Half a mile ahead, the tracks emerged from behind a fenceline and cut west toward the flat timbered ridge-top that dominated these high pastures. They were heading west, maybe for the open draws and foothills leading up toward the Boaz and Grubstake Mine country to the south or to Revenue Flats. If that was their destination, Johnny realized, they were walking right into a trap.

"Twenty-five-six." He called Merlin. "Take the Bronco up the ranch road past the houses and get out there in those west pastures to scout the big open draw behind this high country."

It was Bill Pronovost, riding shotgun with Merlin, who acknowledged Johnny's call. Johnny nodded to the empty snowfield before him, happy that he had two officers as good as Merlin and Bill out ahead to secure his flank. Now all he had to do was stay on this trail before he lost his daylight.

From this vantage point, he saw that there was enough open country on the hillside to the right of the Nicholses' track for him to follow their route from higher ground. That would reduce the chances of a sniper attack, and also give him a better view ahead.

But, he knew, the howl of the snow machine, straining up the slopes, might alert them to his presence. It wouldn't matter much, if that chopper showed up soon. And, if it didn't. . . . He'd cover that possibility when it happened. In a deal like this, an overactive imagination could slow you down.

For about a mile Johnny skirted the Nicholses' tracks, horsing the snow machine along the increasingly steep and rocky slope.

Don and Dan still seemed to be headed straight west, following the bottom of the open pasture below as they climbed toward the scrub pines of the ridgetop ahead. Johnny was so busy watching the tracks in the fading light that he didn't see the rubbly patch of naked rock until he hit it. The snow machine growled and clattered. This was the end of the line.

If he was going to follow their tracks further, it would either be in the helicopter or on foot.

Out to the west, the sky went from plum to rusty apple red. The horizon was streaked with strips of dirty storm cloud. He had forty minutes of daylight, maybe less.

Johnny called the command post. The helicopter, they told him, was supposed to be on its way, carrying Sheriff Onstad and Detective Bob Campbell. But they did not have a firm ETA.

Johnny hit the stop button, killing the throbbing engine. Around him the white slopes seemed unnaturally silent. He knew what he should do, and he knew what he could reasonably expect to accomplish in the remaining daylight. But he really did not give a damn about caution or normal expectations right now. The Nicholses were right out there ahead of him, and he still had daylight. He was not about to sit down and wait for that phantom helicopter. He unslung his rifle and plowed his way down the slope, leaving a wake in the deep powder.

A quarter of a mile ahead, a large herd of mule deer had moved down from the timber to the left and was grazing on the frozen grass they uncovered with their sharp hoofs. He stalked closer to the deer, satisfied that his hooded white parka provided good camouflage in this open snow.

When he got near the deer, they spooked and bounced along to the right, up toward the rocky ridge he'd been following with the snow machine.

The snow was trampled and chopped up where they'd been grazing. Johnny stopped to lean over the tracks. Hot blood rushed to his ears and stinging face. The Nicholses' tracks crossed over those of the deer. Johnny had hunted these hills long enough to realize what this meant. So soon after hunting season, the deer stayed hidden in the timber all day and only moved down to the open like this in the late afternoon. Certainly, they hadn't been grazing in this draw for more than half an hour. So Don and Dan's tracks were fresher than that. They were at most only half an hour ahead.

For sure this time, not just in the flamboyant imagination of some East Coast tracking guru.

"Any ETA on that chopper yet?" Johnny called.

"They're saying 1640 or so," the command post reported.

They'd be here in twenty minutes. Maybe.

The prudent course of action would be for Johnny to wait here in this open draw, so the helicopter could spot him easily. But, even if the chopper did get here in twenty minutes, it would be nightfall, and they'd never find the track in the shadowy timber up ahead. That would mean an overnight stakeout with limited personnel. And it would also mean a dawn assault on these high pastures, with the Nicholses fully aware that they were surrounded. And the lawmen uncertain of the Nicholses' hiding place.

That scenario lead toward a shootout and casualties. He hated to ask deputies to sweep this open, snowy country with Don Nichols holed up someplace high, sighting down with that sniper rifle of his. In the FBI's psychological profiles of the two, Don was described as a potentially suicidal depressive who might welcome a shoot-out.

Johnny made up his mind. "I'm awful close to these guys," he called on his radio. "Their tracks are so fresh I can almost smell them."

He plunged ahead through the snow, up the steepening valley toward the dark pines above. Casting around like a hound on either side of the main track, his head down as he searched the snow, Johnny saw that the Nicholses had adopted a new tactic. From the snow signs, it was clear they were now guarding their back trail, one man staying behind to watch while the other moved ahead a few hundred yards. Then the back-trail guard would leap-frog the next man, and the process would start again. For the first time all afternoon, Johnny recognized that the Nicholses were displaying the caution and cunning they'd grown famous for.

The empty expanse of the draw now seemed dangerously exposed. He cut sharply to his right, trotting through the snow to climb the hillside where he could still see their tracks, but could also find some cover if they sniped at him.

Johnny was winded and sweat steamed beneath the combined layers of parka, flak jacket, and heavy wool shirt. As he forced himself to keep the pace, the ammunition clips clanked dully in the gaping pockets of the parka.

Moving through junipers and wind-stunted limber pines, he felt the first sunset breeze, chill and dry on his sweaty forehead. The breeze brought the drone of an aircraft engine. But it was that spotter Cessna from Belgrade, not the chopper. For a few moments, he caught his breath on the ridgetop, watching the silver Cessna working the country to the west. The plane did not seem to be flying low enough at all, not if they planned to spot tracks. But then, Merlin and the other deputies always said that nobody ever flew low enough to please Johnny.

Five months he'd been hunting these two murderers. He wasn't about to let them slip away in the dark now.

"I'm going to keep poking along here and see what I can find," Johnny advised the command post.

Detective Ron Cutting, the spotter in the Cessna,

came on the frequency and asked if the plane was working the right country.

"Can you see any tracks in that big draw you're over?" Johnny asked.

"Negative," Cutting replied. "We can't see you, either. What's your position?"

"I'm toward the top of the ridge to the north of you, right by a big drift fence."

As Johnny watched, the plane banked toward him and leveled off, about a thousand feet above the ridge.

"Okay," Ron Cutting called. "We see you now, Johnny."

"Try to get a little lower and work that draw again," he told Cutting. "You ought to be picking up some tracks."

The Cessna banked south, and Johnny called again. "No, you're too far south. Come on back and try a little further north. The tracks look like they're headed right into that big draw."

The pilot obeyed, but still seemed too high for effective spotting.

Johnny plowed ahead through the snow, eager to cross the flat table of the ridgetop, so that he could look down into the draw himself before the light was gone. "Merlin," he called as he plunged along, "get your vehicle into the head of that draw and scope the country. See if the tracks come down from here and cross that open stretch."

He could see neither Merlin's Bronco nor the draw itself, but he had a clear mental picture of the landscape he was rushing toward. "Move down that fenceline. You're bound to pick up their tracks if they went out that way."

When Johnny clicked off, the command post came on, advising him that Gary Lincoln had his van on the highway, at the mouth of the big draw, that the other draws were blocked by Dave Schenk and Lee Edmisten, and, most importantly, that the chopper's ETA was now confirmed for ten minutes.

Great, Johnny thought, we're going to get them boxed in, and maybe we'll still have enough daylight to spot them in the open.

He moved past some trees, then kicked through a deep series of drifts. The radio burst with static, followed by a clear voice. It was John Onstad in the approaching helicopter, talking to the command post.

"Is anyone with France?" Onstad asked, his voice hoarse with excitement and worry.

"Negative," the command post answered.

"Twenty-five one," Onstad called, "do you copy?"

Johnny raised his set and replied. But the little walkie-talkie didn't have the range to reach the chopper. He tried again, then asked the command post to relay that he was approaching the summit of the highground, about four miles west of the highway.

He heard Onstad acknowledge, "Ten-four. My ETA ten minutes."

Johnny was in low, open, drifted country now, jogging along the level summit of the ranch's highest elevation. Again, he called the other members of the search team, asking that they relay his message to the helicopter if necessary. "They're probably in the bottom of this big draw. I'm gonna work my way a little closer to this draw here to get a better idea of the situation."

When he released the transmit button of his radio, the set snarled with the garbled squeak of overlapping transmissions. One of the crackling voices sounded like John Onstad. The electronic cacophony seemed horribly loud on this snowy ridge. "I'm gonna be out of radio contact for a little bit here," Johnny advised. The last thing he needed was a squawking radio to tip Don Nichols to his location.

He clearly remembered Kari Swenson's report that it had been Al Goldstein's radio that they'd heard first when he and Schwalbe stumbled through the thick timber around that camp on Moonlight Creek.

The edge of the ridge dropped away ahead of him. Johnny stopped, leaning forward to grip his knees while he tried to catch his wind. Maybe, he ought to wait for Merlin to scope that draw before he went down there.

But the daylight was fading fast now, so he turned down the volume of his radio to minimum, breathed several deep, slow lungfuls of cold air, and moved to the edge of the draw. Ahead the naked summit of Baldy in the Tobacco Roots stood out like a shark's tooth against the sunset. The wings of the Cessna glinted metallic orange as the plane banked. The ground dropped away sharply. Johnny stepped over the lip of the draw warily, conscious of the steep bank and the crumbly pink quartz, exposed where the snow had drifted away. It would be easy to slip and fall on such a slope. This southern flank of the draw was thick with low timber, juniper, pine, and one tall, bushy Douglas fir, about forty feet below.

Johnny tried to focus on the distance, on the open snow fields down there, searching the bottom of the draw for tracks. Cautiously he negotiated the snowy rocks. His parka snagged on a currant bush to his right. As he bent to free it, he saw them.

They were squatted on their heels beneath the snowy overhanging boughs of the big fir tree, thirty feet below, their backs to him as they stared out at the draw, intently watching the Cessna bank toward them. Their dark clothes were ragged, their beards clotted with soot and grease.

They had made a camp just like the one that Tom Heintz had reported. Their green sleeping bags were spread on a leveled platform near the tree trunk, beside a small fire of smokeless squaw wood. There were the three stones of the fire ring. There was their greasy skillet. Johnny saw red venison steaks sputtering in the skillet. He saw their grimy plastic food canisters.

Their rifles stood against the tree trunk, Dan's .22 closest, and Don's heavy scoped .222 Sako resting on a spiky snag that rose from the far side of the fir.

Johnny was not aware of the cold, of the plane's engine, of the sunset. He was aware only of the Nicholses' camp, less than forty feet below him on the snowy hillside. After all these months, he stood on the edge of their camp. They had not yet seen him. His thumb clicked off the rifle's safety; his finger tightened on the icy trigger. He figured he had maybe ten seconds to make a decision before one of them turned and saw him.

The prudent, rational procedure rose in his mind. Back up, climb over the lip of this hill, dash for cover on the far side of the ridgetop, and call in the other officers. However, the crumbly slope of snow and quartz pebbles was too steep for him to climb backwards while he kept them covered with his rifle. He would have to turn his back on them in order to extract himself from this exposed position. From his unconscious sprang the image of Al Goldstein. Only a fool would turn his back on Don Nichols.

If he tried to call on his radio from this position, they would definitely hear the electronic squawking. Besides, the other men were just too far away to make it here before dark. There was no cautious action open to him. Even if he sprinted safely to the ridgetop, twenty feet above, the Nicholses would be spooked. They'd dash away down the slope into the darkening draw and hole up there, like cornered animals, waiting to blast any lawman who tried to take them.

Johnny had no right to expose the others to that danger, not when he was here now, with the means to take control.

There were, he realized, some decisions that were so simple, so obvious and yet so crazy that he would never be able to explain them. Like climbing out the door of that airplane without a parachute. People had said that was crazy. But Tom and that boy from the Forest Service never complained.

Johnny took a deep breath.

When he moved, he moved fast, dropping his radio to the snow and striding free of the snagging brush.

"You fellas seen any coyotes?" His voice seemed to boom under the snowy height of the tree.

The effect was immediate, just as he hoped. Don and Danny spun on their haunches, stunned by Johnny's appearance. Danny stood motionless, suddenly upright under the white fir boughs, his windburned face slack with shock. Don scurried like a startled crab, wheeling to the left in the shadows to grab his rifle.

Johnny sighted down the barrel. For a broken moment, he seemed to have a clear shot on Don's chest, but then Don was shielded by Danny's bulky sheepskin coat. To hit Don, Johnny realized, he'd have to shoot several rounds, right through Danny's body.

Johnny's finger eased on the trigger. He dove downslope, clambering to the right, toward the thin cover of a snaggy deadfall that lay twenty feet from the camp.

Don had his rifle and was hidden behind the thick, rough-barked trunk of the fir tree. Danny had not moved.

This was a classic standoff, almost a scene from the romantic Western novels that Don Nichols so disparaged.

Don had solid cover behind the fir trunk, but Danny was an exposed pawn. If Johnny started shooting with this semiautomatic, the boy would surely be hit.

Johnny knelt in the snow, the rifle raised, his cheek against the cold varnish of the stock. For a second, his mind pulsed with the shocked recognition that this confrontation was an almost exact duplicate of the standoff up on Moonlight Creek five months before.

Then Al Goldstein had menaced Don and his son with a loaded gun. Goldstein had not fired, but Johnny France would not make the same mistake. He hoped there was another way.

"Don," he yelled, "don't do anything stupid. Give that kid a chance to do something with his life. He's not in too deep, Don. He's got something to look forward to. This is no place for him to die." Johnny's words spilled out in a rush. He hadn't planned this speech, but he knew he must appeal to Don's unnatural attachment to the boy if he was going to prevent a shootout.

"Who are you?" Don's voice was outraged, a bully's angry demand.

"I'm the law, Don," Johnny answered, trying to sound calm.

"Go on," Don yelled in the same bully's voice. "Go on, just leave us alone. You know I had to kill that guy."

Johnny saw the butt and muzzle of Don's rifle bobbing on opposite sides of the dark fir trunk as Don maneuvered for a shooting position. But Johnny followed every movement over the peep sights of his own rifle.

"Think of the boy, Don," Johnny pleaded.

"The boy can speak for himself."

Again, the rifle butt bobbed, and the muzzle danced in the shadows.

"Don," Johnny yelled, "I know that you had some mitigating circumstances up there. I think you've got a real good defense." Like any skilled police negotiator, Johnny was trying to win his quarry's trust, to appeal to his wildest hopes, to avoid sending him into a panic. If Don Nichols had asked him for the moon right then, Johnny would have gladly offered it.

There was no reply.

"Come on, Don," Johnny called. "Drop your gun. Let's call it quits. Come on out of there and let's look at this thing like mature adults." He sighted on the right side of the tree, suddenly afraid Don would make a break past the snag. "Let's stop playing these games, Don."

As Johnny spoke, the Cessna roared overhead, right down on the treetops for the first time all afternoon.

Don's words were lost in the blast of the engine.

"Danny," Johnny called to the boy, "I can't hear him."

Now Danny acted as a relay. His voice was thin and quick, clearly close to panic. "He says, 'What guarantees do I have that you won't kill us?'"

"I don't want to kill you, Danny," Johnny reasoned. "And I won't kill you, not unless you make me."

Again the Cessna banked overhead, and Don's words were shredded in the engine noise.

Before Danny could relay again, the hillside was rocked by the blast of the helicopter. It pounded along the ridgetop from the east, then looped north, its rotors clattering above the snowy trees.

"How many guys you got up here?" Don called, his voice still an angry snarl.

The question caught Johnny by surprise. "There's two . . . ," he stuttered. "Uh . . . two more."

Johnny's ears rang from the chopper's roar. He

sweated under the parka and flak jacket, but a chill weight was forming in his gut. Don was stalling for darkness; then he would make his move.

Then Don Nichols spoke. "What do you want me to do?"

Johnny sighed. Don's voice was suddenly weak, deflated. Defeated.

When Johnny spoke, he dropped the tone of the friendly negotiator and assumed the commanding voice of an arresting cop. "I want you to put down that rifle and come out from behind there. . . . And, Don, I want to see your hands at all times."

He knew they both carried pistols, and he surely did not want to get suckered into anything dumb.

Don hesitated a long moment, then stepped from behind the tree trunk. Johnny saw his empty hands, and the butt of the rifle, resting against the roots.

Don hesitated. He was still within grabbing distance of that rifle.

"Go on," Johnny commanded angrily, leveling the rifle at Don's chest.

"You guarantee you're not gonna shoot us?" Don's voice was old, tired . . . and afraid.

"Yes," Johnny answered, letting human feeling enter his voice. "I'm not gonna shoot you. And I can guarantee you some hot water and some hot food and a warm place to sleep."

Don shook his head in disgust. "I don't give a damn about the food or the bed." He moved slowly to the left, to stand a few paces from Danny.

He stared at Johnny, examining his face for the first time. "Who are you?" There was something of the indignant bully in his voice again.

"I'm Johnny France, Sheriff of Madison County."

Don looked skeptical. "Where's those two other

guys?" Again, his voice was gruff, demanding, almost as if he were the captor and Johnny the prisoner.

"Oh, they're around." Johnny yelled into the dusk. "Joe, Bob . . . over here by the big tree."

Don scowled at the surrounding brush, maybe beginning to realize that he had been captured by a single lawman.

Johnny would not give him a chance to dwell on that. "One at a time," he said, resuming his mean cop's voice, "I want you to open your coats, so I can see what's underneath."

Don shrugged. "Oh, we're not carrying any sidearms."

"Just do it," Johnny shouted. "Then we'll all be happy."

Don Nichols and his son complied. They seemed eager now to keep Johnny happy.

They were absolutely filthy, the soot and grease deeply embedded in their hands and faces, like men who had been trapped for weeks in a coal mine.

Johnny herded them away from the dark cover of the camp tree. As he moved past his radio on the hillside, the set squawked. He gingerly stooped to retrieve the radio, feeling for it blindly with his left hand, the muzzle of the rifle held steady on Don's chest.

The helicopter rumbled above the ridgetop to the north, approaching them again.

"John O.," he called, "John F."

"France," Onstad yelled, "where you at?"

Johnny shivered with old adrenaline and licked his lips. He wanted to get some backup in here fast, but he did not want to announce on this open channel that he had captured the Nichols boys. Not yet. It was almost dark, and there was a lot of country to get through before they had these two down on the highway. If the media—which surely had news of the operation by this time—heard him on their police scanners, they'd swarm up this mountainside, interfering with the arresting officers. Worse, there was the danger of an escape or even a hostage situation if a media circus developed.

"John O.," he called, "I got a couple guys down here who need a ride."

"Who you got down there?" Onstad was clearly not in the mood for guessing games.

"A couple of guys who need a ride," he repeated.

"Say again," John Onstad called.

"I've got Don and Dan Nichols in custody, John."

The helicopter swooped over the crest of the hillside, blasting powdery snow with its rotorwash.

Johnny waved casually and smiled, keeping his rifle trained squarely on Don's heart.

To the west, the sun was a cooling ember in the ashes of the snow clouds.

Murray Duffy landed the chopper on the flat ridgetop, and Onstad and Bobby Campbell came plowing down the snowy hillside, their rifles at the ready.

When Campbell saw Johnny guarding the two filthy scarecrows, he slapped Johnny on the back. "Johnny," he yelled, "you are all right."

For Montana, that was a real compliment.

Onstad was grinning broadly. "France," he bellowed, rapping Johnny's shoulder, "you're one of the gutsiest sons of bitches I ever met."

Now Don Nichols realized just how badly he'd been tricked. There had been no deputies, no "Joe" and "Bob" in the trees. "Boy," Don muttered at Johnny. "You're just as dumb as you always were." He shook his head in obvious disgust. "That was real dumb, comin' in alone like that."

Johnny smiled at him. Old Don was confusing Johnny with his Uncle Joe. Well, Johnny thought, that's a kind of compliment too.

As Bob Campbell searched the Nicholses, Johnny told Onstad that he'd not had a chance to read them their rights.

Onstad nodded, then stepped forward. "Obviously," he said, "you're under arrest. Therefore you must understand your rights. . . ."

Danny Nichols stared at the snow, disoriented, as though in shock. Don gazed evenly up at the big sheriff's face, trying to discern if this were another trick of the rotten system he had tried so desperately and so long to escape.

"You do have the right to remain silent," Sheriff Onstad droned, his breath steaming in the rosy dusk. "Anything you say may be used against you in a court of law. If you would like to talk to an attorney. . . ."

Johnny moved away. The cramp was beginning to ease from his shoulders. At this side of the clearing, he could look down the open draw to the distant highway. Tiny red jewels of police pursuit lights twinkled in the winter darkness. He had brought the Nichols boys into the bureaucratic web of justice. The time for guns and violence was over. Now society reasserted its claim on these two renegades. They would not walk these mountains for years to come, if ever.

He breathed the clean night air. It was over, he was tired. It was too soon to really feel anything. His mind returned to practicalities. There wouldn't be room in the chopper for both prisoners and two guards, and he surely did not want them in there with only one officer, not today. Given the darkness, he thought, it probably won't be a good idea to put cuffs on Don and Dan

307

because if they were going to walk them down this draw to the highway, the chances were that they'd slip and fall.

Johnny stepped closer to the dropoff of the hillside to check the slope below. Away to the south, the snowy heights of the Beartrap caught the last pink afterglow of the sunset.

Epilogue

The Madison Range, Montana

Summer, 1985

A YEAR HAD PASSED SINCE THE BIZARRE KIDNAPPING. Now the heat gripped the Madison Range once more, the driest, hottest weather in almost one hundred years.

Out in the valley, the hay crop was burning up, despite around-the-clock irrigation. Hundred-dollar hay was going to put a lot of ranchers out of business, come the fall, according to the old cowboys who drank their mugs of strong black coffee at Bettie's Cafe.

But the heat and drought were not the main topics of conversation that summer. Up in the stately brick courthouse in Virginia City, the second Nichols trial was in progress.

In May, Danny Nichols had faced a jury of twelve of his fellow citizens. They found him guilty of kidnapping and assault, but not of felony murder. District Judge Frank Davis, a crusty old southerner who ran a tight court, had not yet passed sentence. But it was no secret he was annoyed at the verdict; Montana law was quite specific. If the jury found the boy guilty of kidnapping, then they were obliged to also find him guilty of the murder of Al Goldstein, which occurred during the course of the original felony.

But this was rural Montana, not the South Bronx or Miami. Some folks on the jury just couldn't find a kid like Danny guilty of murder, when it had been the old man who pulled the trigger.

Now Danny was out on bail, subpoenaed to testify in his father's trial on the same charges. Danny Nichols was much in evidence the week of his dad's trial. The young man wore a wide, pearl-gray Stetson. His fine blond hair was washed and blow dried daily. His sudden brown stare and angular face made a positive impression on many of the spectators who crammed into the stifling courtroom.

But the Swenson family and Al Goldstein's widow and two brothers were not impressed. The hatred for the Nicholses that radiated from the front row of seats was obvious to all the reporters jammed into the press section at the side of the room. Throughout this second trial, Kari Swenson sat close beside her mother, staring straight ahead, avoiding the eyes of Don Nichols and his son.

Once more, to this new jury, Kari Swenson and Jim Schwalbe gave their detailed recitation of the terrible events of July 15 and 16, 1984. Once more Don Nichols and his boy gave their version. The intense young woman court reporter swayed over her Stenograph in the choking heat to record their exact words.

From the side door of the courtroom, Sheriff Johnny France watched the progress of the trial.

At the end of the week, Don Nichols was found guilty of murder and kidnapping. No one came forward from the front row of courtroom seats to shake Johnny's hand.

Judge Davis passed his sentences.

Danny got the maximum, twenty years and six months. To be served at the hardrock adult prison at Deerlodge, not the youth camp at Swan River.

Later, Judge Davis sentenced Donald Boone Nichols. Eighty-five years, the maximum term under the law. Don Nichols must serve forty-two years before he will be eligible for parole.

According to the Washington *Post*, Kari Swenson resumed full-time training in the autumn of 1985. She jogged through the dry Indian Summer heat of Vermont's Green Mountains, training hard again for international biathlon competition, despite her reported pain and psychological traumas.

But she never ran alone. Even on a crowded campus or in a city park. She bought a guard dog. She will not talk about the crime.

But she has discussed the state of her training. She has regained about seventy percent of her former ability. "I'd love to be as good as I can be," she said wistfully, "but I don't know if I ever will be."

After the trials, Al Goldstein's widow, Dianne, and his two brothers asked Jay Cosgrove if he would lead them up to the clearing on Moonlight Creek that everyone now calls "the crime scene."

On the way up the indistinct game trail, the Goldsteins commented on the thickness of the country, on the surprisingly wild forest, so close to the civilization of Big Sky.

Jay showed them the camp, the three-stone fire ring.

INCIDENT AT BIG SKY

The deadfall where Kari was chained. The tree where Don Nichols fired the shot. The lodgepole where Al fell.

There were alpine asters and Indian paint brush growing on the pine needle floor of the forest where he died.

They huddled close together, and one of the young men took a picture of the delicate flowers.